Copyright: 1991 by Geo. K. Schweitzer
All rights reserved. Except for use in a review,
the reproduction, copying, recording, or
duplication of this work in any form by any means
is forbidden without the written permission
of the author.

ISBN 0-913857-03-3

TABLE OF CONTENTS

Chapter 1. NORTH CAROLINA BACKGROUND 5
  1. North Carolina geography 5
  2. Early Colonial NC 7
  3. Later Colonial NC 9
  4. The Revolutionary War 11
  5. Early statehood 13
  6. The Middle Period 14
  7. The Civil War 15
  8. Reconstruction and after 17
  9. The NC counties 20
  10. Recommended readings 20

Chapter 2. TYPES OF RECORDS 25
  1. Introduction .25
  2. Bible records 26
  3. Biographies .27
  4. Birth records 29
  5. Cemetery records 30
  6. Census records 31
  7. Church records 36
  8. City directories 40
  9. City and county histories 41
  10. Colonial record compilations 41
  11. Court records 45
  12. DAR records 48
  13. Death records 48
  14. Divorce records 49
  15. Emigration and immigration 50
  16. Ethnic records 52
  17. Gazetteers, atlases, and maps 54
  18. Genealogical indexes for NC 56
  19. Genealogical periodicals 57
  20. Genealogical societies 60
  21. Historical societies 62
  22. Land records 64
  23. Manuscripts. 66
  24. Marriage records 68
  25. Military records: Colonial 69
  26. Military records: Revolutionary War 71
  27. Military records: 1812-1860 75
  28. Military records: Civil War 78
  29. Mortuary records 81
  30. Naturalization records 81
  31. Newspaper records 82

```
32. Published genealogies for the US . . . . . . . . . . 85
33. Regional records . . . . . . . . . . . . . . . . . 86
34. Tax lists . . . . . . . . . . . . . . . . . . . . 86
35. Wills and probate records . . . . . . . . . . . 87

Chapter 3.  RECORD LOCATIONS . . . . . . . . . . . . . . 91
     1. Court houses . . . . . . . . . . . . . . . . . . 91
     2. The major facilities . . . . . . . . . . . . . . 92
     3. The North Carolina State Archives . . . . . . . . 92
     4. The North Carolina State Library . . . . . . . . 96
     5. The Library at the University of NC   . . . . . 98
     6. Perkins Library, Duke University . . . . . . . . 99
     7. Family History Library and its Branches  . . . . 100
     8. Regional libraries . . . . . . . . . . . . . . . 104
     9. Local libraries  . . . . . . . . . . . . . . . . 105
    10. Large genealogical libraries . . . . . . . . . . 106

Chapter 4.  RESEARCH PROCEDURE & COUNTY LISTINGS . . . 109
     1. Finding the county . . . . . . . . . . . . . . . 109
     2. Recommended approaches . . . . . . . . . . . . . 110
     3. State-wide records . . . . . . . . . . . . . . . 112
     4. The format of the listings . . . . . . . . . . . 114
     5. Alamance County   . . . . . . . . . . . . . . . 115
     6. Albemarle County . . . . . . . . . . . . . . . . 116
     7. Alexander County . . . . . . . . . . . . . . . . 116
     8. Allegheny County . . . . . . . . . . . . . . . . 117
     9. Anson County . . . . . . . . . . . . . . . . . . 117
    10. Archdale County  . . . . . . . . . . . . . . . . 118
    11. Ashe County  . . . . . . . . . . . . . . . . . . 118
    12. Avery County . . . . . . . . . . . . . . . . . . 118
    13. Bath County  . . . . . . . . . . . . . . . . . . 119
    14. Beaufort County  . . . . . . . . . . . . . . . . 119
    15. Bertie County  . . . . . . . . . . . . . . . . . 119
    16. Bladen County  . . . . . . . . . . . . . . . . . 120
    17. Brunswick County . . . . . . . . . . . . . . . . 120
    18. Buncombe County  . . . . . . . . . . . . . . . . 121
    19. Burke County . . . . . . . . . . . . . . . . . . 121
    20. Bute County  . . . . . . . . . . . . . . . . . . 122
    21. Cabarrus County  . . . . . . . . . . . . . . . . 122
    22. Caldwell County  . . . . . . . . . . . . . . . . 123
    23. Camden County  . . . . . . . . . . . . . . . . . 123
    24. Carteret County  . . . . . . . . . . . . . . . . 124
    25. Caswell County . . . . . . . . . . . . . . . . . 124
    26. Catawba County . . . . . . . . . . . . . . . . . 125
    27. Chatham County . . . . . . . . . . . . . . . . . 125
    28. Cherokee County  . . . . . . . . . . . . . . . . 126
```

29. Chowan County 126
30. Clay County 127
31. Cleveland County 127
32. Columbus County 128
33. Craven County 128
34. Cumberland County 129
35. Currituck County 129
36. Dare County 130
37. Davidson County 130
38. Davie County 131
39. Dobbs County 131
40. Duplin County 131
41. Durham County 132
42. Edgecombe County 132
43. Forsyth County 133
44. Franklin County 133
45. Gaston County 134
46. Gates County 134
47. Glasgow County 135
48. Graham County 135
49. Granville County 135
50. Greene County 136
51. Guilford County 136
52. Halifax County 137
53. Harnett County 138
54. Haywood County 138
55. Henderson County 139
56. Hertford County 139
57. Hoke County 140
58. Hyde County 140
59. Iredell County 140
60. Jackson County 141
61. Johnston County 141
62. Jones County 142
63. Lee County 142
64. Lenoir County 143
65. Lincoln County 143
66. Macon County 144
67. Madison County 144
68. Martin County 145
69. McDowell County 145
70. Mecklenburg County 146
71. Mitchell County 146
72. Montgomery County 147
73. Moore County 147
74. Nash County 148

75. New Hanover County 148
 76. Northampton County 149
 77. Onslow County 149
 78. Orange County 150
 79. Pamlico County 151
 80. Pasquotank County 151
 81. Pender County 152
 82. Perquimans County 152
 83. Person County 153
 84. Pitt County 153
 85. Polk County 154
 86. Randolph County 154
 87. Richmond County 155
 88. Robeson County 155
 89. Rockingham County 156
 90. Rowan County 156
 91. Rutherford County 157
 92. Sampson County 157
 93. Scotland County 158
 94. Stanly County 158
 95. Stokes County 159
 96. Surry County 159
 97. Swain County 160
 98. Transylvania County 160
 99. Tryon County 161
100. Tyrrell County 161
101. Union County 161
102. Vance County 162
103. Wake County 162
104. Warren County 163
105. Washington County 163
106. Watauga County 164
107. Wayne County 164
108. Wilkes County 165
109. Wilson County 165
110. Yadkin County 166
111. Yancey County 166
112. TN records 167

Chapter 1

NORTH CAROLINA BACKGROUND

1. North Carolina geography

The state of North Carolina (hereafter abbreviated NC), one of the thirteen original colonies, is located in the central region of the eastern seaboard of the US. In shape, it resembles a long rectangle with a sizable southeastern protrusion and a smaller southwestern extension (see Figure 1). The state is about 450 miles from east to west, making it the broadest state east of the MS River, and it is about 180 miles wide at its widest point. The highly irregular coast gives NC a coastline of about 300 miles. The state is bordered on the east by the Atlantic Ocean, on the north by VA, on the west by its daughter state TN, and on the south by GA and SC. The capital of the state is located at Raleigh in the north central region, and the state is divided into 100 counties. The principal cities of NC (with their approximate populations in thousands) are Charlotte (314 K), Greensboro (156 K), Raleigh (150 K), Winston-Salem (131 K), Durham (101 K), High Point (63 K), Fayetteville (60 K), Asheville (54 K), Gastonia (47 K), Wilmington (44 K), and Rocky Mount (41 K). Charlotte and Gastonia are in the south central part of the state; Greensboro, Winston-Salem, Durham, and High Point in the north central region; Wilmington and Fayetteville in the southeastern section; Asheville in the southwestern area; and Rocky Mount in the northeastern portion. As it has always been, NC is a rural state, with slightly more than half of its people living in non-urban areas, although most of these are now not farmers.

An understanding of the progressive settlement of the state and the genealogies of its early families is greatly enhanced by an examination of its major geographic regions and features. These are pictured in Figure 1. The first region consists of the Outer Banks, a series of narrow sand dunes, reefs, bars, and islands which rest off the east coast. The Outer Banks form three major projections which thrust outward into the Atlantic: Cape Hatteras (CH) in the north, Cape Lookout (CL) in the center, and Cape Fear (CF) in the south.

Between the Outer Banks and the main shore of the state there is a series of sounds, including two very large ones: Albemarle Sound (AS) in the north, and Pamlico Sound (PS) in the center. The Outer Banks are cut by several narrow inlets which connect the sounds with the ocean, some of the chief ones of these being (from north to south) the Oregon (OI), Hatteras (HI), Ocracoke (OC), and Bogue (BI) Inlets. The treacherous currents, coastal storms, shifting sands, narrow inlets, reef-laden capes, and shallow sounds make the waters of the Outer Banks extremely dangerous and accessible only for small craft navigation. The second region is the

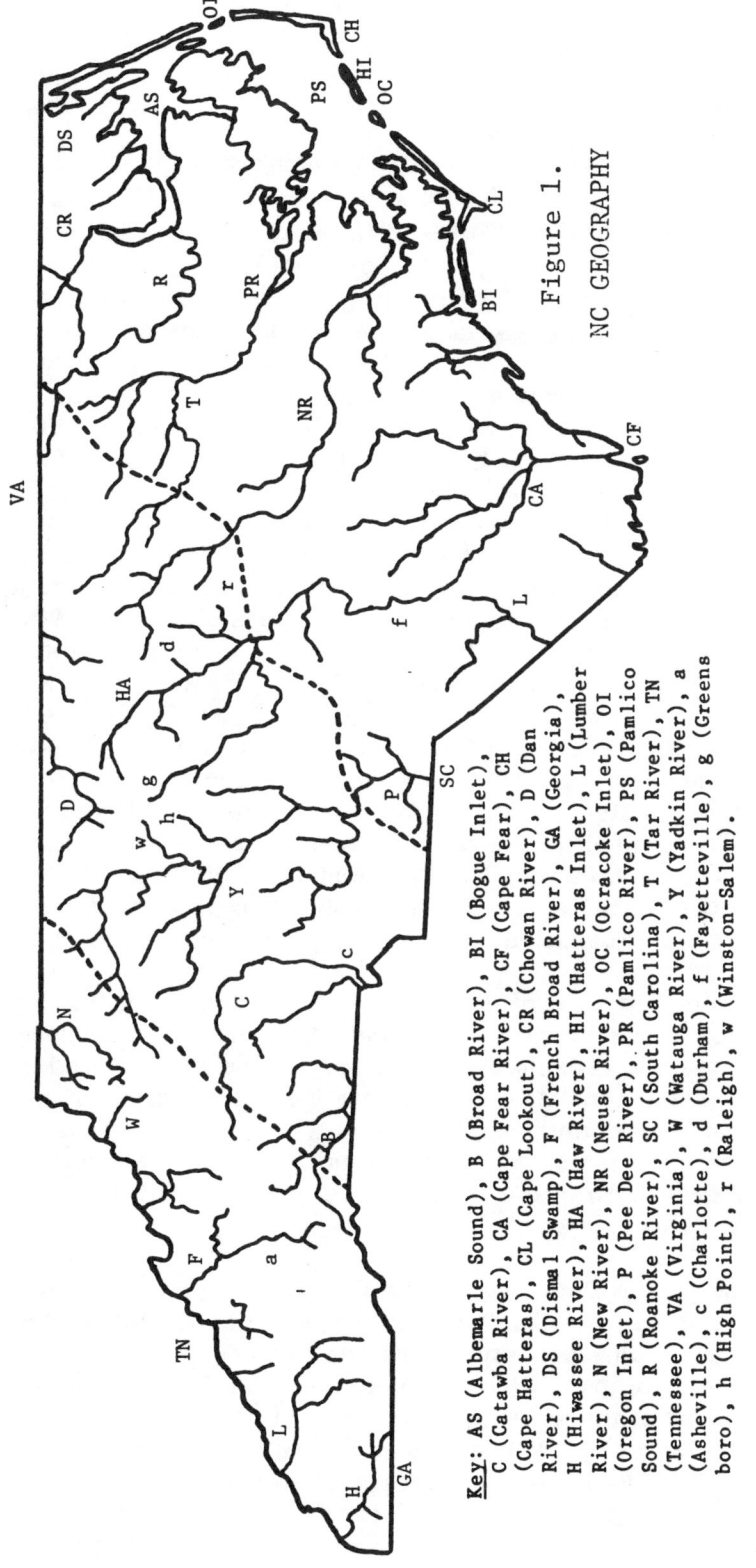

Figure 1.
NC GEOGRAPHY

Key: AS (Albemarle Sound), B (Broad River), BI (Bogue Inlet), C (Catawba River), CA (Cape Fear River), CF (Cape Fear), CH (Cape Hatteras), CL (Cape Lookout), CR (Chowan River), D (Dan River), DS (Dismal Swamp), F (French Broad River), GA (Georgia), H (Hiwassee River), HA (Haw River), HI (Hatteras Inlet), L (Lumber River), N (New River), NR (Neuse River), OC (Ocracoke Inlet), OI (Oregon Inlet), P (Pee Dee River), PR (Pamlico River), PS (Pamlico Sound), R (Roanoke River), SC (South Carolina), T (Tar River), TN (Tennessee), VA (Virginia), W (Watauga River), Y (Yadkin River), a (Asheville), c (Charlotte), d (Durham), f (Fayetteville), g (Greensboro), h (High Point), r (Raleigh), w (Winston-Salem).

Coastal Plain which extends from the seacoast to the fall line of the rivers. This fall line runs roughly from 110 miles inland in the north to 150 miles inland in the south. The area is the largest region of the state and includes about 42 counties. The portion of it near the coast is low and swampy containing several large marshy areas [including Dismal Swamp (DS) in the northeast], numerous natural lakes, an abundance of bays, and several savannahs. The interior segment of the Coastal Plain rises gently toward the fall line. It contains much fertile land and a great deal of timber. West of the fall line is the third region known as the Piedmont Plateau. This area is made up of about 41 counties and extends to the base of the Blue Ridge Mountains. As one moves from the fall line westward, gently rolling country gradually becomes more hilly, and finally quite rugged. About half of the country is timbered and the land is cut by many narrow, swift streams. The fourth area, the Mountain Region is made up of about 17 counties, and consists of two mountain ranges running from the northeast to the southwest with a narrow plateau in between. The first of these ranges is the Blue Ridge Mountains which rise at the end of the Piedmont Plateau. On the west side is the narrow plateau which gives way to other mountains of the Appalachian Chain, the most important of which are the Great Smoky Mountains which rest along the TN border.

Figure 1 also depicts the major rivers of NC. They may be treated in terms of the geographical areas referred to above. The first set of rivers is made up of those which drain the western slopes of the Blue Ridge Mountains: the New (N), Watauga (W), French Broad (F), Little TN (L), and Hiwassee (H) Rivers. The New flows into VA and the others into TN. A second set of rivers consists of those which pick up water from the eastern slopes of the Blue Ridge Mountains and then drain to the southeast into SC: the Yadkin-Pee Dee (Y,P), Catawba (C), and Broad (B) Rivers. The third group of rivers includes the ones which rise in the Piedmont Plateau, then cross the Coastal Plain to flow into the sounds or directly into the Atlantic Ocean: the Chowan (CR), Dan-Roanoke (D,R), Tar-Pamlico (T,P), Neuse (N), Haw-Cape Fear (HA,CA), and Lumber (L) Rivers.

2. Early colonial NC

Human settlement in what is now NC probably dates from about 8000 BC. By 1500, 30 tribes of Indians numbering 35,000 lived in the region. The most important were the Hatteras along the coast, the Catawba, Chowanoc, and Tuscarora in the coastal plain and piedmont, and the Cherokee in the western mountains. Following the voyages of Columbus, the NC region was explored by France, Spain, and England. In 1524, de Verrazano representing France, explored the NC coast and sent reports back. In the 1560s, other French explorations were conducted, but France chose to develop its colonies in Canada and the MS Valley. After some explorations along the Cape

Fear coast in 1525, de Ayllon of Spain planted a 500-person colony by the lower Cape Fear River. Disease and starvation brought about its early failure. The explorer de Soto on his MS River discovery trip of 1539-41 passed through the NC mountain region. However, Spain turned its attention to activity in FL and the southwest. The English were left to do the early colonization of NC. In 1585, Walter Raleigh, acting under the authority of Queen Elizabeth, and on the basis of a favorable report of explorers he had dispatched in 1584, sent 7 ships and over 100 colonists to settle on Roanoke Island. This first English colony in America met with starvation and Indian hostility which forced them to abandon their small settlement in 1586. In the next year, Raleigh dispatched a second group of about 120 to make another attempt to establish a colony on Roanoke Island. Their leader, John White, went back to England for supplies later in the year. When he returned in 1590, after being delayed by a threatened Spanish invasion of England, he found the settlement to have disappeared.

In 1607, a permanent English settlement was established at Jamestown in VA, just about 45 miles north of the present northeastern corner of NC. After a period of struggle, the VA colony began to prosper, more people came into the area, and plantations spread in the country around the village. By 1619 the population had grown to about 2500, by 1635 about 5000, by 1641 about 7500. Traders, trappers, and explorers moved in and out of what is now northeastern NC, but no settlements were made. In 1629, King Charles had granted to Robert Heath what he called the Province of Carolana (land of Charles). The territory consisted of all the property that now makes up NC and SC with the western borders extended to the Pacific Ocean. Heath failed to develop colonies in the area, and in 1638 transferred his grant to the Duke of Norfolk. During his ownership, and in spite of his failure to promote colonization, VA people began to move into the region north of the Albemarle Sound about 1653 and to settle there. A map drawn in 1657 shows the house of Nathaniel Batts at the western end of Albemarle Sound. Batts had come in September 1653. The Virginians who followed him bought land from the Indians and recorded their grants in VA. In 1662, VA sent Samuel Stephens to be commander of the area; he appointed a sheriff to keep order and to collect taxes.

In 1663, eight English entrepreneurs, who saw a good business opportunity in the development of Carolana, persuaded Charles II to grant them the area. These men were known as the Lords Proprietors of Carolina, and in 1664 they established a government in the area northeast of the Chowan River. The region was known as Albemarle County, and the government came to consist of an appointed governor, an appointed advisory council, and an elected general assembly. In 1670, the county was divided into four precincts: Currituck, Pasquotank, Perquimans, and Chowan. The proprietors did many things to encourage settlers including land grants and subsidies, but their law code was oppressive, and their governors were in

general inefficient and corrupt. In 1677, some colonists rebelled against the corruption and ran the county for about a year with their own governor, John Culpepper. Several others of the proprietors' governors were driven out of office by the settlers.

During the period of the proprietors, which lasted until 1729, the colony grew very slowly, and it was plagued with mismanagement, pirate activity, internal dissension, and Indian hostilities. In 1691, governors over the whole Carolina colony took residence in Charleston, and deputy governors were put over the NC section. Because settlement had spread south of Albemarle, a new county called Bath was set up in 1696. In 1705, the first town, also called Bath, was settled by Huguenots who had left VA, and the County of Bath was divided into three precincts: Wickham, Archdale, and Pamptecough. By 1710 settlement had moved as far south as the Neuse River area, and in that year a Swiss land company sponsored a town at the junction of the Neuse and Trent Rivers. The town, called New Bern, was populated by Swiss, German, and English people. In 1711, a rebellion against Governor Cary by oppressed Quakers was put down by force, but the Governor was subsequently removed. His replacement in 1712 was designated as the Governor of NC, this act marking NC as a separate colony. In this same year the three precincts of Bath County underwent a name change to Hyde, Craven, and Beaufort.

The year 1711 also witnessed a 3-day slaughter of colonists in and around New Bern by the Tuscarora Indians. Sporadic attacks continued, but in 1713 the Tuscarora were defeated with the aid of SC militia. A couple of years after that when NC troops went to help SC counter an Indian uprising south of the Cape Fear River, they rediscovered the fertile Cape Fear lands. Over the next decade an increasing number of settlers began to move into the region, many coming up from SC. During the proprietors' period, pirate terrorism along the coast had been broadspread. Efforts by SC and VA to terminate this activity met with success in 1718 when Bonnet was captured and hanged and Blackbeard was killed. A period of growth then set in with the counties of Carteret and Bertie and the town of Edenton being established in 1722. This town became the center of government. In 1729, the British monarch purchased the lands of seven of the eight proprietors (Granville excepted) and took over the governance of the colony. NC thus joined its neighbors VA and SC as a royal colony. At this time, about 36,000 people lived in NC.

3. Later colonial NC

The year 1729, when NC became a crown colony, marked the beginnings of a period of increased settlement and greater prosperity. The population would increase from 35,000 to almost 350,000 in 1775, and settlement would move through the coastal plain, across the piedmont, into the mountains,

and a bit beyond. These expansions were in a large part due to good governors, a policy encouraging settlers, and the availability of an abundance of good, inexpensive land. Most of the NC colonists before 1729 had been English, who had settled in the coastal plain and in the eastern edge of the piedmont. A fair number of them were yeoman farmers and former indentured servants who left VA to come to NC. Many had owned no land in VA and left few legal records in that state. The main exceptions to the English settlements were the French Huguenots who had come into the Neuse and Trent River areas (1686-1708) and the Germans and Swiss who established New Bern (1710).

After 1729, the settlers were chiefly non-English: Highland Scottish, Scotch-Irish, Moravian, and German. Once a port on the Cape Fear River opened, about 20,000 Scottish Highlanders began to arrive from overseas about 1732. An ever-increasing number of them moved steadily up the river, such that the Cape Fear and Lumber valleys came to be known as Little Scotland. While these settlements were being made, two other groups were moving into NC. Approximately 65,000 Scotch-Irish and around 25,000 Germans out of PA, MD, NJ, DE, and several other northeastern states came down the great wagon road from PA through the valley of VA into the piedmont and the mountain region. The Scotch-Irish, Presbyterian in their faith, spread out over the entire western half of the state. The Germans, who were Lutheran, German Reformed, and Moravian, settled in the west-central piedmont. Following 1740, the numbers of blacks rose, as the eastern counties brought them in to work in farming and in industry.

During the period (1729-75) NC troops fought in several wars against the French, the Spanish, and the Indians. Included were Queen Anne's War (1702-13), the defeat of the Yemassee Indians in SC in 1715, the War of Jenkins' Ear (1739-44), King George's War (1744-8), and the French and Indian War (1754-63) with the defeat of the Cherokees in 1760 near present-day Statesville. The Cherokee peace treaty in 1761 opened up very large areas in VA, NC, and SC.

As settlement proceeded through this era, extreme conflict developed between the English-settled east and the non-English-settled west. These two groups had many differences: geographic, ethnic, economic, social, religious, and political. The government was controlled by the east, and the peoples of the back-country suffered exploitation by corrupt officials (land agents, tax collectors, surveyors, sheriffs, politicians). The interests of the east saw to it that the western area continued to be under-represented in the general assembly, thus assuring sustained eastern dominance. The west protested in many ways including local vigilante action against the corruption. This action broke out in a full scale rebellion by a western group called the Regulators. On 16 May 1771 Governor Tryon in command of NC

troops defeated them at the Battle of Alamance. A sizable number of them moved farther west.

Even though the Anglican (Episcopal) Church was the established church of the colony of NC, it never was very strong. As early as 1680 there was a Quaker monthly meeting in the region. In the years before 1700, there were members of several other Protestant groups in NC, but very little organized religious activity. From about 1725 forward, the non-Anglican groups grew rapidly, spread widely, and established many churches. Approximate dates of the first organized activity for various groups are as follows: Quakers (1672 in Perquimans County), Baptists (1727 in Chowan County), Presbyterians (1736 in New Hanover County), Lutheran and German Reformed (1740s in northern Anson County), Moravians (1753 in Rowan County), and Methodists (1772 in Currituck County). At the end of this period, Baptists were the most numerous religious group, with Methodists, Presbyterians, and Lutherans following. At the beginning of this period (1729), NC was the least settled and most isolated colony; at the end of the period (1775), it was the fourth most populated.

4. The Revolutionary War

Following the termination of the French and Indian War (1763), Britain found herself severely in debt, and began to tighten up her trade and taxation policies in the American colonies. Having become used to an independence fostered by British disinterest, the colonies strongly resented the new policies. They protested that their rights to participate in such policy decisions were being ignored, and they began to defy the tax laws. NC, as did other colonies, used force to coerce royal officials and to prevent the enforcement of the regulations. This was done by an armed group called the Sons of Liberty as well as by some other groups. Associations were also organized for the purpose of boycotting British goods and opposing import duties. In 1773 a NC Committee of Correspondence was formed to keep in touch with other such committees in the colonies and to promote unified action and cooperative support. When the British, in reaction to MA's opposition and defiance, blockaded Boston in 1774, NC sent the town supplies and pledged its support, as did other colonies.

As relations between Britain and the 13 colonies continued to decay, NC in 1774 defied the royal governor Martin and held an anti-British provincial congress in New Bern. This assembly endorsed the First Continental Congress and elected three NC delegates to attend the meeting in Philadelphia. When open warfare broke out in April 1775 at Lexington and Concord in MA, Governor Martin left his capital at New Bern, ultimately taking refuge on a British warship stationed off the coast. The government of the colony of NC then came to be administered by the newly-formed provincial congress, a provincial council, and district and local committees

of safety. Public meetings were held in many counties to establish new county governments and to raise military forces. At the fourth meeting of the provincial congress held in Halifax, NC, 12 April 1776, the delegates empowered their representatives to the Continental Congress to concur with the other colonies in declaring independence from Britain. The Declaration of Independence was subsequently drawn up and signed by colonial delegates, including the three from NC. A special assembly which convened at Halifax on 12 November 1776 drafted a constitution for the new independent state of NC.

A sizable fraction of the people in NC were Loyalists (faithful to Britain) during the Revolution, the largest group being Highland Scots. In 1776, the Highland Scots raised military units in their counties and moved to join up with British troops along the coast. They were intercepted by American patriots and defeated in the Battle of Moore's Creek Bridge on 22 February. This ended the threat from Loyalists within NC, and British hopes that they could establish an early foothold in the southern colonies were thwarted.

From this time until late in 1780 there was little battle action in NC except for a few harassments of military operations by Loyalists. However, NC troops were active in the places where the war was actively waged. NC contributed over 6000 men to the Continental Army. In addition, approximately 10,000 NC militia were active at one time or another, mostly in NC and bordering areas. The NC members of the Continental Army constituted 10 regiments which fought under Washington in campaigns across NY, NJ, PA, and VA. Many NC troops were also engaged in subduing the Cherokees. Following the British defeat at Saratoga on 17 October 1777, they moved the focus of their warfare to the south. Both NC Continentals and militia were heavily involved in the remaining major actions of the war, since these actions occurred in NC or in the colonies adjacent (SC, GA, VA). On 29 December 1778, Savannah fell to the British and by February 1779 most of GA was theirs. In May 1779 a British assault on Charleston was repulsed, but an October effort to retake Savannah failed. After several months of siege, American efforts to defend Charleston faltered, and the city was surrendered on 12 May 1790. Over 5000 troops were taken prisoner, including many from NC.

In the fall of 1780, British General Corwallis led an invasion of NC. This was stopped when a contingent of the British army was soundly defeated by militia from western NC on 07 October 1780 at Kings Mountain. In Cornwallis' second invasion of the state, the British troops chased American forces under the crafty General Greene, who pulled the enemy farther and farther away from their supply depots. The forces finally met on 15 March 1781 in the Battle of Guilford Court House. The result of this engagement was that the British ended up in control of the field, but they were

so weakened that Cornwallis had to retreat to the coast at Wilmington. From there he went north into VA finally ending up at Yorktown, where he was surrounded by American and French forces. After a short siege, the British surrendered on 19 October 1781, and the American Revolution was essentially over.

5. Early statehood

In 1776, the colony of NC had adopted a constitution, elected their own governmental officials, and taken New Bern as their capital. The new constitution established legislative, executive, and judicial branches of government, with all important powers in the legislative, and with the executive and judicial branches quite weak. The document provided a bill of rights, gave the vote only to property owners and tax payers, and separated church and state. However, the new constitution perpetuated the inequities in representation which permitted the eastern counties to dominate the western ones. Following the British surrender, the last of their troops left NC on 18 November 1781, but Loyalist bands continued raids until the following spring. The formal peace treaty with Britain was signed on 03 February 1783. The war left numerous problems in NC, but progress was rapid as western settlement continued, churches were organized and reorganized, schools were re-established, newspaper publication was resumed, trade increased, and so did agriculture. The government passed an act of pardon for many Loyalists, and land beyond the western mountains (now TN) was granted to Revolutionary War veterans. Conflicts between the east and the west grew ever more bitter.

During the period 1777-83, NC had established several counties beyond the western mountains: Washington, Sullivan, Greene (now in East TN), and Davidson (now in Middle TN). In 1784, discontented settlers in the first three counties charged NC with neglect and set up an independent government called the State of Franklin. Their efforts gradually failed as NC, VA, and the Continental Congress all refused to recognize them. In 1787, NC sent five delegates to the Constitutional Convention in Philadelphia, all five of them representing the eastern counties. Their contributions to the drafting of the Constitution reflected a favoring of centralization of authority. When the document was submitted to the thirteen states for ratification, NC rejected it at a state convention held in Hillsboro in 1788. Knowledge that most other states had ratified and the promise of a bill of rights prompted a second state convention at Fayetteville in 1789. At this meeting, NC ratified the Constitution and became the 12th state of the US. After much east-west controversy, Wake County was chosen for the new state capital in 1792. A capital building was completed in 1794 at the site which was called Raleigh.

In 1789, the year NC ratified the Constitution, the state also ceded the land beyond the mountains to the US. This area in 1790 became the Territory South of the Ohio River, with Knoxville as its capital. Then in 1796, TN was admitted to the US as the 16th state.

The period 1800-35 in NC was characterized by inertia, lack of progress, economic stagnation, illiteracy, one-party politics, loss of population, low incomes, low standards of living, and provincialism. The government remained undemocratic in form and action as it was almost completely controlled by the ultra- conservative, self-seeking, landed eastern aristocracy. They viewed the common people with disdain and contempt, and did very little to benefit them, especially those in the west. The state's farmers exhausted much land by the growth of corn, wheat, cotton, and tobacco, then moved west to farm fresh land. Thousands of people left the state dropping its population greatly, most of them migrating to TN, AL, and OH. There was a rise in slavery as demand for slave labor on the farms increased. The reluctance of the government to levy taxes for public works resulted in inadequate roads, few cities or towns which functioned as commercial centers, a neglect of elementary education, and the development of very little industry. As a result of these conditions, tensions continued to mount between the oligarchic, status- quo seeking, eastern coastal planters and the democratic, reform-minded, poor, small farmers of the west.

During this period of backwardness (1800-35), the War of 1812 (1812-5) was fought with Britain. Actions of the English in the first decade of the 19th century to encourage Indians to attack the US, plus the searching of American ships and the impressment of US sailors on the high seas led to the War. The War of 1812 was not a popular war and NC, like the US, was divided over it. Even though NC was not solidly behind the War, the state furnished well over 15,000 soldiers. They served on the Canadian and southern frontiers and guarded the coast. The treaty of peace was signed on 24 December 1814. Before word of the treaty reached either side, a native of NC, Andrew Jackson, led Americans to a decisive defeat of the British at New Orleans on 08 January 1815.

6. The middle period

In 1835 the east-west conflicts in NC came to a head when western protests secured a referendum in 1835 for a constitutional convention. This convention marked a turning point in the history of NC. The new constitution that was drafted reapportioned the legislature, giving the west proportional representation. Other reforms were also included which for the most part made the government more democratic. The new document was approved, and the Whig political party began a series of progressive actions. In the years 1836-50, they supported railroad construction, enacted and implemented a public school law, established a school for the deaf, sponsored a state

hospital for the insane, reassessed property, and levied taxes on incomes, licenses, inheritances, and luxuries to finance public projects.

In 1845, US President Tyler's plan for the annexation of TX was accepted by that state. This action, added to previous frictions, was the immediate cause of the Mexican War. When US General Taylor occupied Point Isbel at the mouth of the Rio Grande River, Mexico saw this as an aggressive act. Mexican troops then crossed the river, bombarded Fort Taylor, and the US declared war on 12 May 1846. Taylor drove the Mexican troops back across the Rio Grande, Santa Fe was taken by US General Kearny, and CA switched to American rule. In February 1847, Taylor and Mexican President Santa Anna clashed at Buena Vista, the battle ending in a Mexican withdrawal. The final campaign of the war began in March 1847, when US General Scott landed at Vera Cruz and began a drive on Mexico City, successively taking Cerro Gordo, Contreras, Casa Mata, Molino del Rey, and Chapultepec. US forces entered Mexico City on 14 September 1847, and the treaty of 02 February 1848 provided for Mexico's cession of two-fifths of its land to the US.

In 1850, the Democrat party won the state elections (governor and control of the legislature), and instead of reversing the previous reforms, they improved and extended them. They expanded free suffrage, supported extension of the railway network, improved the school system, gave state aid for the construction of plank roads, and fostered trade and commerce. The decade of the 1850s was one of unprecedented prosperity in NC. In those 10 years, the value of taxable property doubled, tobacco production tripled, cotton production doubled, and wheat production more than doubled. Industrial expansion was also noteworthy, the value of manufactured items almost doubling. There was also a strong revival movement in religion with the membership and influence of the churches increasing markedly.

In the midst of all this prosperity, some shadowed currents began to flow. The 1835 constitution had disenfranchised free blacks, and the prosperity of the 1850s convinced slaveholders of the economic advantage of slavery. The slave code was made harsher, abolitionists were forced out of the state, and many churches expounded biblical arguments for slavery. Even so, there was strong sentiment in NC for not permitting the slavery issue to separate them from their sister states of the north. It should also be recognized that the old east-west split in the state was evidenced by pro-slavery-antislavery tendencies in the regions.

7. The Civil War

For several decades prior to 1860, the Northern and southern States had been progressively becoming divided by a number of issues: sectional rivalry, industrial against agricultural interests, economic and trade regulation, federal centralization

against states' rights, Congressional control, and slavery. Compromises had been worked numerous times, but they became increasingly unsatisfactory as the 1850s wore on, and conflict loomed large. When Lincoln was elected president in 1860, the south clearly remembered his campaign statement that a government cannot endure permanently half slave and half free. Before the inauguration, SC seceded from the Union on 20 December, and by 01 February 1861, had been joined by AL, FL, GA, LA, MS, and TX. During these months many public meetings were held in NC, but no secession sentiment emerged. Neither did the legislature take any action. But gradually the divided, unorganized majority began to weaken and the organized, enthusiastic secessionist minority to strengthen. However, a referendum to call a secession convention failed on 28 February. The secessionists continued their vigorous campaign, on 12 April 1861 Fort Sumter fell to SC forces, and when on the 14th Lincoln called for troops from NC, sentiment for secession became very strong. A state convention which met on 20 May repealed the ordinance of 1789, thus seceding from the US. By the end of the month eleven states (the above plus VA, AR, TN) had joined the Confederacy. The two sides, Union and Confederate, mobilized their men and resources, and four years of horrible conflict began. We will now summarize the war, and then we will look at NC's part in a bit of detail.

The intention of the Union came to be defeat of the Confederacy by invasion and subdual. Five strategies were to be pursued: (1) the blockading or capture of southern ports to cut off supplies, (2) the taking of the Confederate capital Richmond by attack from the north, (3) the splitting of the Confederacy by driving down and up the MS River, (4) the further splitting of the Confederacy by driving from the northwest corner of TN down the TN and Cumberland Rivers to Nashville to Chattanooga to Atlanta to Savannah, and then, if necessary (5) driving north from Savannah into SC, then NC, then assaulting Richmond from the south.

Strategy 1, the sea blockade, was accomplished early in the war with most Atlantic and Gulf ports blockaded or captured by the end of 1862. Strategy 2, the drive toward Richmond from the north, failed again and again, the Confederacy even making two counter-invasions to threaten Washington, until success began to be had by Grant in 1864, Richmond falling on 02-03 April 1865. Strategy 3, the drives to take the MS River, had been completed with the collapse of Port Hudson 09 July 1863. Strategy 4, the drive from northwest TN to Savannah took 34 months, but ended in the capture of Savannah on 22 December 1864. Strategy 5, the drive north from Savannah was accomplished by the taking of Charleston and Columbia in February 1865, then pushing into NC where one of the two remaining major Confederate armies surrendered on 26 April 1865. The other had surrendered after the fall of Richmond at Appomattox on 09 April 1865.

It is obvious from the above account that the major Civil War actions in NC took place under Strategies 1 and 5. Early in the war, NC organized and trained troops, built fortifications, and accumulated supplies, thus turning the state into an armed military camp. By the end of the conflict, NC had furnished over 125,000 combatants. NC men fought on the sea, in NC, in the western states, in practically every major battle, but chiefly in VA. Over 19,000 were killed in battle and over 20,000 died from disease. Eleven battles and over 70 skirmishes were fought in NC. As part of Strategy 1, the blockade of the south, the Union captured Hatteras Inlet (29 August 1861), Roanoke Island (08 February 1862), New Bern (14 March 1862), Washington (21 March 1862), Fort Macon (26 April 1862), and Plymouth (13 December 1862). These bases permitted the Federals to control much of the coast throughout the war and to constantly threaten the interior regions. Wilmington was defended by powerful Fort Fisher, which held out until 15 January 1865. Until then the town was an effective port for blockade runners who brought in supplies. In April 1864, Confederate General Hoke retook Plymouth and Washington, but they were relost when he had to go to VA to reinforce Lee.

In the Union pursuit of **Strategy 5**, Union General Sherman on his drive north from Savannah, GA, crossed from SC to NC on 06 March 1865 near Rockingham. During the previous few weeks, the Federals had taken Wilmington and had pushed inland from there and from other NC coastal bases. During 08-10 March, at the Battle of Kinston, Confederate forces engaged Federals who were moving inland but were unable to stop the advance. Sherman's army occupied Fayetteville on 11 March, and on the 15th moved northeast toward Goldsborough, as other Union forces marched toward the same town from Kinston. Four miles south of Averasborough, on 16 March Sherman's troops drove off Confederates who were blocking their path. Then on 19-21 March the largest NC encounter, the Battle of Bentonville, was fought in a last attempt to stop Sherman, to no avail. On the 20th of March Union General Stoneman left Jonesboro, TN to move eastward into NC, where he would demolish the military prison at Salisbury and destroy railroads, factories, supplies, and food in and around the major towns of the western half of NC. Upon hearing of Lee's surrender at Appomattox, VA (09 April 1865), Confederate General Johnston, commander of the Southern troops in NC, retreated to Raleigh, which was taken the next day by Sherman. On 26 April 1865, Johnston surrendered to Sherman at Durham Station, 3 miles west of Durham, and except for a few minor actions, the war was over.

8. Reconstruction and after

Following Johnston's surrender, NC was put under military occupation and governance headed by Federal General Schofield. President Johnson, who followed the assassinated Lincoln, of-

fered amnesty and pardons to most NC persons and appointed W. Holden as provisional governor. A constitutional convention then repealed the ordinance of secession, outlawed slavery, and repudiated the war debt in a new constitution. In the 1865 elections, J. Worth was voted into office, and NC refused to grant suffrage and schooling for freedmen, and enacted black codes to restrict them. The US Congress subsequently passed the Reconstruction Acts, and NC was placed under military control again. Under this regime the NC Republican Party was formed in March 1867 by three groups: NC natives (scalawags), immigrants (carpetbaggers), and leaders of the black freedmen. They took control of the government, wrote a new constitution, and obtained readmission to the US. This new constitution enfranchised the freedmen, provided for popular election of county and state officials, removed religious restrictions for voting and office holding, and supported the schools. The Ku Klux Klan at this time began its campaign of violence and fear to discourage political activity by blacks and whites sympathetic to them.

In 1870, Conservatives won control of the legislature, impeached Holden, removed him from office, and set out to undo the advances of reconstruction. They neglected the schools, roads, public institutions, welfare services, favored business over farmers and labor, put county government back under the legislature, and came to exercise a dominating control over the election apparatus. They did, however, reduce the state debt and encouraged industrialization. In 1876, they changed their party name to Democrat. In 1887, a strong farmer's group began to lobby for reforms, and by 1890 an alliance of farmers had become effective enough to control the 1891 legislature. A railroad commission resulted, as well as colleges for women and for blacks. In 1892, farmers entered politics as the Populist Party, and in 1894, they combined with the Republicans to defeat the Democrats in the 1894 congressional and legislative elections. In 1895 and 1896, they elected both US senators and state officials. They were able to return county government to local rule and to enact economic reforms. In the Spanish-American War (1898), NC contributed three regiments, two white, one black. The 1st Regiment reached Havana, Cuba, on 11 December after the war was over; the other two never left the state. The only North Carolinians who saw military action were those in the regular services. The Democrats launched a campaign based on race prejudice in 1898, and regained control of the government in 1899. They adopted a suffrage amendment in 1900 which strongly reduced the black vote.

The development of industry was the most important NC economic factor during 1870-1900. The state had a mild climate, abundant water power, cheap labor, and great quantities of cotton, tobacco, and lumber. Governmental support of industry produced rapid increases in factories which produced cotton textiles, tobacco products and furniture. Large fortunes were accumulated by promoters of these industries. The manufac

turing enterprises resulted in a rapid increase in state wealth, numerous banks, railroad construction, and the growth of towns and cities. Unfortunately, NC lagged behind in social, cultural, and educational development. The highly successful industrialists joined the Democratic Party, and the party in turn became the guardian of their vested interests. Some minor labor movements began in 1880-1900, but they wielded little influence, the order of the day for laborers being long hours, low pay, child employment, and company exploitation. Agriculture remained the occupation by which most North Carolinians earned their livelihood. Despite the wartime destruction, lack of capital and credit, loss of slave labor, and high transportation costs, agriculture reached its prewar production levels by about 1875. This abundance resulted in prices which fell steadily from 1875 to 1900, causing much hardship among farmers.

From 1901-60, the Democratic Party dominated NC. In the 1901-17 period, NC's economic growth was great, as both industry and agriculture expanded. This was accompanied by notable improvements in education, newspapers, and cultural activity. In 1917, the US entered World War I, and NC contributed over 86,000 men, several training camp sites, and the manufacture of ships and munitions. After the end of the war in 1918, NC shared the country's materialism, speculative economic policy, and social and moral decay, which gave way to the severe depression of 1929-33. In 1933, the federal government began a broad program of economic recovery, social reform, and poverty relief. Then, in 1941, the US entered World War II. NC contributed sites for camps which trained over two million men, gave over 362,000 military personnel, and supplied vast amounts of war material. After the termination of the conflict in 1945, NC's industrial expansion continued, maintaining the state as the leading industrial state in the southeastern US, and as the world's largest producer of textiles, tobacco products, and wooden furniture.

One of the major ways of seeing the development of NC, and a way of particular interest to genealogists, is to follow the increasing population of the state (given in parentheses in thousands [K] after the years): 1675 (4K), 1701 (5K), 1707 (7K), 1715 (11K), 1729 (35K), 1752 (100K), 1765 (200K), 1771 (250K), 1786 (350K), 1790 (394K), 1800 (478K), 1810 (556K), 1820 (639K), 1830 (738K), 1840 (753K), 1850 (869K), 1860 (993K), 1870 (1071K), 1880 (1400K), 1890 (1618K), 1900 (1894K), 1910 (2206K), 1920 (2559K), 1930 (3170K), 1940 (3572K), 1950 (4062K), 1960 (4556K), 1970 (5084K), 1980 (5874K), 1990 (6656K).

Among the historic sites of genealogical interest are Alamance Battleground (at Alamance), Bennett Place (near Durham), Bentonville Battlefield (near Newton Grove), Brunswick Town (Brunswick), Cornwallis House (Wilmington), Elizabethan Garden (on Roanoke Island), Fort Caswell (near Southport), Fort Fisher (south of Wilmington), Fort Macon (near Beaufort),

Fort Raleigh National Historic Site (on Roanoke Island), Guilford Courthouse National Military Park (near Greensboro), Moore's Creek National Military Park (near Wilmington), Old Salem (Winston-Salem), and Tryon Palace (New Bern).

9. The NC counties

NC has had 116 counties (or precincts as they were called for some time). Three were renamed (Archdale, Pamptecough, Wickham), six were abolished (Albemarle, Bath, Bute, Clarendon, Fayette, Glasgow), and seven were ceded in 1790 to the US Government (Davidson, Greene, Hawkins, Sullivan, Sumner, Tennessee, Washington), later to become the state of TN. The 100 NC counties are shown in Figure 2. To locate a county consult the following alphabetical list, and notice its general region (W for west, WC for west central, C for central, NE for northeast, and SE for southeast). The small map in Figure 2 shows you the general region in which to search for the county. The present counties are: Alamance (C), Alexander (WC), Alleghany (WC), Anson (WC), Ashe (WC), Avery (WC), Beaufort (NE), Bertie (NE), Bladen (SE), Brunswick (SE), Buncombe (W), Burke (WC), Cabarrus (WC), Caldwell (WC), Camden (NE), Carteret (SE), Caswell (C), Catawba (WC), Chatham (C), Cherokee (W), Chowan (NE), Clay (W), Cleveland (WC), Columbus (SE), Craven (SE), Cumberland (C), Currituck (NE), Dare (NE), Davidson (WC), Davie (WC), Duplin (SE), Durham (C), Edgecombe (NE), Forsyth (WC), Franklin (C), Gaston (WC), Gates (NE), Graham (W), Granville (C), Greene (SE), Guilford (C), Halifax (NE), Harnett (C), Haywood (W), Henderson (W), Hertford (NE), Hoke (C), Hyde (NE), Iredell (WC), Jackson (W), Johnston (C), Jones (SE), Lee (C), Lenoir (SE), Lincoln (WC), Macon (W), Madison (W), Martin (NE), McDowell (W), Mecklenburg (WC), Mitchell (W), Montgomery (C), Moore (C), Nash (NE), New Hanover (SE), Northampton (NE), Onslow (SE), Orange (C), Pamlico (SE), Pasquotank (NE), Pender (SE), Perquimans (NE), Person (C), Pitt (NE), Polk (W), Randolph (C), Richmond (C), Robeson (C), Rockingham (C), Rowan (WC), Rutherford (W), Sampson (SE), Scotland (C), Stanly (WC), Stokes (WC), Surry (WC), Swain (W), Transylvania (W), Tyrrell (NE), Union (WC), Vance (C), Wake (C), Warren (C), Washington (NE), Watauga (WC), Wayne (SE), Wilkes (WC), Wilson (NE), Yadkin (WC), Yancey (W).

10. Recommended reading

A knowledge of the history of NC and of its local regions is of extreme importance for the tracing of the genealogies of its former inhabitants. This chapter has been a brief treatment of the history. Your next step should be the reading of one of these exceptionally good, short, one-volumed works:

__W. S. Powell, NC, A HISTORY, University of NC Press, Chapel Hill, NC, 1988.

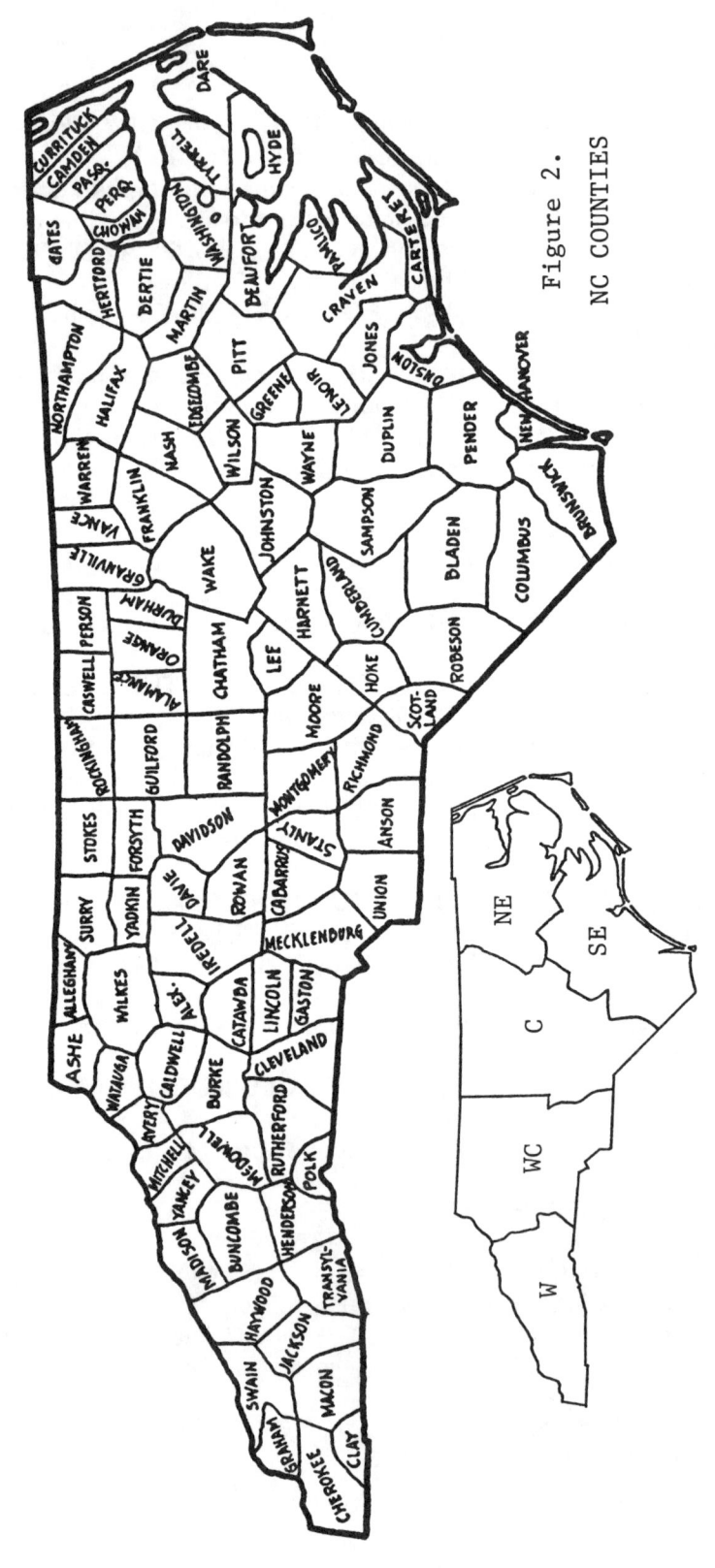

Figure 2. NC COUNTIES

___T. C. Parramore and D. C. Wilms, NC, THE HISTORY OF AN AMERICAN STATE, Prentice-Hall, Englewood Cliffs, NJ, 1983.

After this, it is recommended that you purchase and make good use of one of these one-volumed, detailed histories of the state and its peoples:

___H. T. Lefler and A. R. Newsome, NC: HISTORY OF A SOUTHERN STATE, University of NC Press, Chapel Hill, NC, 1973.
___W. S. Powell, NC THROUGH FOUR CENTURIES, Univ. of NC Press, Chapel Hill, NC, 1989.

If you care to go further, you may wish to employ one or more of the several multi-volumed histories of NC. Among the better ones are:

___S. Nathans, THE WAY WE LIVED IN NC, University of NC Press, Chapel Hill, NC, 1983, 5 volumes.
___H. T. Lefler, HISTORY OF NC, Lewis Historical Publishing Co., New York, NY, 1956, 2 volumes.
___R. D. W. Conner, NC: REBUILDING AN ANCIENT COMMONWEALTH, American Historical Society, Chicago, IL, 1929, 2 volumes.
___S. A. Ashe, HISTORY OF NC, Van Noppen, and Edwards and Broughton, Raleigh, NC, 1908 and 1925, 2 volumes.
___A. Henderson, NC, THE OLD NORTH STATE AND THE NEW, Lewis Publishing Co., Chicago, IL, 1941, 2 volumes.

In order to locate books dealing with certain time periods of NC and/or certain aspects of its history, consult:

___J. F. Steelman in D. C. Roller and R. W. Twyman, THE ENCYCLOPEDIA OF SOUTHERN HISTORY, LA State University Press, Baton Rouge, LA, 1979, pages 926-8.
___H. T. Lefler, A GUIDE TO THE STUDY AND READING OF NC HISTORY, University of NC Press, Chapel Hill, NC, 1969.
___J. J. Crow and L. E. Tise, WRITING NC HISTORY, University of NC Press, Chapel Hill, NC, 1979.

An excellent volume giving much detail about NC historical sites which are well worth visiting is:

___G. Scheer, III, NC, A GUIDE TO THE OLD NORTH STATE, Franklin and Co., New York, NY, 1982.

Details concerning the county formations, court houses, and records may be found in:

___D. L. Corbett, THE FORMATION OF THE NC COUNTIES, 1663-1943, NC State Archives, Raleigh, NC, 1975.
___School of Design, NC State University, 100 COURTHOUSES, University Graphics, NC State University, Raleigh, NC, 1978.
___C. C. Crittenden and D. Lacy, THE HISTORICAL RECORDS OF NC: COUNTY RECORDS, The NC Historical Commission, Raleigh, NC, 1938-9, 3 volumes.
___W. R. Draughon and W. P. Johnson, NC GENEALOGICAL REFERENCE, The Authors, Durham, NC, 1966.

__NC State Archives, GUIDE TO RESEARCH MATERIALS IN THE NC STATE ARCHIVES, SECTION B: COUNTY RECORDS, The Archives, Raleigh, NC. 1990.

Individual county histories will be listed in Chapter 4 of this book, and other historical works dealing with regions, counties, cities, and towns of NC are listed in:

__M. J. Kaminkow, US LOCAL HISTORIES IN THE LIBRARY OF CONGRESS, Magna Carta Book Co., Baltimore, MD, 1975, volume 2.

__P. W. Filby, A BIBLIOGRAPHY OF AMERICAN COUNTY HISTORIES, Genealogical Publishing Co., Baltimore, MD, 1985.

__G. Stevenson, NC LOCAL HISTORY, A SELECT BIBLIOGRAPHY, NCSA, Raleigh, NC, 1984.

LIST OF ABBREVIATIONS

A	=	Agricultural census records
C	=	Civil War Union veterans census records
CH	=	Courthouse(s)
FHC	=	Family History Center(s), Branches of FHL
FHL	=	Family History Library
I	=	Industrial census records
LDU	=	Library, Duke University
LGL	=	Large genealogical library(ies)
LL	=	Local library(ies)
LUNC	=	Library, University of NC
M	=	Mortality census records
N	=	Early NC census-like lists
NA	=	National Archives
NC	=	North Carolina
NCSA	=	NC State Archives
NCSL	=	NC State Library
P	=	Pensioner census records, Revolutionary War
R	=	Regular census records
RBNA	=	Regional Brances of the National Archives
RL	=	Regional library(ies)
S	=	Slaveholder census records

Chapter 2

TYPES OF RECORDS

1. Introduction

The state of North Carolina is relatively rich in genealogical source materials, even though there are notable gaps in the early years, and there are problems with the loss of records in court house (CH) fires, which were fairly common in the 18th and 19th centuries. A great deal of work has been done in accumulating, preserving, photocopying, transcribing, abstracting, printing, and indexing records. The best overall collection in existence is in the building at 109 East Jones Street in Raleigh. This building houses the North Carolina State Archives (NCSA) and the North Carolina State Library (NCSL). They have large holdings of historical, biographical, and genealogical books, microfilms (city records, county records, state records, federal records, Confederate records, newspapers, censuses, military records, manuscripts), Bible records, church records, colonial records, maps and atlases, and original documents, plus numerous indexes and finding aids.

Two subsidiary genealogically-related libraries also deserve mention. The first is the Library at the University of NC in Chapel Hill (LUNC). The second is the Perkins Library at Duke University in Durham (LDU). These libraries have extensive collections of historical and biographical volumes, manuscripts, family, personal, and business papers, newspapers, church records, and several special NC historical collections.

The Family History Library (FHL) in Salt Lake City, the largest genealogical library in the world, holds a large number of books and microfilm copies of books and original records relating to NC. The microfilms are made available to you through the Library's numerous branch Family History Centers (FHC), which are located all over the US. Included among these centers are ten in the state of NC.

In addition to the above collections, there are NC record collections in a number of large genealogical libraries (LGL) around the country, especially those in states near NC. Other collections, usually with an emphasis on a particular section of NC, are located in several good regional libraries (RL) in NC. Almost all of the NC counties have deposited their pre-1868 records (except deed and will books) in the NC State Archives (NCSA). The NC Archives also has microfilm copies of many of these deed and will books plus originals or microfilm copies of many records after 1868. This means that the resources of the FHL (FHC), the NCSA, and the NCSL should be used first, then if necessary, research can be continued in the appropriate county court house (CH). Finally, local libraries (LL) in the county seats and cities which are not county seats often have good materials relating to their

own areas. All of the archives, repositories, and libraries mentioned above will be discussed in detail in Chapter 3.

In this chapter, the many types of records which are available for NC genealogical research are discussed. Those records which are essentially <u>national</u> or <u>statewide</u> in scope will be treated in detail. Records which are basically <u>county</u> records will be mentioned and treated only generally, but detailed lists of them will be given in Chapter 4, where the major local records available for each of the 100 NC counties will be presented.

2. Bible records

During the past two hundred years it was customary for families with religious affiliations to keep vital statistics on their members in the family Bible. These records vary widely, but among the items that may be found are names, dates and places of birth, christening, baptism, marriage, death, and sometimes military service. Compilations of such Bible records have been made by the Daughters of the American Revolution (DAR) and by other agencies and individuals for various NC counties and areas. Bible records in the form of transcriptions, copies, and/or manuscripts are available in several places in NC: NCSA, NCSL, LUNC, LDU, RL, the Library at Wake Forest University in Winston-Salem, and in the collections of several other college, university, and local libraries. Microfilm copies of many of these are in the FHL and may be borrowed through its numerous FHC. In addition, Bible records may appear in published family genealogies and in genealogical periodical articles. These last two types of records, as well as manuscript sources, will be discussed in sections 18, 19, 23, and 32 of this chapter. So, this section will be devoted to Bible record compilations, both those which have been published and those which are gathered together in files or notebooks at various repositories.

Published and manuscript compilations of Bible records are generally found in five main forms: books, typed compilations, hand-written compilations, loose files, and microform copies of all of these. Many of these collections can be located by using the appropriate indexes at several important repositories. The indexes which refer to Bible records may be labelled something different than Bible records, so be sure and look under categories such as family records, genealogical records, manuscripts, name indexes, surname indexes, and don't overlook the listings under the counties.

_NC State Library, NCSL, Raleigh, NC.
_NC State Archives, NCSA, Raleigh, NC.
_Family History Library, FHL, Salt Lake City, UT.
_Family History Centers, FHC, all over the US, and many overseas.
_Southern Historical Collection, Library of the University of NC, LUNC, Chapel Hill, NC.

_Library of Duke University, LDU, Durham, NC.
_Rowan Public Library, Salisbury, NC.
In addition, RL sometimes have Bible record compilations relating to their own areas, as do LL. Also, LGL may have some of the NC Bible record compilations. In Chapter 4, those counties for which extensive Bible record compilations exist are indicated. Instructions regarding locating the repositories and then finding the Bible records in them will be presented in Chapter 3.

Among NC compilations of Bible records, there are some multi-county and state-wide publications. Included among them are:
_M. A. Lester, OLD SOUTHERN BIBLE RECORDS, Genealogical Publishing Co., Baltimore, MD, 1956-62 (1974).
_W. C. Spence and E. M. Shannonhouse, NC BIBLE RECORDS DATING FROM THE EARLY 18TH CENTURY, Shannonhouse, Elizabeth City, NC, 1974.
_NC BIBLE RECORDS, Capital Publishing Co., Cabin John, MD, 1936 (1983), Several series, numerous volumes.
_E. K. Kirkham, AN INDEX TO SOME OF THE FAMILY RECORDS OF THE SOUTHERN STATES, Everton Publishers, Logan, UT, 1980.

3. Biographies

There are several major national biographical works which contain sketches on nationally-prominent North Carolinians. If you suspect or know that your ancestor was that well known, consult:
_NATIONAL CYCLOPEDIA OF AMERICAN BIOGRAPHY, White Co., New York, NY, 1893- present, over 54 volumes, cumulative index for volumes 1-51.
_DICTIONARY OF AMERICAN BIOGRAPHY, Scribners, New York, NY, 1928-37, 20 volumes, cumulative index.
_THE 20TH CENTURY BIOGRAPHICAL DICTIONARY OF NOTABLE AMERICANS, Gale Research, Detroit, MI, 1968, 10 volumes.
_AMERICAN BIOGRAPHY: A NEW CYCLOPEDIA, American Historical Society, New York, NY, 1916-33, 54 volumes, cumulative index for volumes 1-50.
_ENCYCLOPEDIA OF AMERICAN BIOGRAPHY, NEW SERIES, American Historical Co., West Palm Beach, FL, 1934-present, 4 volumes.
Most of these works and about 750 more have been indexed in a multi-volumed set which gives the sources of over 6 million biographies, all arranged in alphabetical order of the names:
_M. C. Herbert and B. McNeil, BIOGRAPHY AND GENEALOGY MASTER INDEX, Gale Research Co., Detroit, MI, 1980-, with annual supplements. Also available for computer access as BIOBASE.
Several good biographical compilations for the state of NC or for sections of it exist. These volumes list persons who have attained some prominence

in the fields of law, agriculture, business, politics, medicine, engineering, science, military, teaching, public service, or philanthropy. Included are:

_S. A. Ashe and others, BIOGRAPHICAL HISTORY OF NC FROM COLONIAL TIMES TO THE PRESENT, Reprint Co., Spartanburg, SC, 1905 17 (1971), 8 volumes.

_M. W. Collier, BIOGRAPHIES OF REPRESENTATIVE WOMEN OF THE SOUTH, 1861-1923, Atlanta, GA, 1920-9, 5 volumes.

_R. D. W. Connor, MAKERS OF NC HISTORY, Thompson, Raleigh, NC, 1911.

_R. D. W. Connor, NC, 1584-1929, Reprint Co., Spartanburg, SC, 1928 (1973), volumes 3-4.

_R. D. W. Connor, W. K. Boyd, J. G. deR. Hamilton, and others, HISTORY OF NC, Lewis Publishing Co., Chicago, IL, 1919, volumes 4-6.

_CYCLOPEDIA OF EMINENT AND REPRESENTATIVE MEN OF THE CAROLINAS OF THE 19TH CENTURY, Reprint Co., Spartanburg, SC, 1892 (1973), volume 2.

_J. Dowd, SKETCHES OF PROMINENT LIVING NORTH CAROLINIANS, Edwards & Broughton, Raleigh, NC, 1888.

_W. H. Foote, SKETCHES OF NC, HISTORICAL AND BIOGRAPHICAL, NC Presbyterian Historical Society, Raleigh, NC, 1846 (1966).

_M. B. Haywood, BUILDERS OF THE OLD NORTH STATE, Raleigh, NC, 1968.

_A. Henderson, NC, THE OLD NORTH STATE AND THE NEW, Lewis Publishing Co., Chicago, IL, 1941, volumes 3-5.

_H. T. Lefler, HISTORY OF NC, Lewis Historical Publishing Co., New York, NY, 1956, volumes 3-4.

_NC BOOKLET, NC Society of the DAR, 1901-26, 23 volumes. [Many biographies.] Index by G. Stowell, NC College for Women Extension Bulletin, volume 1, issue 5, May, 1923, 27 pages.

_W. S. Powell, DICTIONARY OF NC BIOGRAPHY, University of NC Press, Chapel Hill, NC, 1979-, in progress, several volumes now published.

_W. S. Powell, NC LIVES, KY Historical Records Commission, Hopkinsville, KY, 1962.

_L. Rogers, TAR HEEL WOMEN, Warren, Raleigh, NC, 1949.

_J. H. Wheeler, HISTORICAL SKETCHES OF NC FROM 1584-1851, Genealogical Publishing Co., Baltimore, MD, 1851 (1974), 2 volumes.

_J. H. Wheeler, REMINISCENCES AND MEMORIES OF NC AND EMINENT NORTH CAROLINIANS, Genealogical Publishing Co., Baltimore, MD, 1884 (1966).

In the NCSA, there is an extensive biographical index which includes entries from over 12 NC biographical reference works:

_NC Archives, BIOGRAPHICAL INDEX, NCSA, Raleigh, NC.

Indexes in other libraries and archives in NC should be looked into. Likely places are LDU, FHL (FHC), RL (listed in Chapter 3, section 7), college and university repositories, and LL (listed in Chapter 4).

In addition to the above national, state, and regional biographical works, there are county and city biographical volumes which will be indicated under the counties in Chapter 4. Almost all the national, state, regional, county, and city biographical books are available at NCSL, LUNC, and LDU. Many are at FHL and microfilm copies may be borrowed through FHC. Many are also in RL in NC and some are available in LGL, particularly those near NC. The volumes relating to specific counties and cities are usually on the shelves of LL in the corresponding counties and cities.

4. Birth records

NC state law required births to be registered with the state beginning in 1913. Careful enforcement was not practiced, and it was 1917 before the registration reached a 90% complete level. Copies of birth certificates may be obtained from:

_Register of Deeds, County Court House, County Seat (see Chapter 4 for county seat name and zip code).

Copies of birth certificates are also available to family members, attorneys, insurance agencies, and certified genealogists from:

_NC Division of Health Services, Vital Records Branch, PO Box 2091, Raleigh, NC 27602.

Both sources require a fee for this service. When ordering birth records from either source, be sure and give them as many of the following as you can: full name, sex, race, names of parents, maiden name of mother, exact or approximate birth date, exact or approximate place of birth, your relationship to the person, and the reason you want the record (namely, genealogical research).

A few counties and cities of NC kept birth records for various periods of time before 1913, but in most cases, the records are quite incomplete. These pre-1913 records will be indicated in Chapter 4 under the county names. They are available in NCSA, in FHL, and through FHC. In addition, most counties have records of delayed birth certificates. These are certifications of their birth dates filed by persons who were born before 1913.

Birth certificates show some or all of the following: name, date of birth, county of birth, city or town of birth, hospital, residence of mother, sex of child, name of father, age of father, occupation of father, birth place of father, maiden name of mother, age of mother, birth place of mother, name of informant. Prior to the time when NC required birth registration (1913), other records may yield dates and places of birth along with the names of parents: Bible, biographical, cemetery, census, church, DAR, death, divorce, manuscript, marriage, military, mortuary, newspaper, pension, and published records. These are all discussed in other sections of this chapter. The finding of birth record articles in genealogical periodicals is also described in a separate section in this chapter.

5. Cemetery records

If you know or suspect that your ancestor was buried in a certain NC cemetery, the best thing to do is to write the caretaker of the cemetery, enclose an SASE, and ask if the records show your ancestor. If no luck is had, or no official caretaker can be located, try writing the local genealogical society, the local historical society, or the LL, inquiring about records for cemeteries in the area. Addresses for these organizations will be presented under the appropriate county in Chapter 4.

Another important cemetery record source is the numerous collections of cemetery records which have been made. Two very important state-wide indexes to thousands of gravestone inscriptions in NC are located in the NCSA:
_WPA CEMETERY INDEX, NCSA, Raleigh, NC. Also at FHL.
_NC UDC CONFEDERATE SOLDIER BURIAL INDEX, NCSA, Raleigh, NC.
Other collections have been made by the DAR (Daughters of the American Revolution), the state, regional, and local genealogical societies, and individuals. The main sources of NC cemetery records are NCSA, NCSL, the National DAR Library in Washington, DC, FHL, and FHC. In addition, LL often have records of the cemeteries of their own counties, and RL often have those in their regions. Some LGL outside of NC may also have records. The genealogical periodicals published in NC quite frequently carry cemetery listings (see section 19 in this chapter, and listings under counties in Chapter 4). Sizable numbers of compilations have been made by the DAR, but only some of them have been published. Others are still in type-written or handwritten form. The most complete collection of these is in the DAR Library, 1776 D Street, NW, Washington, DC 20006, although NCSA and NCSL has copies of many.

In your investigations in the above repositories, you will encounter several published cemetery record compilations. Among them will be the following:
_Mrs. J. S. Welborn, NC TOMBSTONE RECORDS, The Author, High Point, NC, 1938, 3 volumes.
_L. H. McEachern, NC GRAVESTONE RECORDS, The Author, Wilmington, NC, 1971-81, 10 volumes.
_CEMETERY RECORDS OF NC, Genealogical Society, Salt Lake City, UT, 1947-61, 8 volumes.
In Chapter 4, those counties for which local cemetery record compilations exist in printed, filmed, typed, or written form are indicated. Instructions for locating the above records will be presented in Chapter 3. Instructions for finding cemetery records in genealogical periodical articles are given in section 19 of this chapter.

6. Census records

Excellent ancestor information is available in nine types of census reports which have been accumulated for NC: some early lists in the period 1701-75, NC state (N), regular (R), agricultural (A), industrial (I), mortality (M), slaveholder (S), the special 1840 Revolutionary War pension census (P), and the special 1890 Union Civil War veteran census (C).

The early lists during 1701-75, even though incomplete, are valuable because they provide useful data during the colonial period. Among the most important of these are:
_1701 RESIDENTS, National Genealogical Society Quarterly, volume 53, pages 196-7.
_1740 JURYMEN, Colonial Records of NC, volume 4, pages 516-25.
_1741-52 COLONIAL CENSUS, Journal of NC Genealogy, volumes 12, 13.
_1754 PETITIONERS, Colonial Records of NC, volume 5, pages 164-6.
_1775 PETITIONERS, American Archives, 4th series, volume 3, pages 184-7.
_R. V. Jackson, EARLY AMERICAN SERIES, NC, Accelerated Indexing Systems, Bountiful, UT, 1980-, 7 volumes.

During 1785-7, a NC state census (N) was taken. Compliance with the legislature's mandate was half-hearted, some of the returns were lost, and some have not been identified with certainty. This means that the census is imperfect and incomplete. There are records for only 24 counties (out of 51), and most of these are partial. The surviving records, which list over 14,000 heads of household, have been published.
_A. K. Register, STATE CENSUS OF NC, 1784-7, Genealogical Publishing Co., Baltimore, MD, 1978, indexed.
The counties which are represented in these census records are indicated in the county listings in Chapter 4 by the symbol 1785N. This volume is available in NCSA, NCSL, LUNC, LDU, FHL (thus FHC), most RL, many LL, and some LGL.

Regular census records (R) are available for all NC in 1790, 1800, 1810, 1820, 1830, 1840, 1850, 1860, 1870, 1880, 1900, and 1910. The 1840 census and all before it listed the head of the household plus a breakdown of the number of persons in the household according to age and sex brackets. Beginning in 1850, the names of all persons were recorded along with age, sex, occupation, real estate, marital, and other information, including the state of birth. With the 1880 census and thereafter, the birthplaces of the mother and father of each person are also shown. Chapter 4 lists the regular census records (R) available for each of the 100 NC counties. Census data for 1790 were lost for three counties (Caswell, Granville,

Orange), so tax lists were substituted for them. Two printed transcripts of the 1790 records are available, both being indexed:

_US Bureau of the Census, HEADS OF FAMILIES AT THE FIRST CENSUS OF THE US, 1790, NC, Genealogical Publishing Co., Baltimore, MD, 1908(1978).
_W. Clark, STATE RECORDS OF NC, AMS Press, New York, NY, 1905 (1971), volume 26.

All other censuses cover all existing NC counties except the census records for 1810 (Craven, Greene, New Hanover, and Wake missing) and 1820 (Currituck, Franklin, Martin, Montgomery, Randolph, and Wake missing). Microfilms and transcripts of the original census records are available as:

_R. V. Jackson and G. R. Teeples, NC 1800 CENSUS. Accelerated Indexing Systems, Provo, UT, 1974.
_US Bureau of Census, SECOND CENSUS OF THE US, 1800, NC, The National Archives, Washington, DC, Microfilm M32, rolls 29-34.
_US Bureau of Census, THIRD CENSUS OF THE US, 1810, NC, The National Archives, Washington, DC, Microfilm M252, rolls 38-43.
_D. W. Potter, 1820 FEDERAL CENSUS OF NC, The Author, Tullahoma, TN, 1970-5, 56 volumes.
_US Bureau of Census, FOURTH CENSUS OF THE US, 1820, NC, The National Archives, Microfilm M33, rolls 80-5.
_US Bureau of Census, FIFTH CENSUS OF THE US, 1830, NC, The National Archives, Microfilm M19, rolls 118-25.
_US Bureau of Census, SIXTH CENSUS OF THE US, 1840, NC, The National Archives, Microfilm M704, rolls 354-74.
_US Bureau of Census, SEVENTH CENSUS OF THE US, 1850, NC, The National Archives, Microfilm M432, rolls 619-49.
_US Bureau of Census, EIGHTH CENSUS OF THE US, 1860, NC, The National Archives, Microfilm M653, rolls 886-919.
_US Bureau of Census, NINTH CENSUS OF THE US, 1870, NC, The National Archives, Microfilm M593, rolls 1121-66.
_US Bureau of Census, TENTH CENSUS OF THE US, 1880, NC, The National Archives, Microfilm T9, rolls 950-968.
_US Bureau of Census, TWELFTH CENSUS OF THE US, 1900, NC, The National Archives, Microfilm T623, rolls 1180-1225.
_US Bureau of Census, THIRTEENTH CENSUS OF THE US, 1910, NC, The National Archives, Microfilm T624, rolls 1095-1137.

The 1790 census records are indexed in the published volumes mentioned above, and indexes have been printed for the 1800, 1810, 1820, 1830, 1840, 1850, 1860, and 1870 census records. Chief among these indexes are:
_E. P. Bentley, INDEX TO THE 1800 CENSUS OF NC, Genealogical Publishing Co., Baltimore, MD, 1977.

_R. V. Jackson and G. R. Teeples, NC 1800 CENSUS INDEX, Accelerated Indexing Systems, Bountiful, UT, 1977.
_E. P. Bentley, INDEX TO THE 1810 CENSUS OF NC, Genealogical Publishing Co., Baltimore, MD, 1978.
_D. W. Smith, NC 1810 CENSUS INDEX, Heritage House, Thomson, IL, 1977.
_R. V. Jackson and G. R. Teeples, NC 1810 CENSUS INDEX, Accelerated Indexing Systems, Bountiful, UT, 1976.
_D. W. Potter, INDEX TO 1820 NC CENSUS, SUPPLEMENTED FROM TAX LISTS AND OTHER SOURCES, Genealogical Publishing Co., Baltimore, MD, 1978. [Note supplements for missing counties.]
_R. V. Jackson, G. R. Teeples, and D. Schaefermeyer, NC 1820 CENSUS INDEX, Accelerated Indexing Systems, Bountiful, UT, 1976.
_R. V. Jackson, D. Schaefermeyer, and G. R. Teeples, NC 1830 CENSUS INDEX, Accelerated Indexing Systems, Bountiful, UT, 1976.
_G. M. Petty, INDEX OF THE 1840 FEDERAL CENSUS OF NC, The Author, Columbus, OH, 1974.
_R. V. Jackson and G. R. Teeples, NC 1840 CENSUS INDEX, Accelerated Indexing Systems, Bountiful, UT, 1978.
_R. V. Jackson, G. R. Teeples, and D. Schaefermeyer, NC 1850 CENSUS INDEX, Accelerated Indexing Systems, Bountiful, UT, 1976.
_R. V. Jackson, NC 1860 CENSUS INDEX, Accelerated Indexing Systems, North Salt Lake City, UT, 1991.
_1870 NC CENSUS INDEX (HEADS OF HOUSEHOLDS), Precision Indexing, Bountiful, UT, 1989.

In addition to the above bound indexes, there is a microfilm index which contains only those families with a child 10 or under in the 1880 census. There are also complete microfilm indexes to the 1900 and 1910 censuses. The 1880 and 1900 censuses are indexed by a code called Soundex and the 1910 census is indexed by a code called Miracode. Librarians and archivists can show you how to use these codes. The indexes are:
_US Bureau of Census, INDEX (SOUNDEX) TO THE 1880 POPULATION SCHEDULES: NC, Microfilm T766, rolls 1-79.
_US Bureau of Census, INDEX (SOUNDEX) TO THE 1900 POPULATION SCHEDULES: NC, Microfilm T1063, rolls 1-168.
_US Bureau of Census, INDEX (MIRACODE) TO THE 1910 POPULATION SCHEDULES: NC, Microfilm T1271, rolls 1-178.

The indexes listed in the two previous paragraphs are exceptionally valuable as time-saving devices. However, some of the computer-printed volumes have enough errors in them that you need to use them with caution. If you do not find your ancestor in them, do not conclude that he or she is not in the state; this may mean only that your forebear has been accidentally omitted or that the name has been misread or misprinted. Once you have

located a name in the indexes, you can go directly to the reference in the census microfilms and read the entry. When indexes are not available (partially 1880), it is necessary for you to go through the census listings entry-by-entry. This can be essentially prohibitive for the entire state, so it is necessary for you to know the county in order to limit your search. Both the census records and the indexes are available in NCSA-NCSL, the National Archives in Washington, DC, FHL (thus FHC), and in some LGL, RL, and LL. Other LGL, RL, and LL have the printed indexes but not the microfilmed indexes or censuses. The Regional Branches of the National Archives also have the microfilmed indexes and censuses. They are located in or near Boston, New York, Philadelphia, Chicago, Atlanta, Kansas City, Fort Worth, Denver, San Francisco, Los Angeles, and Seattle. Their exact addresses and telephone numbers can be obtained from telephone directories in these cities or from the leaflet:
_National Archives, REGIONAL BRANCHES OF THE NATIONAL ARCHIVES, the Archives, Washington, DC, latest edition.
Also, the microfilmed census records and the microfilmed census indexes may be borrowed for you by your local library through interlibrary loan [from AGLL, PO Box 244, Bountiful, UT 84010]. There is a charge of a few dollars per roll.

Agricultural census records (A), also known as farm and ranch census records, are available for 1850, 1860, 1870, and 1880 for NC. These records list the name of the owner, size of farm or ranch, value of the property, crops, livestock, and other details. If your ancestor was a farmer (quite likely), it will be worthwhile to seek him in these records. No indexes are available, but you will probably know the county, so your entry-by-entry search should be fairly easy. Microfilm copies of the records are available in NCSA and in the National Archives in Washington, DC.

Industrial census records (I) are available for 1850, 1860, 1870, and 1880. There were fragmentary records of this sort in 1810 (added to the regular census), and a short record was taken in 1820. The records, particularly the later ones (1850, 60, 70, 80), list manufacturing firms which produced articles having an annual value of $500 or more. Given in the later records are the name of the firm, the owner, the product(s), the machinery, number of employees, and other details. No indexes are available, so knowledge of the county is helpful. The microfilmed records are available at NCSA and in the National Archives in Washington, DC.

Mortality census records (M) are available for the one-year periods 01 June (1849, 1859, 1869, 1879) to 31 May (1850, 1860, 1870, 1880). The records give information on persons who died in the year preceding the 1st of June of each of the census years 1850, 1860, 1870, 1880. The data contained in the compilations include name, age, sex, occupation, place of birth, and other information. The original records or

microfilmed copies of them are available at NCSA and in the National Archives in Washington, DC. The microfilms are:
_US Bureau of Census, MORTALITY CENSUS SCHEDULE MICROFILM, 1850, 1860, 1870, 1880: NC, The National Archives, Washington, DC, Microfilm GR1, rolls 1-5.
Indexed forms of the records are:
_NC MORTALITY CENSUS SCHEDULES, 1850, 1860, 1870, 1880, Accelerated Indexing Systems, Salt Lake City, UT, 1990-, 4 volumes.

Slaveholder census records (S) for 1850 and 1860 are available. The records list the names of slaveholders along with the number of slaves, but no names of slaves are given. No indexes have been compiled, so it is important to know the county. The microfilmed records are available in NCSA, the National Archives in Washington, DC, Regional Branches of the National Archives, FHL, FHC, and in some LGL, RL, and LL. The microfilms are:
_US Bureau of Census, SEVENTH CENSUS OF THE US, 1850: NC, National Archives, Washington, DC, Microfilm M432, rolls 650-656.
_US Bureau of Census, EIGHTH CENSUS OF THE US, 1860: NC, National Archives, Washington, DC, Microfilm M653, rolls 920-927.

Revolutionary War pensioners (P) were included in a special census taken in 1840. This compilation was an attempt to list all pension holders, however, there are some omissions and some false entries. The list and an index have been published:
_CENSUS OF PENSIONERS FOR REVOLUTIONARY OR MILITARY SERVICE, SIXTH CENSUS, 1840, INDEXED, Genealogical Publishing Co., Baltimore, MD, 1841 (1965, 1974).
This volume is available in NCSA, NCSL, FHL, FHC, in most LGL, in many RL, and in some LL.

Civil War Union veterans (C) were included in a special census taken in 1890, as were widows of the veterans. A few numerators have also inadvertently listed some Confederate veterans. These records are arranged by county, so it is well if you know your ancestor's county. However, since there is only one roll, it is relatively easy to go through. Microfilm copies of the records are available at NCSA, the National Archives, Branch Libraries of the National Archives, FHL, FHC, most LGL, and some RL. These records show the veteran's name, widow's name (if applicable), rank, company, regiment or ship, and other pertinent military data. The microfilms are:
_Veterans Administration, SPECIAL SCHEDULES OF THE ELEVENTH CENSUS (1890) ENUMERATING UNION VETERANS AND WIDOWS OF THE CIVIL WAR, National Archives, Washington, DC, Microfilm M123, roll 58.

7. Church records

Many NC families were affiliated with a church, and so for these families, there is the possibility of valuable records. The major denominations in 1860 were as follows (with the number of churches and the approximate number of members in thousands in parentheses): Baptist (780, 65K), Methodist (966, 61K), Presbyterian (182, 15K), Lutheran (38, 4K), Episcopal (53, 3K), Christian (44, 3K), Friends (22, 2K), Moravian (10, 2K), German Reformed (15, 2K), Roman Catholic (7, 0.4K). Since 1860, several other denominations have attained sizable memberships: United Church of Christ (previously Congregational, Evangelical, German Reformed, and some Lutheran), Church of God, Pentecostal Holiness, Wesleyan, Seventh Day Adventists, Latter Day Saints of Jesus Christ (Mormons). This gives a total of about 157K church members out of a total population of 993K, which means that about 16% of the population were affiliated with a church. The records of these churches often prove very valuable since they frequently contain information on one or more of the following items: birth, christenings, baptisms, confirmations, marriages, deaths, burials, admissions, dismissals, reprimands, contributions, officers, ministers. The data are particularly important for those years before county or state vital records were kept. Some of the church records have been copied into books or microfilmed, some have been deposited in denominational or state or private archives, but most remain in the individual churches.

Should you have the good fortune to know your ancestor's church, you can write directly. Send an SASE, a check for $5, your ancestor's name, and the pertinent dates, and request a search of the records, or information on the location of the records if they no longer have them. If they neither have nor know where the records are, dispatch a letter of inquiry to the NC denominational depository or headquarters, enclose an SASE, and ask them if they know where the records are. It is also well for you to check the locality catalog at your nearest FHC to see what church records are available for your ancestor's county in the FHL.

If, as is often the case, you do not know your ancestor's church, you will need to dig deeper. Knowing your ancestor's nationality, his NC county, where in the county he lived, and perhaps some other pertinent details, you should make a guess about his denomination. You may then write the NC depository or headquarters of that denomination, enclosing an SASE, and ask them what churches of their denomination were in your ancestor's section of the county during his dates there. Also request from them information on the locations of the records of these churches. If you are not sure of the denomination, you might examine maps of your ancestor's county which show churches. You can then observe the churches which are near your forebear's property, and you can write the churches and/or the appropriate denominations. Suitable maps for this may be found in:

_J. M. Ormond, THE COUNTRY CHURCH IN NC, Duke University Press, Durham, NC, 1931. [Maps of each NC county with church locations as of 1930.]

_G. P. Stout, HISTORICAL RESEARCH MAPS, NC COUNTIES, The Author, 1209 Hill St., Greensboro, NC 27408. [Detailed historical maps of NC counties showing rural churches.]

_Detailed maps of NC counties obtainable from Distribution Branch, US Geological Survey, Box 25286, Federal Center Bldg. 41, Denver, CO 80225. [Write them and ask for the free Index to Topographic Maps of NC; then order from it the maps you need.]

_See section 17, this chapter, for maps of NC counties in previous years.

The names and addresses of the NC denominational depositories or headquarters will now be given for each major denomination, along with pertinent notes concerning the denominations. These denominations will be treated alphabetically.

Baptist churches got their start in NC in 1727, and spread rapidly, this denomination having the largest membership of any since 1750. About this time Baptists split into Free Will Baptists and Regular Baptists, then in the 1830s, the Regular Baptists split into Primitive Baptists and Missionary Baptists. The Missionary Baptists belong to the Baptist State Convention of NC and the Southern Baptist Convention. Most black churches belong to the NC General Baptist Convention, Free Will Baptists have a state conference, but Primitive Baptists have only local associations. Most Baptist records contain only some of these items: membership lists, admissions, reprimands, dismissals, ordinations. The depository of the Missionary Baptists is:

_NC Baptist Historical Collection, Room 207, Smith Reynolds Library, Wake Forest University, Winston-Salem, NC 27109. [Books, manuscripts, records, periodicals, church records, files, indexes.]

The depository of Free Will Baptists is:

_Free Will Baptist Historical Collection, Moye Library, Mount Olive College, Mount Olive, NC 28365. [Books, manuscripts, papers, periodicals, indexes.]

The depository of Primitive Baptists is:

_The Primitive Baptist Library and Archives, Route 2, Elon College, NC 27244. [Books, histories, periodicals, church records, biographies.]

The Christian Church depository is:

_Historical Society of the Southern Convention of Congregational Christian Churches, Library, Elon College, Elon College, NC 27244. [Books, manuscripts, church records, directories, histories, biographies.]

And the depository of the Disciples of Christ denomination is:

_Carolina Discipliana Library, College Library, Atlantic Christian College, Wilson, NC 27893. [Books, periodicals, church records from 1830 forward.]

Episcopal churches, the successors to the Church of England which was the state church of the colony of NC, became organized in 1790. No Church of England parish registers from before the Revolutionary War survive. The records since 1790 contain considerable information, including baptisms, confirmations, marriages, membership lists, and burials. Episcopalians in NC have no denominational depository, each parish keeping its own records. Each of the three dioceses of NC has a historiographer who may be consulted about history and records:
_Diocese of East Carolina, 305 S. Third St., Wilmington, NC 29402.
_Diocese of Western NC, PO Box 368, Black Mountain, NC 28711.
_Diocese of NC, 201 St. Alban's Drive, Raleigh, NC 27619.

Friends or Quakers were probably the earliest religious group to put a missionary in NC, in 1672. Their growth and influence were considerable at first, but their opposition to the Revolution ended that. The church records they kept contain births, marriages, deaths, committee members, removals, and some other items. Many of the earlier data have been published.
_W. W. Hinshaw, ENCYCLOPEDIA OF AMERICAN QUAKER GENEALOGY, Vol 1, Genealogical Publishing Co., Baltimore, MD, 1969.
The denominational depository is:
_The Quaker Collection, Library, Guilford College, Guilford, NC 27410. [Books, church records, manuscripts, periodicals, histories, indexes, materials from 1680 forward.]

German Reformed churches, who came in the 1740s and who united in 1958 with other groups to form the United Church of Christ, have placed many of their records in:
_Records of the Classis of NC, Library, Catawba College, Salisbury, NC 28144.

Lutherans appeared in the 1740s in NC. At the present time, the Lutheran churches of NC belong to three different national groups: the Lutheran Church in America, the American Lutheran Church, and the Lutheran Church – Missouri Synod. The records which Lutherans kept included baptism, confirmation, communion, marriage, death, and burial. The depository of the Lutheran Church in America, to which most NC Lutheran churches belong, is:
_Archives of the NC Synod of the Lutheran Church in America, NC Synod Church House, PO Box 2049, Salisbury, NC 28144. [Church records, biographies of ministers, cemetery records, histories, manuscripts.]

Methodists did not come into NC until 1772, but following that their expansion was rapid. There have been several divisions of Methodists, one in 1792 to produce the Christian Church, but in 1939 a merger brought together most of the churches as the Methodist Church, then the Evangeli-

cal United Brethren were added in 1968 to form the United Methodist Church. Methodist records generally contain membership, baptism, marriage, and deceased member items. Denominational depositories include:
_Commission on Archives and History, The United Methodist Church, 39 Lake Shore Drive, Lake Junaluska, NC 28745. [Books, church agency records, correspondence.]
_NC Conference Depository, Methodist Building, 1307 Glenwood Avenue, Raleigh, NC 27605.
_United Methodist Church Archives, Drew University, Madison, NJ 07940.
_Western NC Conference Archives, The United Methodist Center, Shamrock Drive, Box 12005, Charlotte, NC 28205.

The <u>Moravians</u> (United Brethren) purchased land in NC and began to settle it in what is now Forsyth County in 1753. Their records include births, baptisms, marriages, deaths, funeral memoirs, and burials. The earliest records have been published in an 11-volumed set of books.
_A. L. Fries and others, RECORDS OF THE MORAVIANS IN NC, NCSA, Raleigh, NC, 11 volumes, each indexed.
The denominational depository is:
_Moravian Archives, Southern Province of the Moravian Church in America, 4 East Bank St., Winston-Salem, NC 27108. [Books, manuscripts, church records, letters, maps.]

The <u>Pentacostal Holiness</u> depositories are:
_Historical Commission, The Pentacostal Holiness Church, Falcon, NC 28342.
_Pentacostal Holiness Church, International Headquarters, PO Box 12609, Oklahoma City, OK 73157.
Several books by V. Synan on the history of the church are available from the headquarters.

The <u>Presbyterians</u> first entered NC as the Highland Scots and the Scotch-Irish during 1735-40. Their records include births, baptisms, marriages, deaths, admissions, dismissals, and reprimands. The denominational repository is:
_Historical Foundation of the Presbyterian and Reformed Churches, Montreat Assembly, Montreat, NC 28757. [Books, manuscripts, church histories, clergy papers, card catalog.]

The <u>Roman Catholic</u> NC depository has microfilm copies of all existing church records dating from 1820 to 1968:
_Roman Catholic NC Archives, 300 Cardinal Gibbons Drive, Raleigh, NC 27603.

A good reference volume discusses NC church records in more detail and/or gives other church record sources in NC, including books on the

history of various denominations in NC, official publications of religious groups, and published records:

_H. F. M. Leary and M. Stirewalt, NC RESEARCH: GENEALOGY AND LO-
   CAL HISTORY, NC Genealogical Society, Raleigh, NC, 1980, pages
   476-506.

In addition to the above depositories, other archives in NC have numerous church records: NCSA, LUNC, LDU, and some of those mentioned in sections 23 of this chapter and section 8 of Chapter 3. Remember also that FHL (FHC) has microfilm copies of numerous church records.

Many NC city and county histories contain histories of individual churches. These city and county histories are discussed in section 9 of this chapter. There are also histories of most denominations in NC. These city, county, and denominational histories may be located in NCSL, LUNC, and LDU, some are found in LGL, and those pertaining to their regions are in RL and LL. They may be located by looking under the city, county, and/or denominational name in the card catalogs of these libraries.

8. City directories

During the 19th century many larger cities in the US began publishing city directories. These volumes usually appeared erratically at first, but then began to come out annually a little later on. They list heads of households and workers plus their addresses and occupations. Businesses, institutions, churches, and organizations are also usually listed. The earliest series of directories in NC began in the following years: Asheville (1886), Charlotte (1875), Durham (1887), Greensboro (1884), Raleigh (1891), Wilmington (1875), and Winston-Salem (1884). The two 1884 listings are to a joint Greensboro, Salem, and Winston directory. In 1866, the first in a series of state-wide NC business directories was printed:

_BRANSON'S NC BUSINESS DIRECTORY, Levi Branson, Raleigh, NC,
   1866-96, 8 volumes.

In general, the smaller cities and towns of NC did not begin regular city directories until very late in the 19th century or in the 20th century. Many of these directories are available in the NCSL and the Library of Congress in Washington, DC, and those pertaining to specific regions are available in RL and LL. Those counties having cities with early city directories are listed in Chapter 4.

The telephone was invented in 1876-7, underwent rapid development, and became widespread fairly quickly. By the late years of the century telephone directories were coming into existence. Older issues can often be found in LL, and as the years have gone on, they have proved to be ever more valuable genealogical sources.

9. City and county histories

Histories for many NC counties and numerous NC cities have been published. These volumes usually contain biographical data on leading citizens, details about early settlers, histories, organizations, businesses, trades, and churches, and often list clergymen, lawyers, physicians, teachers, governmental officials, farmers, military men, and other groups. Several works which list many of these histories are:

_M. J. Kaminkow, US LOCAL HISTORIES IN THE LIBRARY OF CONGRESS, Magna Carta, Baltimore, MD, 1975, 4 volumes.
_G. Stevenson, NC LOCAL HISTORY, A SELECT BIBLIOGRAPHY, NCSA, Raleigh, NC, 1984.
_M. L. Thornton, A BIBLIOGRAPHY OF NC, 1598-1956, Greenwood, Westport, CT, 1973.
_P. W. Filby, A BIBLIOGRAPHY OF AMERICAN COUNTY HISTORIES, Genealogical Publishing Co., Baltimore, MD, 1985.

Most of the NC volumes in these bibliographies can be found in NCSL, LUNC, LDU, and the Library of Congress in Washington, DC, and some are usually in LGL. RL and LL are likely to have those relating to their particular areas. In Chapter 4, you will find listed under the counties various recommended county histories. Not all are listed, only the better one(s) for each county. There will also be an indication under each county which has city and/or town histories available.

10. Colonial record compilations

The colonial period for NC extended from 1663 until 1776, during which time the area was a colony either sponsored by or directly related to Great Britain. Many other sections in this chapter describe specific types of records relating to colonial NC, particularly sections 3, 4, 5, 7, 9, 11, 13, 15, 16, 17, 18, 22, 23, 24, 25, 32, 34, and 35. This section, therefore, will be made up of two sub-sections, one dealing with general reference materials to all the colonies (including NC), a second dealing with general reference materials to colonial NC.

Among the important genealogical materials relating to all the colonies are the following. They should be consulted as you search for your colonial NC ancestor. However, some of the volumes must be used with care, since some of the information in them is not from original sources, and is therefore often inaccurate.

_F. A. Virkus, THE ABRIDGED COMPENDIUM OF AMERICAN GENEALOGY, Genealogical Publishing Co., Baltimore, MD, 1968 (1925-42), 7 volumes. [425,000 names of colonial people]

_G. M. MacKenzie and N. O. Rhoades, COLONIAL FAMILIES OF THE USA, Genealogical Publishing Co., Baltimore, MD, 1966 (1907-20), 7 volumes. [125,000 names]

_H. Whittemore, GENEALOGICAL GUIDE TO THE EARLY SETTLERS OF AMERICA, Genealogical Publishing Co., Baltimore, MD, 1967 (1898-1906).

_T. P. Hughes and others, AMERICAN ANCESTRY, Genealogical Publishing Co., Baltimore, MD, 1968 (1887-9), 12 volumes.

_BURKE'S DISTINGUISHED FAMILIES OF AMERICA, Burke's Peerage, London, England, 1948.

_W. M. Clemens, AMERICAN MARRIAGE RECORDS BEFORE 1699, Genealogical Publishing Co., Baltimore, MD, 1867 (1926-30). [10,000 entries]

_C. E. Banks, PLANTERS OF THE COMMONWEALTH, Genealogical Publishing Co., Baltimore, MD, 1972.

_G. R. Crowther, III, SURNAME INDEX TO 65 VOLUMES OF COLONIAL AND REVOLUTIONARY PEDIGREES, National Genealogical Society, Washington, DC, 1964.

_M. B. Colket, Jr., FOUNDERS OF EARLY AMERICAN FAMILIES, Order of Founders and Patriots of America, Cleveland, OH, 1985.

_H. K. Eilers, NSDAC BICENTENNIAL ANCESTOR INDEX, National Society Daughters of American Colonists, Ft. Worth, TX, 1976.

_National Society of Daughters of Founders and Patriots of America, FOUNDERS AND PATRIOTS OF AMERICA INDEX, The Society, Washington, DC, 1975.

_National Society of the Colonial Dames of America, REGISTER OF ANCESTORS, The Society, Richmond, VA, 1979.

_N. Currer-Briggs, COLONIAL SETTLERS AND ENGLISH ADVENTURERS, Genealogical Publishing Co., Baltimore, MD, 1971.

_P. W. Filby and M. K. Meyer, PASSENGER AND IMMIGRATION LIST INDEX, Gale Research Co., Detroit, MI, 1981-, numerous volumes, including supplements. [Almost 2 million entries.]

_W. A. Crozier, KEY TO SOUTHERN PEDIGREES, Southern Book Co., Baltimore, MD, 1953 (1911). [7000 listings]

_G. F. T. Sherwood, AMERICAN COLONISTS IN ENGLISH RECORDS, Sherwood, London, England, 1932, 2 volumes.

_P. W. Coldham, ENGLISH ESTATES OF AMERICAN COLONISTS, Genealogical Publishing Co., Baltimore, MD, 1980-1, 3 volumes.

_P. W. Coldham, ENGLISH ADVENTURERS AND EMIGRANTS, 1609-1773, Genealogical Publishing Co., Baltimore, MD, 1984/5.

_P. W. Coldham, THE COMPLETE BOOK OF EMIGRANTS, 1607-60, Genealogical Publishing Co., Baltimore, MD, 1987.

_P. W. Coldham, THE COMPLETE BOOK OF EMIGRANTS IN BONDAGE, 1614-1775, Genealogical Publishing Co., Baltimore, MD, 1988.

_P. W. Coldham, THE BRISTOL REGISTERS OF SERVANTS SENT TO FOREIGN PLANTATIONS, 1654-86, Genealogical Publishing Co., Baltimore, MD, 1988.
_E. French, LIST OF EMIGRANTS TO AMERICA FROM LIVERPOOL, 1697-1707, Genealogical Publishing Co., Baltimore, MD, 1962.
_M. Ghirelli, A LIST OF EMIGRANTS FROM ENGLAND TO AMERICA, 1682-92, Magna Carta, Baltimore, MD, 1981.
_J. Wareing, EMIGRANTS TO AMERICA, INDENTURED SERVANTS RECRUITED IN LONDON, 1718-33, Genealogical Publishing Co., Baltimore, MD, 1985.
_F. Rider, THE AMERICAN GENEALOGICAL BIOGRAPHICAL INDEX, Godfrey Memorial Library, Middletown, CT, 1942-52, 48 volumes; THE AMERICAN GENEALOGICAL BIOGRAPHICAL INDEX, NEW SERIES, Godfrey Memorial Library, Middletown, CT, 1952-, in progress, over 140 volumes published.
_J. C. Hotten, THE ORIGINAL LISTS OF PERSONS OF QUALITY, Genealogical Publishing Co., Baltimore, MD, 1980 (1874).
_S. P. Hardy, COLONIAL FAMILIES OF THE SOUTHERN STATES OF AMERICA, Genealogical Publishing Co., Baltimore, MD, 1981 (1958).
_National Society Colonial Daughters of the 17th Century, LINEAGE BOOK, The Society, Rotan, TX, 1982 (1979). [2000 names]
_E. K. Kirkham, AN INDEX TO SOME OF THE FAMILY RECORDS OF THE SOUTHERN STATES, Everton Publishers, Logan, UT, 1980.

There are also important genealogical and historical compendia and indexes relating specifically to colonial NC which you should search.
_W. L. Saunders, THE COLONIAL RECORDS OF NC, AMS Press, New York, NY, 1967, 10 volumes, indexed in S. B. Weeks, INDEX TO THE COLONIAL AND STATE RECORDS OF NC, AMS Press, 1971, 4 volumes.
_M. E. E. Parker and W. S. Price, THE COLONIAL RECORDS OF NC, NCSA, Raleigh, NC, 1963-, 2nd series, 8 volumes so far.
_M. M. Hofmann, PROVINCE OF NC, 1663-1729, ABSTRACTS OF LAND PATENTS, Roanoke News Co., Weldon, NC, 1979.
_M. M. Hofmann, COLONY OF NC, 1735-64, 1765-75, ABSTRACTS OF LAND PATENTS, Roanoke News Co., Weldon, NC, 1983-4, 2 volumes.
_M. M. Hofmann, THE GRANVILLE DISTRICT OF NC, 1748-63, ABSTRACTS OF LAND GRANTS, Roanoke News Co., Weldon, NC, 1986-9, 4 volumes.
_MASTER CARD FILE INDEX TO NC LAND GRANTS, 1679-1959, Land Grant Office, Secretary of State, Administration Bldg., Raleigh, NC 27603. [Alphabetically by first letter of surname, then alphabetically by county. Don't fail to look in section entitled "No County Given".]
_ENTRY PAPERS FROM LORD GRANVILLE'S LAND OFFICE, 1729-1776, filed in NCSA, Raleigh, NC.

_1741-1868 NC MARRIAGE BOND INDEX, NCSA, Raleigh, NC. [Alphabetically by grooms and by brides.]

_J. B. Grimes, ABSTRACT OF NC WILLS COMPILED FROM ORIGINAL AND RECORDED WILLS IN THE OFFICE OF SECRETARY OF STATE, Genealogical Publishing Co., Baltimore, MD, 1910 (1980). [Wills during 1663-1760.] See additions in Journal of NC Genealogy, volume 11, pages 1575-7, volume 12, pages 1611-20, and in NC Genealogy, volume 13, pages 1820-3, 1946-8, volume 14, pages 2101-3.

_W. P. Johnson, NC ADMINISTRATION BONDS, 1680-1778, NC Genealogy, volume 17, pages 2639-49, volume 18, pages 2730-7, volume 19, pages 2803-11, volume 20, pages 2950-6, volume 21, pages 3107-9, and NC INVENTORIES AND SALES OF ESTATES, 1712-98, Journal of NC Genealogy, volume 9, pages 1217-29, NC Genealogy, volume 20, page 2943.

_T. W. Mitchell, NC WILLS, A TESTATOR INDEX, 1665-1900, The Author, Raleigh, NC, 1987, 2 volumes.

_NC Secretary of State, NC WILLS, 1663-1783, Records SS839-73, NCSA, Raleigh, NC. [Alphabetical by surname.]

_NC Secretary of State, NC ADMINISTRATOR'S BONDS, Records SS1-20, NCSA, Raleigh, NC. [Alphabetical by surname, from 1680 forward.]

_NC Secretary of State, INVENTORIES AND SALES OF ESTATES, 1733-98, Records SS889-98, NCSA, Raleigh, NC. [Alphabetical by surname.]

_Colonial Court Records, ESTATE RECORDS, 1669-1759, Records CCR180-5, NCSA, Raleigh, NC. [Alphabetical by surname.]

_F. Rider, THE AMERICAN GENEALOGICAL BIOGRAPHICAL INDEX, Godfrey Memorial Library, Middletown, CT, 1942-52, 49 volumes; also F. Rider, AMERICAN GENEALOGICAL BIOGRAPHICAL INDEX, Godfrey Memorial Library, Middletown, CT, new series, 1952-, in process, over 160 volumes published.

_WPA CEMETERY RECORD INDEX, NCSA, Raleigh, NC.

_W. S. Ray, RAY'S INDEX AND DIGEST TO HATHAWAY'S HISTORICAL AND GENEALOGICAL REGISTER, Genealogical Publishing Co., Baltimore, MD, 1945 (1971). [Use caution, somewhat inadequate.]

_R. V. Jackson and G. R. Teeples, EARLY AMERICAN COLONIAL AND PIONEER SERIES: NC, 1600-1789, Accelerated Indexing Systems, Salt Lake City, UT, 1980-6, 7 volumes.

_NC Society of the Colonial Dames of America, REGISTER OF THE NC SOCIETY, The Society, Raleigh, NC, 1955.

_M. B. Smallwood, SOME COLONIAL AND REVOLUTIONARY FAMILIES OF NC, The Author, St. Augustine, FL, 1964-73, 3 volumes.

_W. P. Haun, OLD ALBEMARLE COUNTY, NC, PERQUIMANS PRECINCT BIRTHS, MARRIAGES, DEATHS, AND FLESH MARKS, The Author, Durham, NC, 1980.

_F. L. Weis, THE COLONIAL CLERGY OF VA, NC, AND SC, Society of the Descendants of Colonial Clergy, Boston, MA, 1955.

_Daughters of the American Revolution, DAR PATRIOT INDEX, The Daughters, Washington, DC, 1966, 1979, 2 volumes.
_National Genealogical Society, INDEX OF REVOLUTIONARY WAR PENSION APPLICATIONS IN THE NATIONAL ARCHIVES, The Society, Washington, DC, 1976.

11. Court records

Among the most unexplored genealogical source materials are the court records of NC. They are often exceptionally valuable, giving information that is often unavailable anywhere else. It is therefore of great importance that you carefully examine all available court records. The court records of the state of NC may be conveniently viewed as being of two types: the county records and the state records. As the names imply, the county courts had jurisdiction within counties, and the state courts had regional (district) or state-wide jurisdiction. We will treat these two types of records separately in paragraphs to follow. But before we do, there are two difficulties that need to be faced if you are not to miss data. The first difficulty is that there were several types of courts, some no longer exist, some replaced others, some had their names changed, often their jurisdictions overlapped, and sometimes it is not clear just which court might have the sort of records that you need. The second difficulty is that in some cases the records of certain courts appear in record books, files, or loose papers under various titles and labels. These titles and labels do not always describe everything contained, and it is sometimes the case that various types of records may be intermixed or they may all appear in a single set of books. This is especially true in the early years. Fortunately, there is a simple rule that avoids these difficulties: look for your ancestor in all available court records which are applicable to the county and the times of your forebear. This means looking into all appropriate county records, all district records of your ancestor's district (each district containing many counties), and all statewide records.

Now, let us look at county courts and their records. From 1663-1868, the basic unit of county government was called the County Court (also known sometimes as the Precinct Court or as the Inferior Court of Pleas and Quarter Sessions). These courts usually met quarterly (in January, April, July, October) and conducted their business: wills, estates, probate, local government, minor civil and criminal matters, deeds, appointment of county officials, taxation, licenses, payments for services, roads, juries, petitions, bonds, land entries, inquests, illegitimacies, orphans, apprentices, incompetents, slaves, and other such matters. The proceedings of these courts were recorded in record volumes called minutes. Almost all of the available minute books for the NC County Courts or copies of them are in the NCSA. Many are also in the FHL. They are listed under the counties in Chapter 4. In 1806, NC established what was called a Superior Court in each county. This court dealt with more serious civil and criminal

matters. In 1868, the Superior Courts replaced the County Courts and therefore took over all of their functions. Superior Court minute books are made up of entries describing the matters brought before them. Most of these minute volumes which still exist or copies of them up to about 1900 are in the NCSA. Many are also found in the FHL. They are listed under the counties in Chapter 4. In 1806, another county-based court was established by NC law, the Court of Equity, which lasted for 62 years, it being abolished in 1868. This court had jurisdiction over civil matters such as unpaid debts, breached contracts, land disputes, estate controversies, and the like. Again the equity court minutes which survive or copies are in the NCSA. They are noted under the counties in Chapter 4.

In many court actions, numerous detailed documents having to do with the action were accumulated. They were usually bundled up or placed in an individual file. Many of these papers have been acquired by the NCSA. They have been separated and are filed under the county records as Marriage Records, Land Records, Estate Records, Civil Action Papers, and Criminal Action Papers, each chronologically. When you discover any sort of action in the court minutes, <u>always</u> check these record categories to see if detailed papers exist. You will know the date, which facilitates locating them.

Another type of court records that you need to seek are those known as dockets. A docket is a listing of brief notices of the actions and decisions of a court or a clerk of a court. In a way, they are finding aids to minutes and file papers since they list the cases involving them. Sometimes all kinds of cases are listed in one docket; at other times, separate dockets were kept for each kind of case or action, such as: summons, trial, judgment, indictment, petition, road, orphans, guardians, civil, criminal, lunacy, and so forth. The NCSA has almost all extant dockets or copies of them up to 1868. Those after 1868 are usually in the CH.

Other records kept by the county courts which are in the NCSA and which will be noted in Chapter 4 under the individual counties include: bonds of various types (administrator, guardian, marriage, appeal, road, bridge, ferry, bastardy, apprentice, officeholder, tavern), alien registrations, naturalizations, loyalty oaths, lunacy reports, livestock marks, professional registrations, records of strays, jury lists, and slave records. Some of these are available for every county and are to be found in the NCSA. The specific records for each of the counties are designated in Chapter 4.

<u>State court</u> records will now be discussed. There has been a sizable number of state and district courts in NC during its more than three centuries of history. Among the courts which you may encounter in your ancestor quest are these: General Court (1670–1754), Supreme Courts of Oyer

and Terminer, and General Gaol Delivery (1755-9), District Superior Courts (1760-72, 1778-1806), Courts of Oyer and Terminer (1773-7), Court of Conference (1800-5), Supreme Court (1805-68), Court of Chancery (1670-1775), Court of Ordinary (1665- 1775), Court of Claims (1670-1775), Palatine's Court (1669-1729), and Magistrates and Freeholders Courts (1715-93). Some of the early records have been published in:
_R. J. Cain, THE COLONIAL RECORDS OF NC, NCSA, Raleigh, NC, 1984-, 2nd series, 7 volumes.

The more important of the other records which have survived are in the NCSA, where they are available for searching:
_General Court Records (1670-1754), NCSA, in Record Group CCR.
_Supreme Courts of Oyer and Terminer, and General Gaol Delivery; few records survived; in the DSCR and CCR record groups at NCSA.
_District Superior Courts (1760-72, 1778-1806), involved districts centering at Edenton*, Fayetteville, Halifax, Hillsborough*, Morgan, New Bern, Salisbury*, and Wilmington; about half the records are extant; the districts with an asterisk indicate many surviving records; see records group DSCR and CCR in NCSA.
_Courts of Oyer and Terminer (1773-7), see special finding aid in NCSA for locating these records. Court of Conference and Supreme Court (1800-68); see card index of the original cases in NCSA; all cases since 1804 have been reported in the publication entitled NC REPORTS, Edwards and Broughton, and other publishers, Raleigh, NC, 1900-1, many volumes. [Index at front of each volume.]
_Court of Chancery (1670-1775), see following records in NCSA: CCR101-2, 180-5, 189, 191, SS309, 878, 888, DSCR206.403.1, CR028.929,112, ER7.
_Court of Ordinary (1665-1775), see following records in NCSA: SS1-20, 309.1, 838-873, 889-98, GO110ff.
_Court of Claims (1670-1775), Headrights, Entries, Warrants, and Patents, see the following records in NCSA: SS586-9, 727.3-727.6, 906, 946, 946.1-946.3, 947-8, GO110.
_Palatine's Court (1669-1729), see following records in NCSA: SS874.2, also books by Parker and Price mentioned above.
_Magistrates and Freeholders Courts (1715-93), to be found in county records and in these NCSA record groups: DSCR, SS, GO, and Treasurer and Comptroller's Office; also in DSCR5.002, 206.928.3, SS311, Treasurer and Comptroller Box 8, PC1629, GO128-9, LP2.

Further details on county and state court records along with general descriptions of their contents will be found in
_H. F. M. Leary and M. R. Stirewalt, NC RESEARCH, The NC Genealogical Society, Raleigh, NC, 1980, pages 223-256, 317-341.

When you begin to look into the county and state court records, you will discover a very distressing fact: not too many of them are indexed. This

means that you will need to go through them page-by-page, but the potential rewards are so good, you should take the time required.

12. DAR records

The Daughters of the American Revolution (DAR), in their quests for the family lines linking them to their Revolutionary War ancestors, have gathered many volumes of records of genealogical pertinence, and have published a sizable fraction of them. The NC chapters of the organization have provided a number of county records (chiefly court, deed, marriage, probate, will), Bible records, cemetery records, and family records. Copies of all these volumes (both published and nonpublished) are available in the DAR Library, 1776 D Street, NW, Washington, DC 20006. Many of them will be found in the NCSL, NCSA, FHL, and through FHC. Copies of some are in RL and in LGL, and the volumes of local interest will often be found in LL. Chapter 3 tells you how to locate these records, and in Chapter 4, these records are included in the listings for the various NC counties. Detailed lists of the volumes will be found in:
_DAR, LIBRARY CATALOG, National Society of the DAR, Washington, DC, 1982/8, 2 volumes.

13. Death records

NC law required deaths to be registered with the state beginning in 1913. Careful enforcement was not practiced, and it was about 1917 before the registration reached a 90% complete level. Copies of death certificates are available from three sources. Those for the entire period 1913-present are available from:
_Register of Deeds, County Court House, County Seat (see Chapter 4 for county seat name and zip code).
Copies of death certificates during 1913-29 may be obtained from:
_Archives and Records Section, Division of Archives and History, 109 East Jones Street, Raleigh, NC 27611.
Copies of death certificates from 1930-present are available to family members, attorneys, insurance agencies, and certified genealogists from
_NC Division of Health Services, Vital Records Branch, PO Box 2091, Raleigh, NC 27602.
All three sources require a fee for this service. When ordering death records from any of the sources, be sure and give them as many of the following as you can: full name, sex, race, names of parents, name of spouse, exact or approximate death date, exact or approximate place of death, your relationship to the person, and the reason you want the record (namely, genealogical research). Indexes to these post-1913 records are available at the above agencies and at the FHL (FHC).

A few counties and cities of NC kept death records for various periods of time before 1913, but in most cases, the records are quite incomplete. These pre-1913 records will be indicated in Chapter 4 under the county names. They are available in NCSA, FHL, and through FHC.

Death certificates show some or all of the following: full name, date of death, place of death, length of residence in US and the community, address, military participation, sex, race, marital status, name of spouse, age of spouse, birth date and place, age at death, occupation, parents' names and birth places, name and address of informant, cause of death, physician, undertaker, cemetery of burial or place of cremation, date of registration. Prior to the time NC required death registration (1913), other records may yield dates and places of death along with other details: Bible, biographical, cemetery, census, church, DAR, manuscript, military, mortuary, newspaper, pension, and published records. These are all discussed in other sections of this chapter. The finding of death record articles in genealogical periodicals is also described in a separate section in this chapter.

14. Divorce records

When NC was a colony, with the Church of England being the established religion, divorce was exceedingly rare. After the Revolution, the authority to grant divorce was vested in the General Assembly. However, they did not act very often, there now being only slightly under 300 petitions for divorce and somewhat over 200 petitions from women who sought the right to act independently from their husbands. These petitions and the legislative acts resulting from them will be found in the NCSA in two forms: (1) original records of the General Assembly, and (2) printed volumes which contain the proceedings of the House of Representatives and the Senate. These printed volumes may also be found in LUNC, LDU, and other major university libraries in NC. There are also two journal articles which list some of the records:

_B. R. McBride, DIVORCES AND SEPARATIONS GRANTED BY THE NC ASSEMBLY 1790-1908, NC Genealogical Society Journal, February, 1977.
_H. Roebuck, NC DIVORCE AND ALIMONY PETITIONS, 1813, NC Genealogical Society Journal, April, 1975.

In 1814, the authority to grant divorce was also given to the Superior Courts in the counties. Then, in 1835, new laws were passed which gave divorce-granting power only to the Superior Courts.

Since 1814, then, divorce records have been kept by the clerks of the Superior Courts, and since 1835, only by them. The minutes of these courts have the proceedings of the cases in them, but frequently there are also separate loose papers which describe the details of the case, often

including much genealogical data. The dates for which Superior Court records exist for the various counties are given in Chapter 4.

15. Emigration and immigration

Since NC was one of the thirteen original colonies, many early settlers came in (immigrated), and many of them or their descendants moved out (emigrated), chiefly to the west. Most of the early settlers came in from the other colonies, largely because of the lack of good ports in NC. There are a number of volumes available which list immigrants to the US. You should consult these volumes because they include both people who came directly to NC and people who came to some other colony or state and then to NC. The first set of volumes is an index to hundreds of ship passenger lists and contains almost 2 million entries. Each listing gives the full name of the immigrant, the names of accompanying relatives, ages, the date and port of arrival, and the source of the information. These volumes are:

_P. W. Filby and M. K. Meyer, PASSENGERS AND IMMIGRATION LISTS IN-DEX, Gale Research Co., Detroit, MI, 1981, 3 volumes, plus annual supplements.

Also of importance for locating passenger lists is:
_H. Lancour, R. J. Wolfe, and P. W. Filby, BIBLIOGRAPHY OF SHIP PAS-SENGER LISTS, 1538-1900, Gale Research Co., Detroit, MI, 1981.

Several other books of lists of ships' passengers are:
_J. C. Hotten, ORIGINAL LISTS OF PERSONS OF QUALITY, Genealogical Publishing Co., Baltimore, MD, 1974.
_C. Boyer, SHIP PASSENGER LISTS: THE SOUTH, 1538-1825, The Author, Newhall, CA, 1980.
_US National Archives and Records Service, GUIDE TO GENEALOGICAL RESEARCH IN THE NATIONAL ARCHIVES, The Service, Washington, DC, 1982, pages 41-57. [Includes NC ports of Beaufort (1865), Edenton (1820), New Bern (1820-45), Plymouth (1820, 1823, 1825, 1840), and Washington (1820-48), also nearby ports in VA and SC.]

A very important work for NC immigration and emigration is one which describes the migration routes and patterns for the state:
_M. W. Lewis, THE DEVELOPMENT OF EARLY IMMIGRANT TRAILS IN THE US EAST OF THE MS RIVER, National Genealogical Society, Washington, DC, 1962.

Then you can look into some works dealing exclusively with immigrants to NC. Among these are:
_T. Blethen and C. Wood, Jr., FROM ULSTER TO CAROLINA, THE MIGRA-TION OF THE SCOTCH-IRISH TO SOUTHWESTERN NC, //, 1986.
_C. Cunningham, MIGRATIONS, ACTUAL AND IMPLIED, TO AND FROM NC, Raleigh, NC, 1968.

_G. D. Bernheim, HISTORY OF THE GERMAN SETTLEMENTS AND OF THE LUTHERAN CHURCH IN NC AND SC, Reprint Co., Spartanburg, SC, 1872 (1972).
_D. Dobson, DIRECTORY OF SCOTS IN THE CAROLINAS, 1680-1830, Genealogical Publishing Co., Baltimore, MD, 1985.
_Genealogical Society of the Church of Jesus Christ of Latter Day Saints, INDEX TO INDIVIDUALS BORN OUTSIDE THE US AS ENUMERATED IN THE 1850 CENSUS OF NC, The Society, Salt Lake City, UT, 1972.
_A. Henderson, CONQUEST OF THE OLD SOUTHWEST, EARLY PIONEERS INTO THE CAROLINAS, VA, TN, AND KY, New York, NY, 1920.
_A. W. McLean, A HISTORY OF THE SCOTCH IN NC, Historical Commission, Raleigh, NC, typescript.
_D. G. Meyer, THE HIGHLAND SCOTS OF NC, University of NC Press, Chapel Hill, NC, 1966.
_A. R. Newsome, RECORDS OF EMIGRANTS FROM ENGLAND AND SCOTLAND TO NC, 1774-5, NC Historical Review, volume 11 (1934), numbers 1 & 2.
_W. S. Powell, THE PROPRIETORS OF CAROLINA, Tercentenary Committee, Raleigh, NC, 1963.
_R. W. Ramsey, CAROLINA CRADLE: SETTLEMENT OF THE NORTHWEST CAROLINA FRONTIER, 1747-62, University of NC Press, Chapel Hill, NC, 1964.
_J. W. Sames, FOUR STEPS WEST, THE FIRST DIVIDING LINE BETWEEN VA AND NC, KY AND TN, The Author, Versailles, KY, 1971.
_NC IMMIGRANTS, Family Puzzlers, 02 March 1971, No. 178, page 4.
_A. L. Fries, RECORDS OF THE MORAVIANS IN NC, Edwards & Broughton, Raleigh, NC, 1922.
_EMIGRATION FROM VA TO CAROLINA, William and Mary Quarterly, 2nd series, volume 7, page 235, and volume 14, page 95.
_V. P. Livingston, SOME MIGRATIONS FROM VA INTO NC, NC Genealogical Society Journal, volume 2 (1976), pages 122-9, 192-7; volume 3 (1977), pages 37-8, 108-13, 182-6, 229-32.

In addition to works on immigrants, there are also several volumes on **emigrants**, that is, people who migrated out of NC, to settle areas to the west. Among those that might help you in your search for a migratory NC progenitor are:
_NORTH CAROLINIANS IN GA, GA PIONEERS, volume 2, No. 2, page 24.
_H. B. Johnston, NORTH CAROLINIANS TO SC, GA GENEALOGICAL MAGAZINE, No. 40, Spring 1971, page 191.
_B. G. C. Cartwright and L. T. Gardiner, NC LAND GRANTS IN TN, 1778-91, The Authors, Memphis, TN, 1958 (1973).
_B. R. McBride, MIGRATIONS AS SHOWN BY POWERS OF ATTORNEY, NC Genealogical Society Journal, volume 3 (1977), pages 5-15, 116-27, 166-72, 233-41; volume 4 (1978), pages 52-7, 108-17,

177-87; volume 5 (1979), pages 37-42, 165-72; volume 6 (1980), pages 48-58, 125-34; and continuing.
Other materials on emigration and immigration relating to NC may be found in
_ O. K. Miller, MIGRATION, EMIGRATION, IMMIGRATION, Everton Publishers, Logan, UT, 1974, 1982, 2 volumes.
The above books are almost all in NCSL, LUNC, and LDU. Some are in RL, LGL, and LL. Many are in FHL, and thus are obtainable through FHC.

16. Ethnic records

In addition to the English, many other ethnic groups were involved quite early in the settlement of NC, as Chapter 1 indicated. Since most of these groups adhered to a particular religious affiliation, many publications relating to them need to be sought among church records. Instructions for locating these records were presented in section 7 of this chapter. Among the larger ethnic groups were the Huguenot French (1696-1708), Swiss and German at New Bern (1710), Welsh (1730), Scotch-Irish (1733- 1830), Highland Scotch (1735-55), Moravian German (1752), and other German (1760). Among the useful volumes relating to these groups are:

_ C. W. Baird, HISTORY OF THE HUGUENOT EMIGRATION TO AMERICA, Genealogical Publishing Co., Baltimore, MD, 1885 (1973). [Many genealogical data.]
_ J. P. M. Morand, LIBRARY CATALOG OR BIBLIOGRAPHY OF THE LIBRARY, Huguenot Society of America, Genealogical Publishing Co., Baltimore, MD, 1920 (1971). [Largest Huguenot collection.]
_ C. E. Lart, HUGUENOT PEDIGREES, Genealogical Publishing Co., Baltimore, MD, 1924-8 (1973). [Over 1500 names.]
_ H. F. Lee, THE HUGUENOTS IN FRANCE AND AMERICA, Genealogical Publishing Co., Baltimore, MD, 1843 (1973). [Many families.]
_ G. E. Reaman, THE TRAIL OF THE HUGUENOTS, Genealogical Publishing Co., Baltimore, MD, 1963 (1973).
_ G. D. Bernheim, HISTORY OF THE GERMAN SETTLEMENTS AND THE LUTHERAN CHURCH IN NC AND SC, Reprint Co., Spartanburg, SC, 1872 (1972).
_ C. Hammer, RHINELANDERS ON THE YADKIN, The Author, Salisbury, NC, 1965.
_ C. A. Hanna, THE SCOTCH-IRISH IN NORTH BRITAIN, NORTH IRELAND, AND NORTH AMERICA, Genealogical Publishing Co., Baltimore, MD, 1902 (1968).
_ A. W. McLean, A HISTORY OF THE SCOTCH IN NC, NCSA, Raleigh, NC, typed manuscript.
_ J. P. MacLean, AN HISTORICAL ACCOUNT OF THE SETTLEMENTS OF SCOTCH HIGHLANDERS IN AMERICA, Genealogical Publishing Co., Baltimore, MD, 1900 (1968).

_D. G. Meyer, THE HIGHLAND SCOTS OF NC, University of NC Press, Chapel Hill, NC, 1961 (1966).
_D. Dobson, DIRECTORY OF SCOTS IN THE CAROLINAS, 1680-1830, Genealogical Publishing Co., Baltimore, MD, 1986.
_A. L. Fries and others, RECORDS OF THE MORAVIANS IN NC, NCSA, Raleigh, NC, 1922-69, 11 volumes.
_L. T. Reichel, THE MORAVIANS IN NC, Genealogical Publishing Co., Baltimore, MD, 1857 (1968).
_S. B. and M. E. Henshaw, CAROLINA QUAKERS, Yearly Meeting, Greensboro, NC, 1972.
_W. W. Hinshaw, ENCYCLOPEDIA OF AMERICAN QUAKER GENEALOGY, Genealogical Publishing Co., Baltimore, MD, 1948 (1969), volume 1.

Other useful volumes will be found listed in:
_O. K. Miller, MIGRATION, EMIGRATION, IMMIGRATION, Everton Publishers, Logan, UT, 1974-81, 2 volumes.

These volumes may be found in NCSL, LUNC, and LDU. Many of them are in RL and LGL. Some are in FHL, and thus are available through FHC. Some are also in LL.

The Indians of NC constitute a notable ethnic group. The Tuscarora (up to 1713) and the Cherokee were the major nations. There are a number of federal, state, and county records which are pertinent to genealogical searchers. These records are described in the following:
_National Archives and Records Service, GUIDE TO GENEALOGICAL RESEARCH IN THE NATIONAL ARCHIVES, The Service, Washington, DC, 1982, Chapter 11, pages 159-170.
_D. Spindel, INTRODUCTORY GUIDE TO INDIAN-RELATED RECORDS TO 1876 IN THE NCSA, NCSA, Raleigh, NC, 1977.
_E. E. Hill, GUIDE TO RECORDS IN THE NATIONAL ARCHIVES RELATING TO AMERICAN INDIANS, National Archives and Records Service, Washington, DC, 1982.
_D. W. Siler, EASTERN CHEROKEES, A CENSUS OF THE CHEROKEE NATION IN NC, AL, AND GA IN 1851, Polyanthos, Cottonport, LA, 1972.
_T. G. Mooney, EXPLORING YOUR CHEROKEE ANCESTRY, Cherokee National Historical Society, Tahlequah, OK, 1987.
_S. Hoskins, CHEROKEE BLOOD NEWSLETTER, PO Box 22261, Chattanooga, TN 37422.

The blacks of NC constitute another important ethnic group. Again there are sizable federal, state, county, and private records which are especially pertinent to blacks. Details of many of these records are given in the following:
_National Archives and Records Service, GUIDE TO GENEALOGICAL RESEARCH IN THE NATIONAL ARCHIVES, The Service, Washington, DC, 1982, Chapter 12, pages 173-185.

_T. W. Mitchell, PRELIMINARY GUIDE TO RECORDS RELATING TO BLACKS IN THE NC STATE ARCHIVES, NCSA, Raleigh, NC, 1980.

Excellent manuscript collections are in NCSA, LUNC, and LDU.

17. Gazetteers, atlases, and maps

Detailed information regarding NC geography is exceptionally useful to the genealogical searcher, especially with regard to land records. They usually mention locations in terms requiring an understanding of local geographical features. Several sorts of geographical aids are useful in this regard: gazetteers, atlases, and maps. Gazetteers are volumes which list geographical features (towns, villages, crossroads, settlements, districts, rivers, streams, creeks, hills, mountains, valleys, coves, lakes, ponds), locate them, and sometimes give a few details concerning them. An atlas is a collection of maps in book form. An exceptionally valuable NC gazetteer is:

_W. S. Powell, THE NC GAZETTEER, University of NC Press, Chapel Hill, NC, 1968. [20,000 entries.]

And four useful atlases are:

_J. W. Clay, NC ATLAS, University of NC Press, Chapel Hill, NC, 1975.
_J. C. Gioe, NC, HER COUNTIES, HER TOWNSHIPS, AND HER TOWNS, The Researchers, Indianapolis, IN, 1975.
_W. Thorndale and W. Dollarhide, MAP GUIDE TO THE US FEDERAL CENSUSES, 1790-1920, AGLL, Bountiful, UT, 1986.
_R. E. Lonsdale, ATLAS OF NC, University of NC Press, Chapel Hill, NC, 1967.

A number of earlier atlases are available for NC, its counties, and some of its cities. Many of these are listed in:

_C. E. LeGear, US ATLASES, Library of Congress, Washington, DC, 1950-3, 2 volumes.

Those counties and cities for which atlases before 1900 are available are indicated in Chapter 4.

There are several books which list NC maps and indicate sources of them or which give descriptions of map collections:

_D. S. Clark, INDEX TO MAPS OF NC IN BOOKS AND PERIODICALS, The Author, Fayetteville, NC, 1976.
_F. B. Lavey and K. H. Wood, BIBLIOGRAPHY OF NC GEOLOGY, MINERALOGY, AND GEOGRAPHY, NC Geological and Economic Survey, Raleigh, NC, 1909, pages 268-362. [Lists 784 maps of NC and its counties during 1590-1909.]
_W. P. Cummings, THE SOUTHEAST IN EARLY MAPS, University of NC Press, Chapel Hill, NC, 1962. [Large map bibliography.]
_W. P. Cummings, NC IN MAPS, NCSA, Raleigh, NC, 1966.

_G. Stevenson, MAPS AND OTHER CARTOGRAPHIC RECORDS IN THE NC STATE ARCHIVES, NCSA, Raleigh, NC, 1974. [Over 3000 maps.]
_National Archives and Records Service, GUIDE TO CARTOGRAPHIC RECORDS IN THE NATIONAL ARCHIVES, The Service, Washington, DC, 1971. [Almost 2 million maps, many for NC.]
_J. R. Hebert, PANORAMIC MAPS OF ANGLO-AMERICAN CITIES IN THE LIBRARY OF CONGRESS, The Library, Washington, DC, 1974. [Maps available for Asheville (1891, 1912), Black Mountain (1912), Durham (1891), Greensboro (1891), Hendersonville (1913), Hickory (1907-8), High Point (1913), Raleigh (1872), Rocky Mount (1907), Statesville (1907-8), Wilson (1908), Winston-Salem (1891).]
_R. W. Stevenson, LAND OWNERSHIP MAPS IN THE LIBRARY OF CONGRESS, The Library, Washington, DC, 1967. [County maps which show names of owners on their land: Alamance (1893), Bladen (1885), Brunswick (1864?), Catawba (1886), Cleveland (1886), Davidson (1890), Durham (1887), Hertford (1863), Orange (1891), Wake (1870).]
_D. L. Corbitt, THE FORMATION OF THE NC COUNTIES, 1663-1943, NCSA, Raleigh, NC, 1950 (1975). [Maps of county formation with geographical detail on the boundaries.]

Five sources of detailed maps of NC counties can provide you with excellent assistance as you attempt to locate your progenitor's land and as you look for streams, roads, bridges, churches, cemeteries, towns, and cities in the vicinity. The _first_ of these sources is the US Department of Agriculture Soil Survey Maps of NC Counties. Although these maps are out of print, they are available at NCSA and LUNC. The _second_ of these sources is the US Geological Survey, which has mapped the whole state of NC and has issued a series of hundreds of detailed maps. These maps are available at very reasonable cost. Write the following address and ask for the Index to Topographic Maps of NC and a Map Order Form:
_Distribution Branch, US Geological Survey, Box 25286, Denver Federal Center, Denver, CO 80225.
The _third_ source is the NC Department of Transportation. They have published highway maps of the NC counties, and these are available for purchase from:
_NC Department of Transportation, Division of Highways, Highway Building, Raleigh, NC 27611
The earlier issues of these maps had far more detail of interest to genealogists, but they are out of print, and must be consulted in NCSA and/or LUNC. The _fourth_ and _fifth_ sources of detailed county maps are two private cartographers. They have drawn and reproduced historical maps of the counties which show early settlers, roads, streams, bridges, towns, settlements, churches, cemeteries, and mountains. They are:
_G. P. Stout, HISTORICAL RESEARCH MAPS OF NC COUNTIES, Stout Map Co., 1209 Hill St., Greensboro, NC 27408.

_F. Hughes, NC COUNTY RESEARCH MAPS, PO Box 549, Jamestown, NC 27282.

The two best map collections in NC are those at the LUNC and the NCSA. Each of them has well over 3000 maps. Those available in the NCSA are indicated in the work by Stevenson mentioned in the second paragraph before this one. Most of the volumes mentioned in this section are available in NCSL, LUNC, and LDU. Some of them are generally available in RL, LGL, FHL, and through FHC.

18. Genealogical indexes for NC

There are a number of genealogical indexes for the colony and state of NC which list very large numbers of names. These are of considerable utility because they may save you going through many small volumes as you search for your NC forebears:

_W. R. Draughon and W. P. Johnson, NC GENEALOGICAL REFERENCE, The Authors, Durham, NC, 1966.
_F. Rider, AMERICAN GENEALOGICAL-BIOGRAPHICAL INDEX, Godfrey Memorial Library, Middletown, CT, 1942-52, 1st series, 48 volumes; 1952-, new series, over 150 volumes.
_J. B. Grimes, ABSTRACTS OF NC WILLS, AND NC WILLS AND INVENTORIES, 1663-1760, Genealogical Publishing Co., Baltimore, MD, 1910-2 (1967), 2 volumes.
_F. A. Olds, AN ABSTRACT OF NC WILLS, 1760-1800, Genealogical Publishing Co., Baltimore, MD, 1954 (1978).
_T. W. Mitchell, NC WILLS, A TESTATOR INDEX, 1665-1900, The Author, Raleigh, NC, 1987, 2 volumes.
_CENSUS INDEXES FOR 1785-7, 1790, 1800, 1810, 1820, 1830, 1840, 1850, 1860, 1880, 1900, 1910, see section 6, this chapter.
_SURNAME INDEX and INTERNATIONAL GENEALOGICAL INDEX at FHL and FHC.
_MASTER INDEX OF MARRIAGE BONDS, 1741-1868, NCSA, Raleigh, NC.
_S. B. Weeks, INDEX TO COLONIAL AND STATE RECORDS OF NC, AMS Press, New York, NY, 1909-1914 (1971), volumes 27-30.
_C. E. Ratcliff, NC TAXPAYERS, 1679-1790, Genealogical Publishing Co., Baltimore, MD, 1984/7, 2 volumes.
_R. V. Jackson, EARLY AMERICAN SERIES, NC, Accelerated Indexing, Bountiful, UT, 1980-5, 7 volumes.
_CARD CATALOGS at NCSL, LUNC, and LDU.
_NC Genealogical Society, INDEX OF NC ANCESTORS, The Society, Raleigh, NC, 1981/4, 2 volumes.
_DAR of NC, ROSTER OF SOLDIERS FROM NC IN THE AMERICAN REVOLUTION, Genealogical Publishing Co., Baltimore, MD, 1972.

_M. M. Hofmann, PROVINCE OF NC, 1662-1729, ABSTRACTS OF LAND PATENTS, Roanoke News Co., Weldon, NC, 1979.
_M. M. Hofmann, COLONY OF NC, 1735-64, 1765-75, ABSTRACTS OF LAND PATENTS, The Author, Roanoke Rapids, NC, 1833-4, 2 volumes.
_M. M. THE GRANVILLE DISTRICT OF NC, 1748-63, ABSTRACTS OF LAND GRANTS, Roanoke News Co., Weldon, NC, 1986-9, 4 volumes.
_MASTER INDEX OF NC LAND GRANTS, 1679-1959, Land Grant Office, Secretary of State, Administration Building, Raleigh, NC.
_L. H. Manarin and W. T. Jordan, NC TROOPS, 1861-5, A ROSTER, NCSA, Raleigh, NC, 1966-, 8 volumes, more to follow.
_WPA CEMETERY INDEX, NCSA, Raleigh, NC.
_US War Department, INDEX TO COMPILED SERVICE RECORDS OF VOLUNTEER SOLDIERS WHO SERVED IN THE REVOLUTIONARY WAR FROM NC, National Archives, Washington, DC, National Archives, Washington, DC, Microfilm Publications M257, 2 rolls.
_US War Department, INDEX TO THE COMPILED SERVICE RECORDS OF CONFEDERATE ARMY VOLUNTEERS FROM NC, National Archives, Washington, DC, Microfilm Publication M230, 43 rolls.
_W. S. Ray, INDEX AND DIGEST TO HATHAWAY'S REGISTER, Genealogical Publishing Co., Baltimore, MD, 1971.

19. Genealogical periodicals

Several genealogical periodicals and history periodicals carrying some genealogical data have been or are being published in NC. These journals or newsletters contain genealogies, local histories, genealogical records, family queries and answers, book reviews, and other pertinent information. If you had a NC progenitor, you will find it of great value to subscribe to one or more of the state-wide periodicals, as well as to any periodicals published in the region or county where he/she lived. The major NC state-wide periodicals are:
_NC GENEALOGICAL SOCIETY JOURNAL, NC Genealogical Society, Reprint Co., Spartanburg, NC 29304.
_NC GENEALOGY, edited by W. P. Johnson, Raleigh, NC, 1955-. Originally called THE NORTH CAROLINIAN.
_JOURNAL OF NC GENEALOGY, Raleigh, NC. 1962-6.
_THE CAROLINA GENEALOGIST, Heritage Papers, Danielsville, GA 30633, 1969-.
_NC GENEALOGICAL AND HISTORICAL NEWS, Cumberland Gap, TN 37224, bimonthly.
_NC HISTORICAL AND GENEALOGICAL RECORD, Forest City, NC, 1932-3.
_NC HISTORICAL AND GENEALOGICAL REGISTER, Raleigh, NC, 19003.
_CAROLINAS GENEALOGICAL SOCIETY BULLETIN, 107 Washington St., Monroe, NC 28110, quarterly, 1964-.

_CAROLINA COMMENTS, NC Division of Archives and History, 109 East Jones St., Raleigh, NC 27611, bimonthly, 1952-.
_NC HISTORICAL REVIEW, NC Division of Archives and History, 109 East Jones St., Raleigh, NC 27611, quarterly, 1924-.
_NC BOOKLET, NC DAR, Raleigh, NC, 1901-26.

Periodicals which serve regions in NC include these:
_QUARTERLY REVIEW OF THE EASTERN NC GENEALOGICAL SOCIETY, Eastern NC Genealogical Society, PO Box 395, New Bern, NC 28560, quarterly, 1974-.
_BULLETIN OF THE VA-NC PIEDMONT GENEALOGICAL SOCIETY, The VA-NC Piedmont Genealogical Society, PO Box 2272, Danville, VA 24541, quarterly, 1979-.

Among the better and more useful of the county publications are:
_(Buncombe County) A LOT OF BUNKUM, Old Buncombe County Genealogical Society, PO Box 2122, Asheville, NC 28801, 10 issues annually, 1980-.
_(Burke County) BURKE COUNTY GENEALOGICAL SOCIETY NEWSLETTER, PO Box 661, Morganton, NC 28655, quarterly.
_(Currituck County) JOURNAL OF THE CURRITUCK COUNTY HISTORICAL SOCIETY, Currituck County Historical Society, Currituck, NC 27929, 1973-.
_(Gaston County) GASTON COUNTY HISTORICAL BULLETIN, Gaston County Historical Society, Gastonia, NC 28052, 1954-.
_(Guilford County) GUILFORD GENEALOGIST, Guilford County Genealogical Society, PO Box 9693, Greensboro, NC 27429, 1974-, quarterly.
_(Iredell County) IREDELL TRACKS, PO Box 946, Statesville, NC 28677, quarterly.
_(Iredell County) NEWSLETTER OF THE GENEALOGICAL SOCIETY OF IREDELL COUNTY, Genealogical Society of Iredell County, Rte. 10, Box 178, Statesville, NC 28677, quarterly, 1978-.
_(Johnston County) JOHNSTON COUNTY GENEALOGICAL SOCIETY NEWSLETTER, Johnston County Genealogical Society, Public Library of Johnston County, Smithfield, NC 27577, quarterly, 1975-.
_(Lincoln County) BITS AND PIECES, Lincoln County Historical Association, Rte. 1. Box 315, Denver, NC 28037, quarterly, 1976-.
_(Mecklenburg County) MECKLENBURG GENEALOGICAL SOCIETY QUARTERLY, PO Box 32453, Charlotte, NC 28232.
_(Perquimans County) PERQUIMANS COUNTY HISTORICAL SOCIETY YEARBOOK, (Perquimans County Historical Society, PO Box 652, Hertford, NC 27944, annual, 1958/9- (except for 1960/1 and 1961/ 2).
_(Randolph County) GENEALOGICAL JOURNAL, Randolph County Genealogical Society of the Randolph County Historical Society, 201 Worth Street, Asheboro, NC 27201, quarterly, 1977-.
_(Randolph County) NORTH RANDOLPH HISTORICAL SOCIETY QUARTERLY, North Randolph Historical Society, Randleman, NC, quarterly, 1966-73.

_(Robeson County) ROBESON COUNTY REGISTER, 1012 South Kings Drive, Charlotte, NC 28283, quarterly.
_(Rockingham County) JOURNAL OF ROCKINGHAM COUNTY HISTORY AND GENEALOGY, Rockingham County Historical Society, PO Box 84, Wentworth, NC 27375, semiannual, 1976-.
_(Rowan County) JOURNAL OF THE GENEALOGICAL SOCIETY OF ROWAN COUNTY, PO Box 4305, Salisbury, NC 28144, quarterly.
_(Rowan County) ROWAN COUNTY REGISTER, PO Box 1948, Salisburg, NC 28144, quarterly.
_(Rutherford County) BULLETIN OF THE GENEALOGICAL SOCIETY OF OLD TRYON COUNTY, Genealogical Society of Old Tryon County, PO Box 938, Forest City, NC 28043, quarterly, 1973-.
_(Wilkes County) WILKES GENEALOGICAL SOCIETY BULLETIN, Wilkes Genealogical Society, PO Box 1629, North Wilkesboro, NC 28659, quarterly, 1973-.
_(Wilkes County) BULLETIN OF GENEALOGICAL SOCIETY OF THE ORIGINAL WILKES COUNTY, North Wilkesboro, NC, 1967-72.
_(Yadkin County) YADKIN COUNTY HISTORICAL AND GENEALOGICAL SOCIETY JOURNAL, PO Box 1250, Yadkinville, NC 27055.
_(Yancey County) FAMILIES OF YANCEY COUNTY, PO Box 1035, North Highlands, CA 95660, quarterly.

Most of the above periodicals will be found in NCSL and LUNC, some in LDU and FHL (and thus through FHC), some in LGL and RL, and those pertaining to local areas in LL.

Not only do articles pertaining to NC genealogy appear in the above publications, they are also printed in other genealogical periodicals. Fortunately, indexes to major genealogical journals are available:
_For periodicals published 1858-1952, consult D. L. Jacobus, INDEX TO GENEALOGICAL PERIODICALS, Genealogical Publishing Co., Baltimore, MD, 1973.
_For periodicals published 1957-62, consult the annual volumes by I. Waldenmaier, ANNUAL INDEX TO GENEALOGICAL PERIODICALS AND FAMILY HISTORIES, The Author, Washington, DC, 1957-8-9-60-1-2.
_For periodicals published 1962-9 and 1974-, consult the annual volumes by various editors, E. S. Rogers, G. E. Russell, L. C. Towle, C. M. Mayhew, and others, GENEALOGICAL PERIODICAL ANNUAL INDEX, various publishers, most recently Heritage Books, Bowie, MD, 1962-9, 1974-.
_For periodicals published 1847-1985, then annually 1986-present, consult Allen County Public Library Foundation, PERIODICAL SOURCE INDEX, The Foundation, Fort Wayne, IN, 1986-.

These index volumes will be found in NCSL, LUNC, and FHL (available through FHC), most LGL, some RL, and a few LL. In them, you should consult all general NC listings, then all listings under the counties which

concern you, as well as listings under family names (if included in the indexes).

20. Genealogical societies

In the state of NC various societies for the study of genealogy, the accumulation of data, and the publication of the materials have been organized. The state and regional societies include:

_(State-wide) NC GENEALOGICAL SOCIETY, PO Box 1492, Raleigh, NC 27602.
_(State-wide) CAROLINAS GENEALOGICAL SOCIETY, 107 Washington St., Monroe, NC 28110.
_(Regional) BROAD RIVER GENEALOGICAL SOCIETY, PO Box 2261, Shelby, NC 28150.
_(Regional) EASTERN NC GENEALOGICAL SOCIETY, PO Box 395, New Bern, NC 28560.
_(Regional) GENEALOGICAL SOCIETY OF OLD TRYON COUNTY, PO Box 938, Forest City, NC 28043.
_(Regional) SOUTHWESTERN NC GENEALOGICAL SOCIETY, 101 Blumenthal, Murphy, NC 28906.
_(Regional) VA-NC PIEDMONT GENEALOGICAL SOCIETY, PO Box 2272, Danville, VA 24541.

There are also genealogical societies whose interests are more local, most usually county-wide. Some of the organizations publish regular journals or newsletters containing data they have gathered, queries from their members, book reviews, and items of general interest.

The members of regional and local societies are generally well informed about the genealogical resources of their regions, and often can offer considerable help to non-residents who had progenitors in the area. Among the major county genealogical societies are:
_(Alamance County) ALAMANCE COUNTY GENEALOGICAL SOCIETY, PO Box 3052, Burlington, NC 27215.
_(Albemarle County) ALBEMARLE GENEALOGICAL SOCIETY, PO Box 87, Currituck, NC 27929.
_(Alexander County) ALEXANDER COUNTY GENEALOGICAL SOCIETY, Route 2, Box 331, Hiddenite, NC 28636.
_(Allegheny County) ALLEGHANY HISTORICAL-GENEALOGICAL SOCIETY, PO Box 817, Sparta, NC 28675.
_(Beaufort County) BEAUFORT GENEALOGICAL SOCIETY, PO Box 1089, Washington, NC 27889.
_(Buncombe County) OLD BUNCOMBE COUNTY GENEALOGICAL SOCIETY, PO Box 2122, Asheville, NC 28802.
_(Burke County) BURKE COUNTY GENEALOGICAL SOCIETY, PO Box 661, Morganton, NC 28655.

_(Caldwell County) CALDWELL COUNTY GENEALOGICAL SOCIETY, PO Box 2476, Lenoir, NC 28645.
_(Catawba County) CATAWBA COUNTY GENEALOGICAL SOCIETY, PO Box 2406, Hickory, NC 28603.
_(Cumberland County) CUMBERLAND COUNTY GENEALOGICAL SOCIETY, PO Box 53299, Fayetteville, NC 28305.
_(Davidson County) GENEALOGICAL SOCIETY OF DAVIDSON COUNTY, PO Box 1665, Lexington, NC 27292.
_(Davie County) DAVIE COUNTY HISTORICAL AND GENEALOGICAL SOCIETY, 371 North Main St., Mocksville, NC 27028.
_(Duplin County) DUPLIN COUNTY HISTORICAL SOCIETY, PO Box 130, Rose Hill, NC 28458.
_(Forsyth County) FORSYTH COUNTY GENEALOGY SOCIETY, PO Box 5715, Winston-Salem, NC 27113.
_(Guilford County) GUILFORD COUNTY GENEALOGICAL SOCIETY, PO Box 9693, Greensboro, NC 27408.
_(Harnett County) HARNETT COUNTY GENEALOGICAL SOCIETY, PO Box 474, Dunn, NC 28334.
_(Henderson County) HENDERSON COUNTY GENEALOGICAL AND HISTORICAL SOCIETY, 432 N. Main St., Hendersonville, NC 28793.
_(Hyde County) HYDE COUNTY HISTORICAL SOCIETY, Genealogical Committee, Route 1, Box 74, Fairfield, NC 27826.
_(Iredell County) GENEALOGICAL SOCIETY OF IREDELL COUNTY, PO Box 946, Statesville, NC 28677.
_(Johnston County) JOHNSTON COUNTY GENEALOGICAL SOCIETY, Public Library of Johnston County, Smithfield, NC 27577.
_(Lee County) LEE COUNTY GENEALOGICAL AND HISTORICAL SOCIETY, PO Box 547, Broadway, NC 27505.
_(Mecklenburg County) OLDE MECKLENBURG GENEALOGICAL SOCIETY, PO Box 32453, Charlotte, NC 28232.
_(Montgomery County) MONTGOMERY COUNTY HISTORICAL SOCIETY, PO Box 161, Mt. Gilead, NC 27306.
_(Moore County) MOORE COUNTY GENEALOGICAL SOCIETY, PO Box 56, Carthage, NC 27327.
_(Pasquotank County) PASQUOTANK HISTORICAL AND GENEALOGICAL SOCIETY, PO Box 523, Elizabeth City, NC 27909.
_(Randolph County) RANDOLPH COUNTY GENEALOGICAL SOCIETY OF THE RANDOLPH COUNTY HISTORICAL SOCIETY, 201 Worth St., Asheboro, NC 27203.
_(Richmond County) RICHMOND COUNTY HISTORICAL SOCIETY, PO Box 1056, Rockingham, NC 28379.
_(Rowan County) GENEALOGICAL SOCIETY OF ROWAN COUNTY, PO Box 4305, Salisbury, NC 28144.
_(Stanley County) STANLEY COUNTY GENEALOGICAL SOCIETY, PO Box 31, Albemarle, NC 28001.

_(Surry County) SURRY COUNTY GENEALOGICAL ASSOCIATION, PO Box 997, Dobson, NC 27017.
_(Tryon County) GENEALOGICAL SOCIETY OF OLD TRYON COUNTY, INC., Box 938, Forest City, NC 28043.
_(Wake County) WAKE COUNTY GENEALOGICAL SOCIETY, PO Box 17713, Raleigh, NC 27619.
_(Wilkes County) WILKES GENEALOGICAL SOCIETY, PO Box 1629, North Wilkesboro, NC 28659.
_(Yadkin County) YADKIN HISTORICAL SOCIETY, PO Box 1250, Yadkinville, NC 27055.

It is advisable for you to join the NC GENEALOGICAL SOCIETY as well as any regional and/or county organization which is in your ancestor's area. All correspondence with such societies should be accompanied by an SASE.

21. Historical societies

In addition to genealogical societies, NC has numerous historical societies. Some of these societies, but not all, deal with genealogical interests in addition to their historical pursuits. Even if they do not carry out much genealogical work as such, their efforts will be of considerable interest to you, since they deal with the historical circumstances through which your ancestor lived. It is often well for you to dispatch an SASE and an inquiry to one or more asking about membership, genealogical interests if any, and publications. Among the historical societies are to be found the following. Those listed are ones which maintain at least one of these: library, book collection, archives, manuscript collection, genealogical projects.
_(State-wide) NC LITERARY AND HISTORICAL ASSOCIATION, 109 East Jones St., Raleigh, NC 27611.
_(State-wide) HISTORICAL SOCIETY OF NC, 109 East Jones St., Raleigh, NC 27611.
_(Allegheny County) ALLEGHENY HISTORICAL-GENEALOGICAL SOCIETY, PO Box 817, Sparta, NC 28675.
_(Anson County) ANSON COUNTY HISTORICAL SOCIETY, 210 East Wade St., Wadesboro, NC 28170.
_(Brunswick County) LOWER CAPE FEAR HISTORICAL SOCIETY, INC., 126 S. 3rd St., Wilmington, NC 28401.
_(Camden County) CAMDEN COUNTY HISTORICAL SOCIETY, Camden, NC 27921.
_(Carteret County) BEAUFORT HISTORICAL ASSOCIATION, 138 Turner St., Beaufort, NC 28516; and CARTERET HISTORICAL RESEARCH ASSOCIATION, PO Box 1722, Beaufort, NC 28516.
_(Caswell County) CASWELL COUNTY HISTORICAL ASSOCIATION, PO Box 278, Yanceyville, NC 27379.

_(Catawba County) CATAWBA COUNTY HISTORICAL ASSOCIATION, 1716 South College Dr., Newton Grove, NC 28658.
_(Cleveland County) CLEVELAND COUNTY HISTORICAL ASSOCIATION, PO Box 1335, Court Square, Shelby, NC 28150.
_(Cumberland County) CUMBERLAND COUNTY HISTORICAL SOCIETY, 312 DeVane St., Fayetteville, NC 28305.
_(Davidson County) DAVIDSON COUNTY HISTORICAL ASSOCIATION, 1 South Main St., Lexington, NC 27292.
_(Duplin County) DUPLIN COUNTY HISTORICAL SOCIETY, 416 East Main St., Wallace, NC 28466.
_(Guilford County) GREENSBORO HISTORICAL MUSEUM, 130 Summit Ave., Greensboro, NC 27401.
_(Halifax County) HALIFAX COUNTY HISTORICAL ASSOCIATION, 301 West Burnette Ave., Enfield, NC 27823.
_(Hyde County) HYDE COUNTY HISTORICAL SOCIETY, PO Box 159, Engelhard, NC 27824.
_(Johnston County) JOHNSTON COUNTY HISTORICAL SOCIETY, 305 Market St., Smithfield, NC 27577.
_(Jones County) JONES COUNTY HISTORICAL SOCIETY, PO Box 219, Trenton, NC 28585.
_(Madison County) MADISON COUNTY HISTORICAL SOCIETY, PO Box 236, Marshall, NC 28753.
_(Mecklenburg County) MECKLENBURG HISTORICAL ASSOCIATION, PO Box 35032, Charlotte, NC 28235; and MINT MUSEUM OF HISTORY, 2700 Randolph Rd., Charlotte, NC 27601.
_(Moore County) MOORE COUNTY HISTORICAL ASSOCIATION, PO Box 324, Southern Pines, NC 28387.
_(Nash County) NASH COUNTY HISTORICAL ASSOCIATION, 4009 Lochinvar Ln., Rocky Mount, NC 27801.
_(Onslow County) ONSLOW COUNTY HISTORICAL SOCIETY, PO Box 5203, Jacksonville, NC 28540.
_(Orange County) CHAPEL HILL HISTORICAL SOCIETY, PO Box 503, Chapel Hill, NC 27514.
_(Pasquotank County) PASQUOTANK HISTORICAL AND GENEALOGICAL SOCIETY, PO Box 523, Elizabeth City, NC 27909.
_(Perquimans County) PERQUIMANS COUNTY HISTORICAL SOCIETY, PO Box 652, Hertford, NC 27944.
_(Person County) PERSON COUNTY HISTORICAL SOCIETY, PO Box 887, Roxboro, NC 27573.
_(Pitt County) PITT COUNTY HISTORICAL SOCIETY, PO Box 5063, Greenville, NC 27834.
_(Randolph County) RANDOLPH COUNTY HISTORICAL SOCIETY, 201 Worth St., Asheboro, NC 27203.
_(Rockingham County) ROCKINGHAM COUNTY HISTORY SOCIETY, PO Box 84, Wentworth, NC 27375.

_(Sampson County) SAMPSON COUNTY HISTORICAL SOCIETY, PO Box 422, Clinton, NC 28328.
_(Stanly County) STANLY COUNTY HISTORICAL SOCIETY, 813 West Main St., Albemarle, NC 28001.
_(Stokes County) STOKES COUNTY HISTORICAL SOCIETY, PO Box 250, Germanton, NC 27019.
_(Yadkin County) YADKIN COUNTY HISTORICAL SOCIETY, East Main St., Yadkinville, NC 27055.

Useful compilations of historical organizations of NC are:
_A DIRECTORY OF NC HISTORICAL ORGANIZATIONS, NC Department of Cultural Resources, Raleigh, NC, latest edition.
_DIRECTORY OF HISTORICAL AGENCIES IN THE US AND CANADA, American Association of State and Local History, Nashville, TN, latest edition.

22. Land records

One of the most important types of NC genealogical records is that type which deals with land. This is because NC throughout most of its history has been predominantly an agricultural state with its population largely rural. In addition, land up until the present century was widely available and quite inexpensive. This means that the great majority of North Carolinians owned land and therefore their names appear in land records. There are basically two kinds of land records in NC. (1) The _first_ kind involves the transactions by which the government originally transferred the land to its first private owner. These transactions made use of documents and records called entries, warrants, surveys, plats, grants, and patents. (2) The _second_ kind of land records are those by which one private owner transferred the land to another private owner. These transactions were evidenced by documents and records called deeds and mortgages.

The _first_ category of land records (transfers from the proprietary, colonial, or state government to the first private owner) dates from 1669. In the period 1669-1729 the eight proprietors of Carolina granted land, during 1729-1776 land was granted by the Crown Colony of NC and the agents of Earl Granville, a proprietor who had refused to sell to the Crown, and from 1778-present land has been granted by the state. The steps in the granting process were as follows. (1) The person desiring land made application (a land entry) to a land office for the piece of property he wanted. (2) The land officer then issued the applicant a warrant for the land, the warrant being an order to the surveyor to survey and describe the land. The land officers were the Secretary of State (1669-1776), or Granville's agents (1729-1776), or the County Entry Taker (1778-present). (3) The surveyor surveyed the land, drew a map (plat) of it, and sent copies to the Secretary of State or Granville's agent (for the Granville section). (4) The Secretary of State or Granville's agent (for the Granville section) then re-

corded the grant (also called patent) and/or kept a copy, and returned the original to the new owner. After 1777, the new owner had to record his grant with the Register of Deeds in his county.

Fortunately, the land grants themselves can be readily found because of an excellent index in the Land Grant Office of the NC Secretary of State:
_MASTER CARD FILE INDEX TO NC LAND GRANTS, 1679-1959, Land Grant Office, Secretary of State, New Legislative Bldg., Raleigh, NC 27603.
This index is arranged by first letter of the surname, then under that letter alphabetically by county. Also be sure to look for your progenitor in the section of the index labelled NO COUNTY NAME GIVEN. Basic information concerning the grant will be found on the index card (grantee, county, acres, date of entry, date of grant, patent book and page where grant is recorded, and file number). The file number on the index card will direct you to a folder containing the warrant and the surveyor's plat. There is also a separate index designated Lord Granville and a finding aid for further Granville records, both of which you must use:
_LORD GRANVILLE INDEX, Land Grant Office, NC Secretary of State, New
_GRANVILLE GRANT CARD FILE, NCSA, Raleigh, NC.Legislative Bldg., Raleigh, NC.
Nine excellent recent books publish abstracts of land patents (grants) for the period 1663-1775:
_M. M. Hofmann, PROVINCE OF NC, 1663-1729, ABSTRACTS OF LAND PATENTS, Roanoke News Co, Weldon, NC, 1979.
_M. M. Hofmann, COLONY OF NC, 1735-64, ABSTRACTS OF LAND PATENTS, Roanoke News Co., Weldon, NC, 1983.
_M. M. Hofmann, COLONY OF NC, 1765-75, ABSTRACTS OF LAND PATENTS, Roanoke News Co., Weldon, NC, 1984.
_M. M. Hofmann, THE GRANVILLE DISTRICT OF NC, 1748-63, ABSTRACTS OF LAND GRANTS, Roanoke News Co., Weldon, NC, 1986-9, 5 volumes.
_C. N. Smith, BRITISH COLONIAL LAND GRANTS IN NC, Westland Publications, McNeal, AZ, 1981.

In addition to state land-grant records, there are also some county records relating to land grants. Some land entries were recorded in County Court Minutes before 1775, but after 1777, all land entries had to be taken to and recorded by the County Entry Taker, and had to be surveyed by the County Surveyor. Sometimes the Clerk of the County Court acted as the Entry Taker, and after 1869, the Register of Deeds often assumed this function. These officials recorded their transactions in books usually entitled LAND ENTRIES and RECORDS OF SURVEYS. The surveyor's maps (plats) may be included in these books or they may be separately recorded in books entitled PLAT BOOK, MAP BOOK, or RECORD OF PLATS. In

Chapter 4 under the county listings, the dates for which these records are available will be given.

From about 1768-96, settlers from NC and VA were making their way into what is now TN, but which was then NC territory. During the time period 1778-90, NC issued land grants (patents) to persons in the following NC counties which would end up in the state of TN: Davidson, Greene, Hawkins, Sullivan, Sumner, Tennessee, Washington. TN land records, both purchased land grants and military grants, are indexed in a card file in the Land Grant Office:

_CARD INDEX TO TN LAND GRANT RECORDS, Land Grant Office, NC Secretary of State, New Legislative Bldg., Raleigh, NC.

The cards in this index are arranged under the county name (those above plus Carter, Giles, Grainger, Jefferson, Knox, Robertson, Sevier, Smith, Williamson, and Wilson), the Eastern, Middle, and Western TN Districts, and a heading NO COUNTY GIVEN. Each card refers to a grant book and page and a file number, which will lead you the grant record and to a folder with original records. Land records relating to previous NC counties now in TN, are also abstracted in the books:

_G. F. Burgner, NC LAND GRANTS IN TN, 1778-91, Southern Historical Press, Easley, SC, 1981.
_B. G. C. Cartwright and L. T. Gardiner, NC LAND GRANTS IN TN, 1778-91. The Authors, Memphis, TN, 1958 (1973).
_THE TN BEE-HIVE, OR EARLY 1778-91 NC LAND GRANTS IN THE VOLUNTEER STATE, Washington, DC, 1948.

The second category of land records (transfers between individual private persons or groups) consists of deeds, land divisions, land suits, mortgages, processions, real estate conveyances, and tax records. These records were kept by the NC counties. They are indicated under the county listings in Chapter 4 along with the dates for which they are available. The NCSA has microfilm copies or originals for all records before 1868 and for many after 1868. The CH in the counties have original deed records up to the present and other types of land records from 1868 up to now. Microfilm copies of many of the records are held by FHL, and are therefore available through FHC. Some of the records have been transcribed and published. These are available in NCSL, and some are in FHL (FHC), RL, and LGL. Microfilm copies and/or published transcript copies are sometimes available in LL for their own counties.

23. Manuscripts

One of the most useful and yet one of the most unused sources of genealogical data are the various manuscript collections relating to NC. These collections will be found in state, regional, and private libraries, archives, museums, and repositories located in numerous places in NC, including universities and colleges.

Manuscript collections consist of all sorts of records of religious, educational, patriotic, business, social, civil, professional, governmental, and political organizations; documents, letters, memoirs, notes, and papers of early settlers, ministers, politicians, business men, educators, physicians, dentists, lawyers, judges, and farmers; records of churches, cemeteries, mortuaries, schools, corporations, and industries; works of artists, musicians, writers, sculptors, photographers, and architects; and records, papers, letters, and reminiscences of participants in various wars, as well as records of military organizations and campaigns. The major sources of manuscripts relating to NC are NCSA, LUNC, and LDU. The holdings of these repositories, as well as the holdings of many other smaller repositories in NC, are described in the following volumes:

_P. M. Hamer, A GUIDE TO ARCHIVES AND MANUSCRIPTS IN THE US, Yale University Press, New Haven, CT, 1961.

_US National Historical Publications and Records Commission, DIRECTORY OF ARCHIVES AND MANUSCRIPT REPOSITORIES IN THE US, The Commission, Oryx Press, New York, NY, 1988.

_US Library of Congress, THE NATIONAL UNION CATALOG OF MANUSCRIPT COLLECTIONS, The Library, Washington, DC, 1959-. (Many volumes, index of names, places, and historical periods in each.)

_E. Altham and others, INDEX TO PERSONAL NAMES IN THE NATIONAL UNION CATALOG OF MANUSCRIPT COLLECTIONS, 1959-84, Chadwyck-Healey, Arlington, VA, 1988, 2 volumes.

_J. B. Howell, SPECIAL COLLECTIONS IN LIBRARIES OF THE SOUTHEAST, Southeastern Library Association, Jackson, MS, 1978.

_B. T. Cain, E. Z. McGrew, and C. E. Morris, GUIDE TO PRIVATE MANUSCRIPT COLLECTIONS IN NCSA, The Archives, Raleigh, NC, 1983.

_S. S. Blosser and C. N. Wilson, Jr., THE SOUTHERN HISTORICAL COLLECTION: A GUIDE TO MANUSCRIPTS, University of NC Library, Chapel Hill, NC, 1970; and E. H. Smith, III, THE SOUTHERN HISTORICAL COLLECTION: SUPPLEMENTARY GUIDE TO MANUSCRIPTS, 1970-5, University of NC Library, Chapel Hill, NC, 1976.

_R. C. Davis and L. A. Miller, GUIDE TO THE CATALOGED COLLECTIONS IN THE MANUSCRIPT DEPARTMENT OF THE PERKINS LIBRARY, DUKE UNIVERSITY, Clio Books, Santa Barbara, CA, 1980.

_J. L. Harper, GUIDE TO DRAPER MANUSCRIPTS, State Historical Society of WI, Madison, WI, 1983.

Included in the smaller, but nonetheless important, repositories in NC are the RL mentioned in Chapter 3, section 8.

The reference books mentioned in the previous paragraph are available in NCSL, LUNC, LDU, and in many larger libraries, including LGL and RL. If you find in these volumes materials which you suspect may relate to your ancestor, write to the appropriate repository asking for details. Don't forget to send an SASE and to ask them for the names of researchers if you cannot go in person. In NCSA, LUNC, LDU, and many other NC manuscript

repositories there are special indexes and other finding aids which facilitate your search. In some cases, there are several indexes, not just one, so you need to be careful to examine all of them.

24. Marriage records

During 1669-1741, NC marriages were performed officially by Anglican clergymen or the governor or his council members, and unofficially (disregarding the law) by other clergymen or by mutual consent. Very few were recorded, and of these, very few records survive. In 1741, NC law extended marrying authority to magistrates, and required one of two things for the marriage to be official. Either banns had to be posted (three notices at a church), or the groom had to post a bond with the Clerk of the County Court and obtain a license (which the groom kept). The law continued to be ignored quite often as clergy of other denominations performed marriages. In 1776, NC authorized all ministers to conduct marriages. In 1851, a law required that the marriage licenses be returned to the Clerk of the County Court along with a certificate that the marriage had been solemnized. Then, in 1868, new laws made the Register of Deeds the issuer of marriage licenses, and made the license the only official record of the marriage. In short, the time spans and the county marriage records that you can expect to find in them are as follows: 1669-1741 (very few), 1741-1851 (marriage bonds), 1851-68 (marriage bonds, licenses, and certificates), 1868-present (marriage licenses). In addition, many counties kept books which summarized and/or indexed marriages called RECORD OF MARRIAGES and/or MARRIAGE REGISTER. Only if a couple posted bond, obtained a license, and/or presented a certificate to the county official would their marriage be recorded in the county records. Many marriages involved none of these, some never being put in writing, some being recorded in church records, and some being shown only in family Bibles.

Fortunately, NCSA has taken all existing marriage bonds for all the counties of NC from 1741 to 1868 and has indexed them in a set of microfiche:
_MASTER INDEX OF NC MARRIAGE BONDS, 1741-1868, NCSA, Raleigh, NC. [About 170,000 entries.]
This index is arranged alphabetically according to groom's names and bride's names. The references in the index will lead you to the original bonds and/or to abstracts of them. You need to remember that a marriage bond only declared a couple's intention to marry. The bonds usually carry groom's name, bride's name, bondsman's name, bond amount, date of bond (not the marriage), county, witnesses' names, and sometimes other items. These marriage bonds are indexed (along with other records) in:
_INTERNATIONAL GENEALOGICAL INDEX, FHL, Salt Lake City, UT, latest edition. Available at FHL and every FHC.

The FHL also has the original bonds on microfilm. They can be borrowed through any FHC. Several other sources into which you should look for early marriage record compilations are:

_G. C. Johnson, NC MARRIAGE BONDS, 1741-78, North Carolinian, volume 2 (1956), pages 231-44, volume 3 (1957), pages 269-77, 299-308, volume 4 (1958), pages 405-10, 459-66, volume 5 (1959), pages 589-95, 626-34.

_M. M. Clemens, NC AND SC MARRIAGE RECORDS FROM THE EARLIEST COLONIAL DAYS TO THE CIVIL WAR, Genealogical Publishing Co., Baltimore, MD, 1927 (1973). [7500 records, 15,000 names]

_W. P. Haun, OLD ALBEMARLE COUNTY, NC, PERQUIMANS PRECINCT BIRTHS, MARRIAGES, DEATHS, AND FLESH MARKS, The Author, Durham, NC, 1980.

In Chapter 4, you will find listed under each county the dates for which marriage records (bonds, licenses, certificates, record books, registers, indexes) are available. These marriage records may be found in NCSA and in many CH, and some of them are in FHL (thus being available through FHC). Transcriptions of some of the marriage records for some counties have been made, some being published and others remaining in manuscript form. Most of these are in NCSL and LUNC, some may be found in LDU, FHL (FHC), RL, and LGL. Those pertaining to individual counties are likely to be in their LL. Other records which often yield marriage dates and places include Bible, biographical, cemetery, church, mortuary, newspaper, obituary, pension, and published genealogical records. All of these are discussed in other sections of this chapter. In addition, the location of marriage data in genealogical periodicals has been discussed in section 19.

25. Military records: colonial

Before going into detail on sources of military records (sections 25, 26, 27, 28), you need to understand the types of records which are available and what they contain. There are five basic types which are of value to genealogists: (a) service, (b) pension, (c) bounty land, (d) claims, and (e) military unit history. Service records contain a number of the following: name, rank, military unit, personal description, plus dates and places of enlistment, mustering in, payrolls, wounding, capture, death, imprisonment, hospital stay, release, oath of allegiance, desertion, promotion, battles, heroic action, re-enlistment, leave of absence, mustering out, and discharge. Pension records (applications and payment documents) contain a number of the following: name, age, rank, military unit, personal description, name of wife, names and ages of children, residences during pension period, plus dates and places of service, wartime experiences, birth, marriage, pension payments, and death. Bounty land records (applications and awards of land) contain the same sort of data that

pension records do. Claims of military participants for back pay and of civilians for supplies or services contain some of the following: name, details of claim, date of claim, witnesses to claim, documents supporting claim, action on claim, amount awarded. Military unit history records trace the detailed events of the experiences of a given military unit throughout a war, often referring to officers, enlisted personnel, battles, campaigns, deaths, plus dates and places of organization, mustering in, reorganization, mustering out and other pertinent events. Now, with this background, you are ready to learn where these records may be found.

Beginning in earliest colonial times, each NC county maintained a military unit (usually a regiment) of its own male citizens called the militia. These regiments were parts of the overall state militia and were subject to call by the governor. In times of disaster, insurrection, riot, or invasion, the militia could be employed. Very few data, such as rolls or lists of militia members, are available. Some few rolls from the period 1747-73 may be found in:
_W. Clarke, STATE RECORDS OF NC, State of NC, Goldsboro, NC, 1895-
  1907, volume 22, pages 160-7, 306-99, indexes in volumes 27-30.
The court minutes and miscellaneous records of some counties report some militia information, often including officer appointments, pay records, accounts of purchases, and courts martial. Some of the tax collection lists of counties are often arranged in terms of the militia organizations of the counties. During wartime, militia records were often kept with more care, and therefore there are numerous wartime militia records. These will be discussed under the appropriate wars in sections to follow.

Not too many records survive from the wars of the colonial period. As you will remember, the major ones were the Tuscarora Indian War (1711-5), the Spanish Alarm (1739-48) which was made up of two wars called the War of Jenkins' Ear and King George's War, the French and Indian War (1755-63), and the War of the Regulation (1768-71). For the Tuscarora Indian War (1711-5), essentially no records of military participants remain. The major remaining records are lists of those who were taxed or who were levied to support the war, and those who filed claims for reimbursement for supplies they had provided. These materials are in the NCSA:
_Colonial Court Records, Taxes and Accounts, 1679-1754, CCR190,
  folders labelled Corn Lists 1715-6, Claims 1713-20, Public Accounts
  1694-1739, NCSA, Raleigh, NC.
Records which are extant for the Spanish Alarm (1739-48) include some muster rolls and troop lists. These are in the NCSA filed under Military Collection, Spanish Invasion 1742-8, and most of them are published in
_W. Clark, STATE RECORDS OF NC, State of NC, Goldsboro, NC, 1895-
  1907, volume 22, pages 262-86, indexes in volumes 27-30.

The French and Indian War (1755-63) records which have been preserved consist mostly of military action on the frontiers of NC, very few relating to NC soldiers serving elsewhere. Troop lists and pay records may be found in the following files in the NCSA:
_Military Collection, a box labelled Frontier Scouting and Indian Wars, 1758-78, NCSA, Raleigh, NC.
Some financial records relating to claims, certificates of service, and treaty and military expenses will also be found in NCSA:
_Treasurer's and Comptroller's Records, Indian Affairs and Lands, T & C Indians 1; and Treasurer's and Comptroller's Records, Military Papers, T & C Mil 1; NCSA, Raleigh, NC.
Most of the records of the War of the Regulation (1768- 71) were destroyed in a fire at the former governor's house. However, there are some pay rolls, enlistment documents, claims, and order books in the NCSA:
_Military Collection, WAR OF THE REGULATION, 1768-79, NCSA, Raleigh, NC.

Most of these NC colonial military records are included and indexed in a very useful volume:
_M. J. Clark, COLONIAL SOLDIERS OF THE SOUTH, 1732-74, Genealogical Publishing Co., Baltimore, MD, 1983.

26. Military records: Revolutionary War

As mentioned in Chapter 1, NC had a heavy involvement in the American War of Independence, particularly in the latter years. About 7300 NC patriots fought with the Continental (united colonies) Army and over 4000 militia members participated on the home front. Quite a large number of records, which you should investigate, are available for this War: national service records, national pension records, national bounty land records, state service records, state pension records, state bounty land records, state civilian service records, state records on supplies that were requisitioned, and county records. As you begin your quest, one very important thing that you need to realize is that you will find both national and state records on Continental personnel, but there are mostly state records (very few national ones) on the militia.

The first step you should take in searching for your NC ancestor who served in this War (or gave public service or provided supplies in support of the War) is to employ the following nation-wide record sources and look for him in them:
_National Archives, GENERAL INDEX TO COMPILED SERVICE RECORDS OF REVOLUTIONARY WAR SOLDIERS, The Archives, Washington, DC, Microfilm Publication M860, 58 rolls. [Continental mainly; copies in

NCSA. National Archives. Regional Branches of the National Archives, FHL (FHC)].

_National Archives. INDEX TO COMPILED SERVICE RECORDS OF AMERICAN NAVAL PERSONNEL DURING THE REVOLUTIONARY WAR, The Archives. Washington. DC. Microfilm Publication M879. 1 roll. [Also includes Marines: copies in NCSA, National Archives. Regional Branches of the National Archives. FHL (FHC)].

_National Genealogical Society, INDEX OF REVOLUTIONARY WAR PENSION APPLICATIONS IN THE NATIONAL ARCHIVES. The Society. Washington. DC. 1976. [Also includes bounty land records; copies in NCSA. NCSL. LUNC. LDU. LGL. some RL, FHL (FHC)].

_F. Rider. AMERICAN GENEALOGICAL INDEX, Godfrey Memorial Library, Middletown. CT. 1942-52. 48 volumes; and F. Rider, AMERICAN GENEALOGICAL AND BIOGRAPHICAL INDEX, Godfrey Memorial Library, Middletown. CT, 1952-84, over 150 volumes, more to come. [Continental and militia.]

_US Pay Department, War Department, REGISTERS OF CERTIFICATES ISSUED BY JOHN PIERCE TO OFFICERS AND SOLDIERS OF THE CONTINENTAL ARMY, Genealogical Publishing Co., Baltimore, MD, 1973.

If you discover from these sources that your forebear served in the Continental forces, then you may proceed to obtain his records from the National Archives. Write them at the following address and ask for copies of Form NATF-80:

_Reference Services Branch (NNIR), National Archives, Washington, DC 20408.

Upon receiving the form, fill it out, check the box asking for military service records, and if you found pension or bounty land references for your ancestor, use separate forms for the pension and/or bounty land record requests. Then, mail the form back, enclosing no money (you will be billed lated). The Archives staff is very busy, and thus the filling of your request may be slow. If you want faster service, you can go to the National Archives in person, or you can hire a researcher in Washington, DC, to do the work for you. Researchers and their addresses may be found in:

_V. N. Chambers. editor. THE GENEALOGICAL HELPER, Everton Publishers. Logan. UT. latest September-October issue.

The _second_ step that you should take, especially if you failed to find your progenitor in the first step is to look into state sources. If you did find your ancestor in the first step, you should not neglect this second possible source of data. The printed sources in which your ancestor may appear are:

_W. Clark, STATE RECORDS OF NC. State of NC, Goldsboro, NC, 1895-1901, volume 16, pages 1002-1197. [Officers omitted, some regimental assignments erroneous.]

_DAR of NC, ROSTER OF SOLDIERS FROM NC IN THE AMERICAN REVOLUTION, Genealogical Publishing Co., Baltimore, MD, 1932 (1977).
_W. L. Saunders, NC TROOPS IN THE CONTINENTAL LINE 1776-82, Secretary of State of NC, Raleigh, NC, 1884. [Officers of NC regiments.]
_J. T. Maddox and M. Carter, NC REVOLUTIONARY SOLDIERS, SAILORS, AND PATRIOTS, GA Pioneers, Albany, GA, 1979, 2 volumes.
_B. G. C. Cartwright and L. J. Gardiner, NC LAND GRANTS IN TN, 1778-- 91, Harper, Memphis, TN, 1958.
_G. F. Burgner, NC LAND GRANTS IN TN, 1778-91, Southern Historical Press, Easley, SC, 1981.

Two very good books describing NC's Continental Army regiments and their histories and the overall War activities of the state are:
_H. F. Rankin, NC CONTINENTALS, University of NC Press, Chapel Hill, NC, 1971.
_P. Russell, NC IN THE REVOLUTIONARY WAR, Heritage Printers, Charlotte, NC, 1965.

Numerous original state War records are available in NCSA and in the NC Land Grant Office which is part of the NC Secretary of State's Office. These records are described in detail in the three following works:
_H. F. M. Leary and M. R. Stirewalt, NC RESEARCH GENEALOGY AND LOCAL HISTORY, NC Genealogical Society, Raleigh, NC, 1980, pages 342-89.
_C. F. W. Coker and D. R. Lennon, NC'S REVOLUTIONARY WAR PAY RECORDS, Archives Information Circular No. 1, NCSA, Raleigh, NC, 1976.
_G. Stevenson, Jr., NC REVOLUTIONARY WAR RECORDS OF PRIMARY INTEREST TO GENEALOGISTS, Archives Information Circular No. 13, NCSA, Raleigh, NC, 1975.

The major indexes and the original records to which they lead, as well as alphabetically arranged original records, will now be listed. Those which deal with military service (both Continental and militia) are:
_REVOLUTIONARY WAR PAY VOUCHERS, 50,000 vouchers, alphabetically arranged, NCSA, Raleigh, NC. COMPREHENSIVE INDEX TO REVOLUTIONARY ARMY ACCOUNT BOOKS, SERIES 1, NCSA, Raleigh, NC, 3 volumes of typescript, which lead to REVOLUTIONARY WAR ARMY ACCOUNT BOOKS, SERIES 1 (12 volumes labelled I, II, III, IV, V, VI, VII, VIII, IX, X, XI, XII), microfilm copies in NCSA.
_SEPARATE INDEXES TO EACH OF THE VOLUMES OF REVOLUTIONARY ARMY ACCOUNT BOOKS, SERIES 2, 3, 4, 3 volumes of typescript, which lead to REVOLUTIONARY WAR ARMY ACCOUNT BOOKS, SERIES 2 (10 volumes labelled A, B, C, D, E-G, H, J, K, W-1, W-2), SERIES 3 (4 volumes labelled 1-6, 19, 28, 30), SERIES 4 (2 volumes, one entitled THE RECEIPT BOOK, the other entitled ABSTRACTS OF THE ARMY ACCOUNTS OF THE NC LINE), microfilm copies in NCSA.

_FINAL SETTLEMENT PAPERS, Treasurer's and Comptroller's Records, Military Papers, T & C Mil 14-20, about 600 folders alphabetically arranged.
_TROOP RETURNS, 1747-1893, in Military Collection, Boxes 3 and 7 (Militia records), Boxes 4, 5, 6 (Continental line records), NCSA, Raleigh, NC, indexed under county names in the NCSA card catalog.

The major indexes which relate to state bounty land awards are as follows. Please remember that there were also national bounty land awards as listed in the National Genealogical Society index mentioned in the second paragraph of this section. Your forebear could have received land under both programs.
_TN LAND RECORD CARD FILE, Land Grant Office, NC Secretary of State, Administration Bldg., Raleigh, NC, includes military bounty land grants, leads to the records.
_CARD INDEX TO BOUNTY LAND WARRANT CLAIM DEPOSITIONS AND PROOFS, Secretary of State Records, Revolutionary Military Papers, NCSA, Raleigh, NC, leads to records.
_CARD INDEX TO REVOLUTIONARY WAR LEGISLATIVE PETITIONS, NCSA, Raleigh, NC, leads to Petitions to the NC Assembly for land warrants, war benefits to disabled veterans and widows.
_CARD AND MICROFILM INDEXES TO TN LAND GRANT RECORDS, TN State Library and Archives, Archives Search Room, Nashville, TN.

There are also records in NCSA relating to Loyalists (those remaining loyal to Britain) in the Revolution. These records consist both of those kept by NC and quite a number kept by the British government. Details on these records may be found on pages 383-8 in the volume by Leary and Stirewalt mentioned above and in the following reference aid:
_R. J. Cain, PRELIMINARY GUIDE TO THE BRITISH RECORDS COLLECTION, Archives Information Circular No. 16, NCSA, Raleigh, NC, 1983.

There are also two volumes which list Loyalist participants:
_R. Demond, LOYALISTS IN NC DURING THE REVOLUTION, Genealogical Publishing Co., Baltimore, MD, 1979.
_M. J. Clark, LOYALISTS IN THE SOUTHERN CAMPAIGN OF THE REVOLUTIONARY WAR, Genealogical Publishing Co., Baltimore, MD, 1980, volume 1.

During and after the Revolutionary War, there were several Indian War campaigns involving NC participants. Included were the Cherokee Indian Expedition (1779), the First, Second, and Third Chickamauga Expeditions (1779, 1782, 1787), and the Cumberland Battalion actions (1786-9). Details of the surviving records (which are in NCSA) will be found on pages 389-94 of the book by Leary and Stirewalt mentioned in the third paragraph of this section.

For much more detail on Revolutionary War genealogical research and records, consult:
_Geo. K. Schweitzer, REVOLUTIONARY WAR GENEALOGY, $9 postpaid from Geo. K. Schweitzer, 407 Regent Court, Knoxville, TN 37923-5807.

27. Military records: 1812-60

In the period 1812-60, the US was involved in two major foreign wars: the War of 1812 (1812-5) and the Mexican War (1846-8). In addition, there was a series of conflicts which began during this period called the Indian Wars (1817-98). A number of NC men were participants in the War of 1812. As was the case with the Revolutionary War, three types of national records should be sought: military service, pension, and bounty land. To obtain these records, request a NATF Form 80 from:
_Reference Services Branch (NNIR), National Archives, Washington, DC 20408.

Upon receiving it, fill it out, giving your ancestor's name and state (NC), as much other information as you can, check one request box on each of three different forms (service, pension, bounty land), attach notes asking for all records, and then mail it back. They will check the indexes, then will send you a request for payment if they are found. Because of their very heavy backlog, the National Archives is often slow. If you want faster service, hire a researcher in Washington, DC, to do the search for you. Such researchers may be found in:
_V. N. Chambers, editor, THE GENEALOGICAL HELPER, Everton Publishers, Logan, UT, latest September-October issue.

Among the microfilm indexes and alphabetical files which the National Archives employees will search or which your hired researcher should search are:
_National Archives, INDEX TO COMPILED SERVICE RECORDS OF VOLUNTEER SOLDIERS WHO SERVED DURING THE WAR OF 1812, Microfilm Publication M602, The Archives, Washington, DC, 234 rolls.
_National Archives, INDEX TO WAR OF 1812 PENSION APPLICATION FILES, Microfilm Publication M313, The Archives, Washington, DC, 102 rolls.
_National Archives, WAR OF 1812 MILITARY BOUNTY LAND WARRANTS (WITH INDEXES), 1815-58, Microfilm Publication M848, The Archives, Washington, DC, 14 rolls.
_National Archives, POST-REVOLUTIONARY WAR BOUNTY LAND WARRANT APPLICATION FILE, arranged alphabetically, National Archives, Washington, DC.

Copies of the three microfilm publications mentioned above may be available in some LGL, NCSA, and the FHL (FHC).

Among published <u>national</u> sources for War of 1812 information are:
_F. I. Ordway, Jr., REGISTER OF THE GENERAL SOCIETY OF THE WAR OF 1812, The Society, Washington, DC, 1972.
_E. S. Galvin, 1812 ANCESTOR INDEX, National Society of US Daughters of 1812, Washington, DC, 1970.
_C. S. Peterson, KNOWN MILITARY DEAD DURING THE WAR OF 1812, The Author, Baltimore, MD, 1955.

In addition, there is a very useful published state source volume for NC:
_NC Adjutant General's Office, MUSTER ROLLS OF THE SOLDIERS OF THE WAR OF 1812: DETACHED FROM THE MILITIA OF NC IN 1812 AND 1814, Genealogical Publishing Co., Baltimore, MD, 1851 (1981). [Be careful, book contains many errors.]

The four volumes mentioned above may be found in NCSL, LUNC, LDU, and FHL, (thus being obtainable through FHC). The first three are likely to be found in many LGL. The NCSA has available a number of alphabetized record series and several indexes leading to original records of participation of both military men and civilians in the War of 1812. Among those which you should use are:
_INDEX TO NC WAR OF 1812 MUSTER ROLLS, leads to entries in 6 volumes of muster rolls, NCSA, Raleigh, NC.
_INDEX TO NC WAR OF 1812 ACCOUNT BOOKS, leads to military and civilian claims in 11 account books, NCSA, Raleigh, NC.
_INDEX TO NC WAR OF 1812 PAY AND RECEIPT ROLLS, leads to entries in 77 payroll and receipt lists, NCSA, Raleigh, NC.
_NC WAR OF 1812 PAY VOUCHERS, almost 5000 vouchers listed alphabetically, NCSA, Raleigh, NC.

For considerably more detail about genealogical information which can be derived from War of 1812 records, you may consult a book especially dedicated to this:
_Geo. K. Schweitzer, WAR OF 1812 GENEALOGY, $9 postpaid from Geo. K. Schweitzer, 407 Regent Court, Knoxville, TN 37923-5807.

This volume goes into detail on local, state, and national records, discusses service, pension, bounty land, and claims records, and treats the subjects of regimental histories, hospital records, courts-martial, prisoners, militia activity, battle sites, museums, officer biographies and many other related topics.

During the <u>Indian Wars</u> period (1817-98), some NC personnel were involved in several of the conflicts. The National Archives has military service, pension, and bounty land application records, plus indexes to all three. NATF Form 80 should be obtained and used or a researcher hired in accordance with the previously-given instructions (1st paragraph, this section). The National Archives indexes which lead to the records and some alphabetized records are as follows:

_National Archives, INDEX TO COMPILED SERVICE RECORDS OF VOL-
UNTEER SOLDIERS WHO SERVED DURING INDIAN WARS, Microfilm
Publication M629, The Archives, Washington, DC, 42 rolls.
_National Archives, INDEX TO INDIAN WARS PENSION FILES, Microfilm
Publication T318, The Archives, Washington, DC, 12 rolls.
_National Archives, INDEX TO COMPILED SERVICE RECORDS OF NC
VOLUNTEERS IN THE CHEROKEE DISTURBANCES AND REMOVAL,
Microfilm M256, The Archives, Washington, DC, 1 roll.
_National Archives, POST-REVOLUTIONARY WAR BOUNTY LAND APPLI-
CATION FILE, arranged alphabetically, National Archives, Washington,
DC.

The Mexican War was fought 1846-8. As before, NATF Form 80 should be obtained and used or a researcher hired as indicated in previously-given instructions (1st paragraph, this section). Again, military service, pension, and bounty land records should be asked for. The National Archives indexes which lead to the records and some alphabetized records are:
_National Archives, INDEX TO THE COMPILED SERVICE RECORDS OF
VOLUNTEER SOLDIERS DURING THE MEXICAN WAR, Microfilm Publi-
cation M616, The Archives, Washington, DC, 41 rolls.
_National Archives, INDEX TO MEXICAN WAR PENSION FILES, Microfilm
Publication T317, The Archives, Washington, DC, 14 rolls.
_National Archives, POST-REVOLUTIONARY WAR BOUNTY LAND APPLI-
CATION FILE, arranged alphabetically, National Archives, Washington,
DC.
An exceptionally valuable publication is a complete roster of both regular and volunteer troops in the Mexican War:
_W. H. Roberts, MEXICAN WAR VETERANS, 1846-8, Washington, DC,
1887.
Also useful is:
_C. S. Peterson, KNOWN MILITARY DEAD DURING THE MEXICAN WAR,
The Author, Baltimore, MD, 1957.
The NCSA has among its Mexican War materials two items which may be of some further use to genealogical researchers:
_NC Adjutant General's Office, LISTS OF MEXICAN WAR VOLUNTEERS,
AG11, NCSA, Raleigh, NC, unindexed list of those who volunteered, but
not all were accepted.
_NC Adjutant General, ROSTER OF NC TROOPS IN THE WAR WITH MEXI-
CO, State of NC, Raleigh, NC, 1887, accompanied by a separate index
in NCSA.

28. Military records: Civil War

Records which are available for NC participants in the Civil War (1861-5) include national service records (both Union and Confederate), national pension records (Union only), NC state pension records, NC Civil War militia officer records, NC Confederate gravestone records, federal pardon records, and NC state bounty payrolls (not to be confused with bounty land records). No bounty land awards were made by either the federal or the state government for service in the Civil War.

Several major indexes lead to NC service records (both Union and Confederate) which are in the National Archives:
_National Archives, INDEX TO THE COMPILED SERVICE RECORDS OF VOLUNTEER UNION SOLDIERS WHO SERVED IN ORGANIZATIONS FROM THE STATE OF NC, Microfilm Publication M391, The Archives, Washington, DC, 2 rolls.
_National Archives, INDEX TO THE COMPILED SERVICE RECORDS OF CONFEDERATE SOLDIERS WHO SERVED IN ORGANIZATIONS FROM THE STATE OF NC, Microfilm Publication M230, The Archives, Washington, DC, 43 rolls.

These indexes lead to the compiled service records which have been reproduced on microfilm. In addition, service records of Confederate naval and marine personnel may be readily found, because they are arranged alphabetically in the third item below:
_National Archives, COMPILED SERVICE RECORDS OF VOLUNTEER UNION SOLDIERS WHO SERVED IN ORGANIZATIONS FROM THE STATE OF NC, Microfilm Publication M401, The Archives, Washington, DC, 25 rolls.
_National Archives, COMPILED SERVICE RECORDS OF CONFEDERATE SOLDIERS WHO SERVED IN ORGANIZATIONS FROM THE STATE OF NC, Microfilm Publication M270, The Archives, Washington, DC, 580 rolls.
_National Archives, (SERVICE) RECORDS RELATING TO CONFEDERATE AND MARINE PERSONNEL, Microfilm Publication M260, The Archives, Washington, DC, 7 rolls, arranged alphabetically by name.

These indexes and records may be examined in the National Archives, their Regional Branches, FHL (FHC), or in the NCSA. Or you may write for NATF Form 80 and use it, or hire a researcher in Washington, DC, to look into these records for you. Details for these procedures were given previously (1st paragraph, section 27). However, do not request Confederate pension records or bounty land records, since they were not given by the US. The federal pension records (Union only) are indexed in:
_National Archives, GENERAL INDEX TO PENSION FILES, 1861-1934, Microfilm Publication T288, The Archives, Washington, DC, 544 rolls.

This index leads to the original pension application files in the National Archives. The files often contain considerable genealogical information. You may use NATF Form 80 to request the data, you may make a personal visit, or you may hire a researcher.

There are several published state sources for information on NC Confederate veterans or military units. The most important of these are the following:
_J. W. Moore, ROSTER OF NC TROOPS IN THE WAR BETWEEN THE STATES, State of NC, Raleigh, NC, 1882, with alphabetically arranged extracts in NCSA. [Lists over 104,000 soldiers, about 70% of those who served.]
_L. H. Manarin and W. T. Jordan, NORTH CAROLINA TROOPS, 1861-5, A ROSTER, NCSA, Raleigh, NC, 1966-, many volumes. [Military service details on each of about 8000 soldiers in each volume.]
_W. Clark, HISTORIES OF THE SEVERAL REGIMENTS AND BATTALIONS FROM NC IN THE GREAT WAR, 1861-5, State of NC, Raleigh, NC, 1901, 5 volumes. [Regimental histories, not much on individuals.]
These volumes are in NCSA, NCSL, LUNC, LDU, FHL (FHC), many LGL, many RL, and some LL. A microfilm copy of the alphabetical extracts from Moore (which is in NCSA) is at LUNC.

Among the state of NC records are the very important Confederate pension records and a number of others which supplement the national records mentioned above. All of these are in NCSA. Those which you should not fail to examine are:
_INDEX TO 1885 CONFEDERATE PENSION APPLICATIONS, NCSA, Raleigh, NC, leads to over 5000 pension applications filed by incapacitated veterans and widows.
_INDEX TO 1901 CONFEDERATE PENSION APPLICATIONS, NCSA, Raleigh, NC, leads to over 39,000 pension applications filed by veterans and widows.
_ROSTER OF THE MILITIA OFFICERS OF NC, 1861-3, Adjutant General's Records, AG129, NCSA, Raleigh, NC. [Records of officers serving in the various home guard units, unindexed. Very few records of enlisted militia members exist.]
_CARD INDEX TO CONFEDERATE GRAVESTONE RECORDS, NCSA, Raleigh, NC, leads to 13 volumes listing Confederate gravestones and their locations.
_CARD INDEX TO NC PETITIONS FOR PARDON, NCSA, Raleigh, NC, leads to almost 2000 applications for pardon made by influential, high-ranking, and affluent NC citizens to the US.
_REGIMENTAL AND UNIT RECORDS, Civil War Collection, CWC42-6, 5 boxes, over 200 muster, descriptive, and pay rolls; arranged by regiment, therefore to be used after you learn that for your progenitor.

Details of further Civil War records in the National Archives and in NCSA will be found in:

_National Archives Staff, GUIDE TO GENEALOGICAL RESEARCH IN THE NATIONAL ARCHIVES, The Archives, Washington, DC, 1982, Chapters 4-10, 16.

_C. F. W. Coker, NC CIVIL WAR RECORDS: AN INTRODUCTION TO PRINTED AND MANUSCRIPT SOURCES, Archives Information Circular No. 4, NCSA, Raleigh, NC, 1977.

_GUIDE TO CIVIL WAR RECORDS IN NCSA, NCSA, Raleigh, NC, 1966.

For a detailed in-depth discussion of Civil War records as genealogical sources, consult:

_Geo. K. Schweitzer, CIVIL WAR GENEALOGY, $9 from Geo. K. Schweitzer, 407 Regent Court, Knoxville, TN 37923-5807.

This work treats local, state, and national records, service and pension records, regimental and naval histories, enlistment rosters, hospital records, court-martial reports, burial registers, national cemeteries, gravestone allotments, amnesties, pardons, state militias, discharge papers, officer biographies, prisons, prisoners, battle sites, maps, relics, weapons, museums, monuments, memorials, deserters, black soldiers, Indian soldiers, and many other topics.

There is in the National Archives an index to service records of the Spanish-American War (1898-9).

_National Archives, GENERAL INDEX TO COMPILED SERVICE RECORDS OF VOLUNTEER SOLDIERS WHO SERVED FROM NC DURING THE WAR WITH SPAIN, Microfilm Publications M413, The Archives, Washington, DC, 2 rolls, leads to service records.

Again a properly submitted NATF Form 80 (see lst paragraph of section 27 for instructions) will bring you both military service and pension records (there were no bounty land awards). Or you may choose to hire a researcher, or even go yourself. The pension records are indexed in:

_National Archives, GENERAL INDEX TO PENSION FILES 1861-1934, Microfilm Publn. No. T288, The Archives, Washington, DC, 544 rolls.

A volume which you should not overlook is:

_NC Adjutant General's Office, ROSTER OF NC VOLUNTEERS IN THE SPANISH-AMERICAN WAR, State of NC, Raleigh, NC, 1900.

Records for World War I and subsequent wars may be obtained from:

_National Personnel Records Center, GSA (Military Records), 9700 Page Blvd., St. Louis, MO 63132.

For veterans whose records were lost in a 1973 fire in St. Louis, a special instruction leaflet has been prepared:

_MILITARY PERSONNEL RECORDS IN NCSA, 1918-64, Archives Information Circular No. 11, NCSA, Raleigh, NC, 1973.

29. Mortuary records

Very few NC mortuary records have been transcribed or microfilmed, even though a few are to be found in manuscripts. This means that you must write directly to the mortuaries which you know or suspect were involved in burying your ancestor. Sometimes a death certificate will name the mortuary; sometimes it is the only one nearby; sometimes you will have to write several to ascertain which one might have done the funeral arrangements. You may discover that the mortuary that was involved is now out of business, and so you will have to try to discover which of the existing ones inherited the records. Mortuaries for NC with their addresses are listed in the following volume:

_C. O. Kates, editor, THE AMERICAN BLUE BOOK OF FUNERAL DIRECTORS, Kates-Boyleston Publications, New York, NY, latest issue.

This reference book will usually be found in the offices of most mortuaries. In all correspondence with mortuaries be sure to enclose an SASE.

30. Naturalization records

In the early colonial period (1607-1700), the major immigrants to the territory that later became the US were English, and since the colonies were British, they were citizens. This was especially so in NC, very few persons of any other nationality coming in. Shortly after the turn of the century, when immigrants of other nationalities began to arrive, English traditions, customs, governmental structures, and language had become firmly established. In spite of this English dominance, many early foreign NC settlers simply did not bother to change their citizenships. This was particularly the case in frontier areas and when foreigners set up separate communities of their own as several did in NC. However, those who chose to do so could swear loyalty to the British sovereign and thereby become official citizens. Others never went through a formal procedure and functionally became citizens simply by conforming to the laws and entering into community activity. In 1740, the English Parliament passed a law which set requirements for naturalization: 7 years residence in one colony plus an oath of allegiance to the Crown. The oath was sometimes certified by a court.

In 1776-7, early in the Revolution, NC passed two laws requiring an oath of allegiance to the new state from officials and merchants, and a bit later from militiamen. Some of these records may be found among the court records of the counties. In general, those who were loyal to the rebellion automatically became citizens of NC. In 1778, the Articles of Confederation made all citizens of states citizens of the new nation. The US Congress in 1790 enacted a national naturalization act which required one year's state residence, two years' US residence, and a loyalty oath taken in a court. In 1795, a five years' residence came to be required, and in 1798,

a 14 years' residence plus a declaration of intention 5 years before the oath. Revised statutes of 1802 called for one year's state residence, 5 years' US residence, and a declaration 3 years before the oath. The declaration and oath could be carried out in any circuit or district court of the US or any court of record of a state. Wives and children of naturalized males usually became citizens automatically. And persons who gave military service to the US and received an honorable discharge also received citizenship.

In 1906, the Bureau of Immigration and Naturalization was set up, and this agency has kept records on all naturalizations since then. Thus, if you suspect your ancestor was naturalized after September 1906, write to the following address for a Form 6641 which you can use to request records:

_Immigration and Naturalization Service, 425 I St., Washington, DC 20536.
For naturalization records before October 1906, you need to recall that the process could have taken place in any US, state, or local court. You need also to recall that most immigrants to NC came from other colonies, not from overseas, so they may have been made citizens before coming into NC. Unfortunately, locating naturalization records before 1906 means going through all possible court records for the time period you think proper. The most likely places to find these records are in the Superior Court minutes and in the US Court records. Only a few NC counties have separated some records: Durham (1882-1904), Forsythe (1891-1906). Records of the US Courts at the following cities are in the Federal Archives and Records Center, 1557 St. Joseph Ave., East Point, GA 30344: Asheville (1871-1906), Charlotte (1872-1906), Elizabeth City (1801-1906), Greensboro (1872-1906), New Bern (1832-1906), Raleigh (1866--1906), Statesville (1878-1906), Wilmington (1858-1906). For further information on naturalization records, you may consult:

_J. C. and L. L. Neagles, LOCATING YOUR IMMIGRANT ANCESTOR: A GUIDE TO NATURALIZATION RECORDS, Everton Publishers, Logan UT, 1975.

_National Archives, PRE-1840 FEDERAL DISTRICT AND CIRCUIT COURT RECORDS, Special List No. 31, The Archives, Washington, DC, 1970.

31. Newspaper records

A number of original and microfilmed newspapers are available for towns, cities, and counties of NC. There were relatively few NC newspapers before the Civil War, most of them being 4-paged weeklies. This situation was largely due to the high illiteracy rate in NC during these years. The existing newspapers contain information on national news, local news, and carry ads, but it was not until about 1820 that they began to include data on local marriages and deaths, the obituaries often containing much genealogical information. The largest NC collection of newspapers is in

NCSA. Others are in LUNC, LDU, and in many RL and LL. Some of these have been partially indexed. The following article lists the locations of these indexes:

_W. R. Griffin and J. L. Rasmussen, A COMPREHENSIVE GUIDE TO THE LOCATION OF PUBLISHED AND UNPUBLISHED NEWSPAPER INDEXES IN NC REPOSITORIES, in NC LIBRARIES, volume 32 (1974), pages 11-25.

The extensive collection of microfilmed and original newspaper records in NCSA is described in:

_R. C. Jones, NC NEWSPAPERS ON MICROFILM (IN NCSA), NCSA, Raleigh, NC, 1982.

Other important guides to NC newspapers in NC repositories and in a number of places outside the state include:

_H. G. Jones and J. H. Avant, UNION LIST OF NC NEWSPAPERS, 1751--1900, NCSA, Raleigh, NC, 1963.

_Library of Congress, NEWSPAPERS IN MICROFILM, The Library, Washington, DC, 1973, supplements 1978, 1979, and further.

_C. S. Brigham, HISTORY AND BIBLIOGRAPHY OF AMERICAN NEWSPAPERS, 1690-1820, American Antiquarian Society, Worcester, MA, 1961, 2 volumes.

_W. Gregory, AMERICAN NEWSPAPERS, 1821-1936, H. W. Wilson Co., New York, NY, 1937.

All the above publications are located in NCSL, LUNC, LDU, LGL, FHL, many RL and some LL. A few LL have newspapers and/or newspaper indexes which are not listed in the above works, so it is always important to look.

As was mentioned above, after 1820 many NC newspapers began to list marriages and deaths. Quite a number of indexes and abstracts have been published. Among the books you should seek in NCSL, LUNC, LDU, FHL, (FHC), LGL, RL, and LL are:

_BIBLICAL RECORDER (BAPTIST) INDEX, 1834 forward, Wake Forest University Library, Winston-Salem, NC, 1976-, 3 volumes.

_BIBLICAL RECORDER (BAPTIST) OBITUARY NOTICES, 1835- 1904, Unpublished typescript, NCSA, Raleigh, NC, 3 volumes.

_C. L. Broughton, MARRIAGE AND DEATH NOTICES FROM RALEIGH REGISTER (AND OTHER RALEIGH NEWSPAPERS), 1799-1893, Genealogical Publishing Co., Baltimore, MD, 1944-52 (1966-75), 3 volumes.

_R. P. Fouts, ABSTRACTS FROM THE STATE GAZETTE OF NC, The Author, New Bern and Edenton, NC, 1982, 3 volumes,

_R. P. Fouts, ABSTRACTS FROM THE NC GAZETTE OF NEW BERN, 1751-98, Genrec Books, Cocoa, FL, 1983, 2 volumes.

_R. P. Fouts, ABSTRACTS FROM NEWSPAPERS OF EDENTON, FAYETTEVILLE, AND HILLSBOROUGH, NC, 1782-1800, Genrec Books, Cocoa, FL, 1984.

R. P. Fouts, ABSTRACTS FROM NEWSPAPERS OF WILMINGTON, NC, 1765-1816, Genrec Books, Cocoa, FL, 1984-7, 5 volumes.

R. P. Fouts, ABSTRACTS FROM THE NC JOURNAL OF HALIFAX, NC, 1792-, Genrec Books, Cocoa, FL, 1989.

R. L. Grantham and C. Haywood, MARRIAGE AND DEATH NOTICES FROM THE MECKLENBURG JEFFERSONIAN, CHARLOTTE, NC, 1841-9: AN INDEX, Public Library, Charlotte, NC, 1966.

L. P. Hall, MARRIAGE NOTICES, OBITUARIES, AND ITEMS OF GENEALOGICAL INTEREST IN THE CAPE FEAR RECORDER, THE PEOPLES PRESS, AND THE WILMINGTON ADVERTISER, 1829-33, Linprint, Wilmington, NC, 1958.

C. Haywood and R. L. Grantham, MARRIAGE AND DEATH NOTICES FROM THE WESTERN DEMOCRAT, CHARLOTTE, NC, 1853-70, AN INDEX, Public Library, Charlotte, NC, 1966, 4 volumes.

I. D. Kellam, MARRIAGE AND DEATH NOTICES IN NEWSPAPERS PUBLISHED IN WILMINGTON, NC, 1797-1842; MARRIAGE CONTRACTS OF NEW HANOVER COUNTY CITIZENS, 1728-1855, Wilmington, NC, 1959.

K. K. Kendall, MARRIAGE AND DEATH NOTICES FROM MILTON NEWSPAPERS, CASWELL COUNTY, 1818-54, in NC Genealogical Society Journal, Volume 4 (1978), pages 35-7.

H. Lu and G. Neumann, NC SPECTATOR AND WESTERN ADVERTISER (1830-5), RUTHERFORD COUNTY, NC, ABSTRACTS, The Authors, Dallas, TX, 1982.

S. E. Lucas, Jr., and B. Holcomb, MARRIAGE AND DEATH NOTICES FROM RALEIGH, NC, NEWSPAPERS, 1796-1826, Reprint Co., Spartanburg, SC, 1977.

W. R. Navey, MARRIAGE AND DEATH NOTICES FROM THE CHARLOTTE JOURNAL, CHARLOTTE, NC, 1835-51, Charlotte, NC, 1964.

L. S. Neal, ABSTRACTS OF VITAL RECORDS FROM RALEIGH, NC, NEWSPAPERS, 1799-1915, Reprint Co., Spartanburg, SC, 1979-, several volumes, others to be published.

R. L. Topkins, MARRIAGE AND DEATH NOTICES FROM EXTANT ASHEVILLE, NC, NEWSPAPERS, 1840-70: AN INDEX, NC Genealogical Society, Raleigh, NC, 1977.

R. L. Topkins, MARRIAGE AND DEATH NOTICES FROM THE WESTERN CAROLINIAN, SALISBURY, NC, 1820-42: AN INDEX, The Author, Raleigh, NC, 1975.

R. L. Topkins, MARRIAGE AND DEATH NOTICES FROM THE IREDELL EXPRESS, STATESVILLE, NC, 1858-65: AN INDEX, in NC Genealogical Journal, volume 3(1977), pages 197-212, 242-53.

R. L. Topkins, MARRIAGE AND DEATH NOTICES FROM EXTANT LINCOLNTON NEWSPAPERS, 1836-53, in NC Genealogical Journal, volume 2 (1976), pages 62-84, 136-47.

32. Published genealogies for the US

There are many published indexes, microfilm indexes, and card indexes which list large numbers of published genealogies at the national level. The most important indexes dealing exclusively with NC were listed in section 18. These listings included the card catalogs in NCSL, LUNC, LDU, FHL, and FHC. This paragraph sets out further indexes to genealogies all over the US. These indexes contain many references to North Carolinians and therefore you must not fail to look into them. Among the larger ones are:

_F. Rider, AMERICAN GENEALOGICAL INDEX, Godfrey Memorial Library, Middletown, CT, 1942-52, 48 volumes. [Millions of references.]
_F. Rider, AMERICAN GENEALOGICAL & BIOGRAPHICAL INDEX, Godfrey Memorial Library, Middletown, CT, 1952-83, over 150 volumes. [Millions of references.]
_The Newberry Library, THE GENEALOGICAL INDEX OF THE NEWBERRY LIBRARY, G. K. Hall, Boston, MA, 1960, 4 volumes. [500,000 names.]
_The NY Public Library, DICTIONARY CATALOG OF THE LOCAL HISTORY & GENEALOGY DIVISION OF THE NEW YORK PUBLIC LIBRARY, G. K. Hall, Boston, MA, 1974, 20 volumes. [318,000 entries.]
_J. Munsell's Sons, INDEX TO AMERICAN GENEALOGIES, 1711-1908, reprint, Genealogical Publishing Co., Baltimore, MD, 1967. [60,000 references.]
_M. J. Kaminkow, GENEALOGIES IN THE LIBRARY OF CONGRESS, Magna Carta, Baltimore, MD, 1972, 4 volumes, with COMPLEMENT, 1981. [over 25,000 genealogies]

These volumes are available in NCSL, LUNC, LDU, FHL (FHC), LGL, some RL, and some LL.

Also available at NCSL, LUNC, LDU, FHL (FHC), LGL, and in some RL and LL are several regional volumes which can lead you to genealogical information on NC families:

_Z. Armstrong, NOTABLE SOUTHERN FAMILIES, Lookout Publishing Co., Chattanooga, TN, 1918-33, 6 volumes.
_J. B. Boddie, HISTORICAL SOUTHERN FAMILIES, Pacific Coast Publishers, Redwood City, CA, 1957-80, 23 volumes.
_M. W. Collier, BIOGRAPHIES OF REPRESENTATIVE WOMEN IN THE SOUTH, 1861-1920, The Author, Atlanta, GA, 1920-9, 5 volumes.
_W. A. Crozier, A KEY TO SOUTHERN PEDIGREES, Southern Book Co., Baltimore, MD, 1953.
_E. K. Kirkham, INDEX TO SOME OF THE FAMILY RECORDS OF THE SOUTHERN STATES, Everton, Publishers, LOGAN, UT, 1979.

33. Regional records

In addition to state and local publications, there are some valuable regional publications which should not be overlooked by any NC researcher. These publications apply to specific regions which are made up of a few or many NC counties. Among them are the newspaper volumes which were mentioned in the latter portion of section 31. Other books which are to be recognized and used include:

_J. P. Arthur, WESTERN NC: A HISTORY, 1730-1913, Reprint Co., Spartanburg, SC, 1914 (1973).
_W. P. Haun, OLD ALBEMARLE COUNTY, NC, PERQUIMANS DISTRICT PRECINCT BIRTHS, MARRIAGES, DEATHS, AND FLESH MARKS, The Author, Durham, NC, 1980.
_C. L. Hunter, SKETCHES OF WESTERN NC, Genealogical Publishing Co., Baltimore, MD, 1877 (1970). [1500 names from Mecklenburg, Rowan, Lincoln, and adjacent counties.]
_M. W. Lambeth, MEMORIES AND RECORDS OF EASTERN NC, The Author, Nashville, TN, 1957. [Family genealogies, tax lists.]
_R. W. Ramsey, CAROLINA CRADLE: SETTLEMENT OF THE NORTHWEST CAROLINA FRONTIER, 1747-62, University of NC Press, Chapel Hill, NC, 1964.
_W. S. Ray, COLONIAL GRANVILLE COUNTY AND ITS PEOPLE, Genealogical Publishing Co., Baltimore, MD, 1945 (1973).
_W. S. Ray, OLD ALBEMARLE AND ITS ABSENTEE LANDLORDS, Genealogical Publishing Co., Baltimore, MD, 1947 (1968). [1200 surnames.]
_W. S. Ray, THE MECKLENBURG SIGNERS AND THEIR NEIGHBORS, Genealogical Publishing Co., Baltimore, MD, 1946 (1966). [Early south central NC.]
_A. D. Smith, WESTERN NC, HISTORICAL AND BIOGRAPHICAL, The Author, Charlotte, NC, 1890.
_W. C. Spence, TOMBSTONES AND EPITAPHS OF NORTHEASTERN NC, Gateway Press, Baltimore, MD, 1973. [Beaufort, Camden, Chowan, Currituck, Gates, Hyde, Pasquotank, Perquimans, and Washington Counties.]

These volumes will be found in NCSL, LUNC, and FHL (FHC). Some of them are in LGL, RL, and some LL.

34. Tax lists

Tax lists of various sorts (assessments, land, personal property, poll, delinquent) are exceptionally valuable records for establishing the year-to-year locations of ancestors. Basically, two categories of taxes were levied on NC people in the 18th and 19th centuries: (1) taxes on persons which were called poll taxes and the persons were called polls, tithables, or taxables, and (2) taxes on property, usually land, but sometimes personal property. The responsibility during these centuries for levying and collecting taxes rested with the counties. Up until 1777, the poll

tax was the only taxation used in NC, but after that year both poll and property taxes were collected well into the 20th century. Each year, each county kept a record of its taxations in the form of tax lists, one list being compiled for each section into which the county was divided. Sometimes the lists were alphabetized, sometimes not; sometimes the lists were combined; sometimes not. Basically tax lists contain a date, the tax district, the names of taxpayers, the polls (number of taxable persons), the amount of property, the value, and the total tax due.

Very few tax lists have survived for the period before the American Revolution. Those which have survived (both before and after 1777) and are available in the NCSA are listed for each county under the county names in Chapter 4. In order to locate the tax records for a given county, all you need to do is to look into the NCSA search room card file under the name of the county. Many of these records are on microfilm in FHL and hence available through FHC. Two volumes have been published which list taxpayers from all known NC tax lists dating before 1790:

_C. E. Ratcliff, NC TAXPAYERS, 1679-1790, Southern Historical Press, Easley, SC, 1984/7, 2 volumes.

35. Will and probate records

When a person died leaving any property (an estate), it was necessary for the governmental authorities to see that the property was properly distributed according to law. If a will had been written, it was usually presented to a county court who ascertained its authenticity, then it was presented to a probate authority whose job it was to see that the stipulations of the will were carried out. This probate authority approved or appointed an executor who did the actual work of distributing the estate. Prior to 1760, a will could be presented to any of the following probate authorities: colonial court of ordinary (the governor), colonial general court, colonial district superior court, or county court of pleas and quarter sessions. The will was then filed with the Secretary of State. After 1760, only wills probated before the governor were filed with the Secretary of State; those probated in a county court of pleas and quarter sessions remained there. After 1777, the only permissible probate authorities were the county courts, and when they were abolished in 1868, the superior courts in the counties took over. When wills were filed, they were usually collected in files and often copied into bound volumes generally called will books. If no will had been written (intestate), the probate authority appointed an administrator who distributed the estate according to law.

The majority of wills during 1663-1760 are in the Secretary of State's Records in NCSA. They are in a large series of alphabetically arranged folders and in several will books. Most of these wills are abstracted in:

_J. B. Grimes, ABSTRACT OF NC WILLS, Genealogical Publishing Co., Baltimore, MD, 1980. [Well indexed, but many errors.]
_F. A. Olds, AN ABSTRACT OF NC WILLS, 1760-1800, Genealogical Publishing Co., Baltimore, MD, 1978. [Incomplete.]
_J. R. B. Hathaway, NC HISTORICAL AND GENEALOGICAL REGISTER, Genealogical Publishing Co., Baltimore, MD, 1900 (1979), volume 1 [many errors]; indexed by F. Rider, THE AMERICAN GENEALOGICAL-BIOGRAPHICAL INDEX, Godfrey Memorial Library, Middletown, CT, 1952-.
_W. P. Johnson, GRIMES WILLS: MAJOR ADDITIONS AND CORRECTIONS, Journal of NC Genealogy, volume 11 (1965), pages 1575-7, volume 12 (1966), pages 1611-20, volume 13 (1967) 1820-3, 1946-8, volume 14 (1968), pages 2102-3.

During 1760-1868, most wills were placed in the records of the county court of pleas and quarter sessions. The originals were usually put in file folders and there were also bound volumes into which wills were copied. Practically all will records or copies for this period of time are now in NCSA. Those available for the various counties are listed in Chapter 4. In the time span 1868-1966, wills were filed, copied, recorded, and indexed in the county superior courts. Some are in NCSA and some are in the counties. Those available in the NCSA are listed in Chapter 4. Most will indexes contain an alphabetical list of those making wills (devisors, testators, decedents) and an alphabetical list of those receiving property (devisees, heirs, beneficiaries). A valuable overall index to NC wills during 1665-1900 has been published:

_T. W. Mitchell, NC WILLS, A TESTATOR INDEX, 1665-1900, The Author, Raleigh, NC, 1987, 2 volumes.

In the various actions by which executors and administrators distributed the property of a person who had died, many records were generated because accounting to the probate authority was required. These records include executors' and administrators' appointments, bonds, papers, accounts, inventories, sales, settlements, allowances for widows, guardian records, orphan records, petitions, land divisions, and others. These records may be found loose or in bound volumes under various titles. In the early years, they may be intermingled with deed records or they may appear in county court minutes. Prior to 1760, these records can be located in the Secretary of State Records (NCSA) and in the county records. After 1760, they are almost all in the county records. The holdings of the NCSA for the various counties are listed under the counties in Chapter 4. Probate and will records are usually very valuable genealogically because they are a primary source linking one generation decisively to another. Children are named and information is often provided regarding their ages, order of birth, marriages, places of residence, deaths, and grandchildren. Spouses are named and information regarding age, the marriage, and previous residences sometimes is given.

A number of will and probate records for selected years in individual counties has been abstracted and published. Most of these may be found in NCSL and LUNC; many are available in LDU, LGL, and FHL (FHC), and some are in RL and LL.

LIST OF ABBREVIATIONS

A	=	Agricultural census records
C	=	Civil War Union veterans census records
CH	=	Courthouse(s)
FHC	=	Family History Center(s), Branches of FHL
FHL	=	Family History Library
I	=	Industrial census records
LDU	=	Library, Duke University
LGL	=	Large genealogical library(ies)
LL	=	Local library(ies)
LUNC	=	Library, University of NC
M	=	Mortality census records
N	=	Early NC census-like lists
NA	=	National Archives
NC	=	North Carolina
NCSA	=	NC State Archives
NCSL	=	NC State Library
P	=	Pensioner census records, Revolutionary War
R	=	Regular census records
RBNA	=	Regional Brances of the National Archives
RL	=	Regional library(ies)
S	=	Slaveholder census records

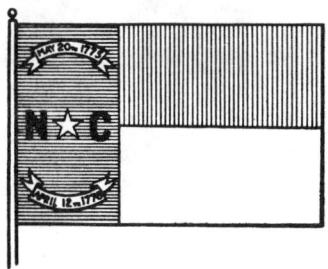

Chapter 3

RECORD LOCATIONS

1. Court houses (CH)

Practically all NC county records of any genealogical importance for the years 1663-1868 are held by NCSA either as the originals or as microfilm copies. In addition, they also hold a large number of original or microfilm copies of numerous county records during the period from 1868 up to and/or into the 20th century (1900s). All original records after 1910 have been retained by the counties, but copies of many are in NCSA. In short, only if you are interested in county records after 1910 should you consider starting your work at the local CH. Even in this case, you will find microfilm copies of numerous county records after 1910 in NCSA. For example, here are the dates up to which NCSA has certain records for Mecklenburg County: apprentice(1920), incorporation (1965), partnership (1967), superior court (1960), election (1920), accounts (1965), administrator (1964), assignment (1960), index to estates (1965), executor (1964), guardian (1925), settlement (1965), deed (1959), marriage (1962), vital statistics index (1947), orders and decrees (1960), will (1965). Chapter 4 lists the county records available for each county, and the following volume provides even more detail on them:

_NC State Archives Staff, GUIDE TO RESEARCH MATERIALS IN THE NC STATE ARCHIVES, SECTION B: COUNTY RECORDS, The Archives, Raleigh, NC, latest edition.

Thus, you can see that once you have located the county of your NC ancestor, it is not usually a good idea to go there first. It is best to first explore the original and microfilm copies of the records in NCSA and the transcribed and published copies of the records in NCSL and LUNC. If you are not near NCSA, NCSL, and LUNC, you should examine the NC records held by the FHL, which are available through FHC. Only after you or your hired researcher have exhausted the resources of NCSA and NCSL (or of FHL [FHC], then NCSA and NCSL) should you visit or send a hired researcher to look into the CH records. And this should only be done after a letter of inquiry to the Clerk of the Superior Court in the county has been answered to the effect that there are records there which NCSA does not have. Write a very brief letter (less than a half page), give the dates you are interested in, ask about specific types of records you want, and enclose an SASE.

Briefly, you need to remember that NC county records (bonds, court, deed, divorce, estate, land, marriage, probate, tax, will) before 1910 should be sought in NCSA. For those after 1910 you should first go to NCSA, then if necessary to CH. Many of these records are in microfilm

form in the FHL and thus available through FHC. The major NC <u>state records</u> (court, estate, land, marriage, military, will) are to be found in NCSA and the FHL (FHC). Please note that there are both county and state court, estate, land, marriage, and will records. Many of the major NC <u>federal records</u> (bounty land, census, military, pension) are in NCSA, but more are available at the National Archives in Washington, DC, in the Regional Branches of the National Archives, and in the FHL (FHC). The major NC <u>non-governmental records</u> (Bible, biographical, cemetery, church, directory, DAR, genealogical compilations, genealogical periodicals, historical, manuscript, mortuary, newspaper) are located in NCSA, NCSL, LUNC, LDU, FHL (FHC), LGL, church archives, RL, and LL.

2. The major facilities

The best overall place in the world to do NC genealogical research is in Raleigh, NC. This city contains the two most heavily stocked NC genealogical resource collections in existence: the NC State Archives (NCSA), and the NC State Library (NCSL). Just a few blocks away are the Land Grant Office of the NC Secretary of State and the Vital Records Branch of the NC State Division of Health Services. Within 35 miles of Raleigh there are two other important facilities: the Library at the University of NC (LUNC) in Chapel Hill, and the Library at Duke University (LDU) in Durham.

In Salt Lake City, UT, is the largest genealogical library in the world, the Family History Library (FHL). This facility has microfilm copies of many of the records in NCSA and NCSL. The library (FHL) has over 250 branch libraries called Family History Centers (FHC) located all over the US. The vast microfilm holdings of FHL can be borrowed through its branches. Each branch has copies of three exceedingly large indexes to the holdings of FHL. Included among the FHC are ones in Raleigh, Charlotte, Fayetteville, Goldsboro, Greensboro, Hickory, Kinston, Skyland (Asheville), Wilmington, and Winston-Salem.

3. The NC State Archives (NCSA)

The Archives and Records Section of the Division of Archives and History of the Department of Cultural Resources (of NC), referred to in this volume as the NC State Archives (NCSA), is located on the second floor of the Archives and History-State Library Building at 109 East Jones St., Raleigh, NC 27611. The mail address is NC State Archives, 109 East Jones St., Raleigh, NC 27611, and the telephone number is 919-733-3952. The location is in the historic downtown area of Raleigh just one block north of the Capitol. There is an underground parking garage provided for visitors to NCSA and NCSL beneath the NC Museum of History located in the block directly southwest of the Archives Building. At this writing, the NCSA is open 8:00

am-5:30 pm Tuesday- Friday and 9:00 am-5:00 pm Saturday. It is closed on all Sundays and Mondays, on holidays, on some days surrounding holidays, and for two inventory days in January. But times change, so don't dare go without calling ahead. The nearest motels, which are within walking distance, are the Holiday Inn Downtown, 320 Hillsborough St., Raleigh, NC 27601 (800-238-8000), the Friendship Inn, 309 Hillsborough St., Raleigh, NC 27603 (919-833-5771), and the Journey's End Motel, 300 North Dawson, Raleigh, NC 27603 (919-828- 9081). Several other motels are within a short drive including the Brownstone Hotel, 1707 Hillsborough St., Raleigh, NC 27605 (1 1/2 miles away, 919-828-0811), and the Velvet Cloak Inn, 1505 Hillsborough St., Raleigh, NC 27605 (1 1/2 miles away, 919-828-0333). And a fairly long walk or a short drive away (3/4 mile) is the Radisson Plaza Hotel, 420 Fayetteville Street, Raleigh, NC 27605 (919-834-9900).

The NCSA is located in the west end of the second floor of the building. Upon entering, turn to your left, walk to the elevator, and then take it to the second floor. Enter the Archives door and you will find yourself in the entry office. Show the security officer behind the desk some identification, fill out the form, store all your materials except pencils and note-taking paper in the lockers, and ask for a copy of the regulations. Enter the search room, find a seat, carefully read the regulations, and then glance around a bit. You will discover that all materials are to be handled with exceptional care; record volumes are to be placed on special reading racks for use; removal, mutilation, or writing on records is a crime; only pencils are to be used; food, drink, and smoking are not permitted; records are to be requested by filling out a call slip; microfilms are located in an adjacent room along with readers; and the walls are lined with reference volumes, finding aids, indexes, and important published books and periodicals. Beginning with the east wall, you will find a large card file case in the southeastern section of it. This contains the:
_WPA NC GRAVES INDEX, Pre-1914, alphabetical by name.
_WPA NC GRAVES INDEX, Post-1914, alphabetical by name.
_NC CONFEDERATE GRAVESTONE RECORDS, alphabetical by name.
    Referenced volumes nearby.
In the southeastern corner, you will find the volumes which contain the official field reports of the Civil War, both for the Armies and for the Navies (Union and Confederate). Then, on the south wall, you will discover the NC Historical Review (with 50-year index, 1924-73), Records of Moravians in NC, numerous volumes of papers (Iredell, Blount, Ruffin, Mangum, Graham, Vance, others), the Colonial and State Records of NC, books on the laws of NC, the House and Senate Journals, numerous volumes of NC legislative documents, and the NC Higher Court Reports. In the nook at the west end of the south wall there are located the finding aids to the records of the British Public Records Office. There is also an alphabetized card file to NC Confederate soldiers as taken from the book by J. W. Moore:

_CARD ABSTRACTS FROM MOORE'S ROSTER, alphabetized by name.
In the same nook and also in the northwest corner, you will discover microfiche indexes to NC marriage bonds (1741-1868):
_INDEX TO NC MARRIAGE BONDS, 1741-1868, state-wide, alphabetical by groom and by bride.

Along the north wall there are shelved books on NC biography and history, county histories, volumes on the Revolutionary War, War of 1812, Mexican War, Civil War, Spanish-American War and other wars, genealogical and historical periodicals, the National Union Catalog of Manuscript Collections, and numerous published and typescript records relating to counties, the state, and taken from old newspapers. Placed in with these you will find several typescript indexes:
_INDEXES TO REVOLUTIONARY WAR ACCOUNTS, typescript volumes (see section 26, Chapter 2).
_INDEX TO WAR OF 1812 VOUCHERS, typescript, alphabetical by name.
_INDEX TO WAR OF 1812 MUSTER ROLLS, typescript, alphabetical by name.
Just around the corner of the right end of the north wall is a shelf containing censuses, census indexes, typescript county marriage bond records, DAR compilations, transcribed cemetery records, and finding aids to private manuscripts and state agency records. When you remove a book from the open shelves and use it, do not return it to the shelf. Leave it on a nearby table for an attendant to replace.

In a large nook in the northeast corner of the Archives Search Room, there is a card file case containing finding aids to many of the major records in the archives:
_CARD INDEX TO COUNTY RECORDS, alphabetical by county.
_CARD INDEX TO STATE COURT RECORDS, alphabetical by court name and by location.
_CARD INDEX TO CHURCH HISTORIES, alphabetical by church name and by denomination.
_CARD INDEX TO CEMETERY RECORDS, alphabetical by county, then by name of cemetery.
_CARD INDEX TO BIBLE RECORDS, alphabetical by name.
_CARD INDEX TO SECRETARY OF STATE RECORDS, alphabetical by type.
_CARD INDEX TO SECRETARY OF STATE REVOLUTIONARY MILITARY PAPERS, alphabetical by name.
_CARD INDEX TO GRANVILLE LAND GRANTS, alphabetical by name.
_CARD INDEX TO GOVERNOR'S PAPERS, three different indexes, one 1688-1775, one 1775-1835, one 1836-58, all alphabetical by name.
_CARD INDEXES TO GENERAL ASSEMBLY RECORDS.
_CARD INDEXES TO NC MAP COLLECTION, 4 separate indexes, one chronologically by date, one alphabetically by waterway, one alphabetically by county, one alphabetically by town or city.

_CARD INDEX TO GEOLOGICAL SURVEY MAP COLLECTION, alphabetical by quadrangle (location).
_CARD INDEX TO APPLICATIONS FOR PARDON, 1865, alphabetical by name.
_CARD INDEXES TO PRIVATE MANUSCRIPT COLLECTION, three separate indexes, one alphabetical by autograph, one alphabetical by subject, one alphabetical by county.
_CARD INDEX TO NEWSPAPER CLIPPINGS, alphabetical by subject and name.
_CARD INDEX TO JOHNSTON COUNTY ESTATES, alphabetical by name.
_CARD INDEX TO FINDING AIDS FOR RECORDS OF STATE AGENCIES, alphabetical by agency, subject, location.

When you locate a reference to materials you want, fill out a call slip, being careful to record all the numbers in the upper left hand corner of the file card. Present this to an attendant at the desk (just opposite the card index case), and your records will be brought to the desk in a short time.

Occupying a sizable segment of the northwest corner of the Archives Search Area is the Microfilm Room. When you enter you will see a small card file case on your left, and the rest of the room occupied with microfilm cabinets and microfilm readers. The thousands of microfilms are listed in a series of card indexes located in the card file case. These include:
_CARD INDEX TO NC COUNTY RECORD MICROFILMS, alphabetically by county.
_CARD INDEX TO NC STATE AGENCY RECORD MICROFILMS, alphabetically by agency.
_CARD INDEX TO NC MUNICIPAL RECORD MICROFILMS, alphabetical by city.
_CARD INDEX TO NC CHURCH RECORD MICROFILMS, alphabetical by county.
_CARD INDEX TO NC NEWSPAPER MICROFILMS, alphabetical by city.
_CARD INDEX TO NC MISCELLANEOUS RECORD MICROFILMS, includes private collections, cemeteries, and state military records.
_CARD INDEX TO FEDERAL RECORD MICROFILMS RELATING TO NC (in drawer with STATE AGENCY RECORDS), includes census records, compiled service records and indexes for Revolutionary War, War of 1812, Cherokee Disturbances, Civil War, Spanish-American War.

When you locate microfilms that you wish to examine, copy the numbers on the left side of the index card, then use these numbers to locate your film in the cabinets. You may then place your film on a reader and examine it. If you are not familiar with the readers, ask an attendant to assist you. When you have finished with a microfilm return it to its box, and then place it on a table top by the microfilm card indexes. Do not return it to the cabinet; leave that for an attendant to do.

There are several finding aids that are kept behind the desk which you may ask for. These include:
_NC CENSUS INDEXES, alphabetical by name.
_APPLICATIONS FOR CONFEDERATE PENSIONS INDEX, alphabetical by name.
_INDEX TO MUSTER ROLLS OF THE WAR OF 1812, alphabetical by name.
_INDEX TO NC BIOGRAPHIES, names taken from many works, alphabetical by name.
Don't overlook discussing your search with an archivist to make sure that you do not miss relevant materials.

The staff of NCSA cannot do genealogical research for you by mail. They are kept busy serving the State an the patrons who come to them in person. They will provide you with a list of researchers if you cannot make a personal visit. Dispatch them a request and an SASE. Though doing no research, they will provide for you the answer to one very specific question which can be answered by taking a brief look at an index. You must include the following in your request: (1) full name of person, (2) name of county, (3) specific document desired, and (4) approximate date.

4. The NC State Library (NCSL)

The Genealogical Services Branch of the Division of State Library of the Department of Cultural Resources (of NC), referred to in this volume as the NC State Library (NCSL), is located on the mezzanine floor of the Archives and History – State Library Building at 109 East Jones St., Raleigh, NC 27611. It is thus in the same building as NCSA. The mail address is Genealogical Services Branch, NC State Library, 109 East Jones St., Raleigh, NC 27611 and the telephone number is 919-733-7222. The parking facilities for NCSL are the same as those for NCSA. The NCSL is open 8:00 am-5:30 pm Monday-Friday, and 9:00 am-5:00 pm Saturday. It is closed on all Sundays and holidays and some days surrounding holidays. But times change, so be sure and call before you go.

The NCSL is located in the southwest section of the mezzanine level of the building. Upon entering, sign the register on the small side table, and leave all brief cases and coats on the rack. Go in, find a seat, and remind yourself of the general rules for libraries (careful handling of all materials, removal or defacing materials is a crime, no food or drink or smoking, work quietly, no pens, only pencils). A medium-sized card file case is located near the entrance. It contains several individual indexes. The first is the main card catalog of the NCSL collection (Author-Title-Subject). Then, there is an extensive card index to family names (in both books and loose papers), and the NC Periodical Index (which indexes the NC Genealogical Society Journal, NC Genealogy, NC Historical and Genealogical Register,

NC Historical Society Quarterly, the Researcher, and several other periodicals by name and county). The main stack area where most of the books are shelved occupies the western-most third of the library. Here you will find a large majority of the published works mentioned in Chapter 2. Along the east wall, you will find genealogical periodicals relating to NC counties, regions, the state of NC, other states, and those of national scope. On the south wall are shelved important national and NC reference works. Along the north wall (just under the windows) are many census indexes, including those of NC. A set of file cabinets containing loose papers on many families (indexed by the card index to family names mentioned above) is located in the southeast corner of the library. These papers are arranged alphabetically by family name and county. A copying machine stands near the stack area.

Begin your work by proceeding to the main card catalog, and start to look for materials of interest to your research by remembering the word SLANT. S stands for subject, so look under various subject headings. The titles of the sections in Chapter 2 will give you a good idea of the sort of things you need to search, but you will not find them all. Other subject headings that you must not overlook are: Registers of births, etc. (vital records may be found here), Epitaphs, Genealogy, Obituaries, and Probate Records. L stands for locality, therefore examine all cards under the heading North Carolina, then all under the name of the county, then all under the names of cities and/or towns in the county which might be pertinent. A stands for author, thus examine the author listings for any books mentioned in Chapters 2 and 4 which you might want to find. N stands for name, which reminds you to look under all the surnames which you are searching for to see if there are books which might be relevant. T stands for title, and hence your final step is to look under the titles of books, periodicals, and agencies (such as Daughters of the American Revolution, United Daughters of the Confederacy, Works Progress Administration, US National Archives) which sponsored publications. The word SLANT is simply a memory device, and does not indicate the best order to look for things in. To shorten your research time, it is recommended that you do N (name) first, then L (locality) [county first, then state], then S (subject), then A (author), and finally T (title). This procedure will give you good coverage of the library holdings which are indexed in the card catalog. Among them you will find almost all of the published materials mentioned in Chapters 2 and 4.

When you run across pertinent materials, write the call numbers down (upper left corner of the card). Then go directly to the stack area and find your book under the call numbers. When you finish with a volume, do not return it to the stacks. Place it on one of the carts designated for this purpose, so that an attendant can re-shelve the book. Your next step is to look into the other indexes mentioned above:

_CARD INDEX TO FAMILY NAMES, leads to family records, both books in the stacks, and loose papers in the vertical file.
_CARD INDEX TO NC PERIODICALS.
There is another item you need to give attention to: a file box on the registration table. This box contains notices left by persons searching given surnames. You should look under its alphabetically arranged notices for the surnames of your ancestors to see if others should be contacted. You are also encouraged to leave your own notices. Do not fail to talk to the librarian about your search and be sure to ask about any other special indexes which might help you.

The staff at NCSL cannot do genealogical research for you by mail. They are kept busy serving the State and the patrons who come to them in person. They will provide you with a list of researchers if you cannot make a personal visit. Dispatch them a request and an SASE. They will provide for you the answer to one very specific question which can be answered by taking a brief look at an index. You must include the following in your request: (1) full name of person, (2) name of county, (3) specific document desired, and (4) approximate date. For example, a specific question might be: Is a George W. STUBBLEFIELD(1) mentioned in the Caswell County(2) census index(3) for 1850(4)? Questions less specific than this will require a personal visit or a hired genealogical researcher.

5. The Library of the University of NC (LUNC)

The Wilson Library at the University of NC (LUNC), Chapel Hill, NC 27514 [919-962-0114] is of exceptional value to every NC genealogist and local historian. Its value consists of two major aspects: (1) the NC Collection of published materials, and (2) the Southern Historical Collection of manuscripts and papers. You should carefully explore the resources of these two collections for materials relating to each and every one of your NC ancestors. Times when both these collections are available for use are 8:00 am-5:00 pm Monday through Friday and 9:00 am-1:00 pm Saturday. However, since times can change (especially between terms), don't fail to call before you go.

The NC Collection of published materials is located in the Wilson Library in Room 506. Practically all of the printed works listed in Chapters 2 and 4 will be found in this collection. As you enter, you will find a very helpful guide on the reference side shelf:
_J. Cotten, A GUIDE FOR BIOGRAPHICAL AND GENEALOGICAL RESEARCH IN THE NC COLLECTION, The Collection, Chapel Hill, NC, 1976.
After looking through this guide, you may then proceed to examine two catalogs: (1) the main card catalog which lists entries under subject, author,

and title categories, and (2) the biography card file, which lists entries under names. Both should be carefully gone through, keeping the S-L-A-N-T categories in mind especially for the main catalog. The call numbers on the cards will lead you directly to the volumes.

The Southern Historical Collection of manuscript materials is located in the Wilson Library in Room 901 on the 4th floor. The collection is an exceedingly large one and should not be overlooked by anyone doing in-depth genealogical research in NC. There are three major finding aids available for this collection. The first is a two-volume set:
_S. S. Blosser and C. N. Wilson, Jr., THE SOUTHERN HISTORICAL COLLECTION: A GUIDE TO MANUSCRIPTS, University of NC Library, Chapel Hill, NC, 1970; and E. H. Smith, III, THE SOUTHERN HISTORICAL COLLECTION: SUPPLEMENTARY GUIDE TO MANUSCRIPTS, 1970-5, University of NC Library, Chapel Hill, NC, 1976.
In addition, there is a card catalog which lists manuscript materials under names of individuals and places, as well as under subjects. Once you find a useful entry in these finding aids, the designations on the card will lead you to a survey description of the manuscript which will permit you to select the portions of it which are relevant to your research. Upon application, the archivist will bring the requested materials out to you.

6. Perkins Library, Duke University (LDU)

The main library at Duke University, Durham, NC 27706 is known as the Perkins Library (LDU). The telephone number of the Reference Department is 919-684-2373 and that of the Special Collections Department Manuscript Reading Room is 919-684-3372. Times when the Reference Department is open are 8:30 am-8:30 pm Monday through Thursday, 8:30 am-5 pm Friday, 12 Noon through 4 pm Saturday, and 1 pm-4:45 pm Sunday. Times when the Special Collections Department is open are 8:00 am-5:00 pm Monday through Friday and 9:00 am-12:30 pm Saturday. However, since these times can change (especially between terms), be sure and call before going. In this excellent very large library, there are two major areas that genealogists need to make use of. The first is the main card catalog area located near the circulation desk on the first floor. Consult also in the same area the online catalog, a computerized catalog known as the Bibliographic Information System (BIS), that contains records of everything cataloged since 1979. All manual catalogs are being converted to this system. You will find two card catalogs there which list the major published holdings of LDU, one arranged by author and title, the other arranged by subject. LDU has many of the printed volumes mentioned in Chapters 2 and 4 and a few of the microfilms. Using the acronym SLANT, as described in section 4 of this chapter, you need to look into both of these card catalogs. When you find pertinent materials, copy

down the call numbers from the upper left hand corners of the cards, and then proceed into the stack areas where you will find your volumes according to these call numbers.

The second area into which you need to go at LDU is the Special Collections Department Manuscript Reading Room located on the third floor in Room 344. There are two major finding aids to assist you in locating materials in this department. The first is a guidebook to the holdings:
_R. C. Davis and L. A. Miller, GUIDE TO THE CATALOGED COLLECTIONS IN THE MANUSCRIPT DEPARTMENT OF THE PERKINS LIBRARY, DUKE UNIVERSITY, Clio Books, Santa Barbara, CA, 1980.
This volume has an extensive index, and you should look into it for all locations (regions, counties, cities), all names, and all subjects in which you have interest. When you locate materials, the archivist on duty will help you obtain the manuscripts. This guidebook is supplemented by an extensive card catalog in the Manuscript Reading Room. The catalog is made up of four principal card files: title file, autograph file, subject file, and geographical (locality) file. There are far more listings in these card files than in the guidebook. Thus, you must not fail to go through them carefully.

7. Family History Library (FHL) and Its Branches (FHC)

The largest genealogical library in the world is The Family History Library of the Church of Jesus Christ of Latter-Day Saints (FHL), often referred to as Mormon Library or the LDS Library. This repository holds well over 1.7 million rolls of microfilm plus more than 175,000 books, all genealogical material. It is located at 35 North West Temple, Salt Lake City, UT 84150. The library opens every day except Sunday and holidays at 7:30 am. It closes at 5 pm Saturday, 6 pm Monday, and 10 pm Tuesday through Friday. The general telephone number is 1-(801)-521-0130. The basic key to the library is a massive index called the Family History Library Catalog (FHLC), a set of microfiche (with five sections: surname, locality, subject, author-title, foreign-language-locality). In addition to the main library, the Church maintains a large number of branches called Family History Centers (FHC) all over the world. Each of these has microfiche copies of the Family History Library Catalog (FHLC), plus several other major indexes, plus forms for borrowing microfilm copies of the records at FHL. This means that the astonishingly large holdings of the FHL are available on loan through each of its numerous FHC (Family History Centers or Branch Libraries of the FHL).

The FHC in NC are as follows:
_Charlotte Stake, 3020 Hilliard Dr., Charlotte, NC 28218 [704535-0238]

_Fayetteville Stake, 3200 Scotty Hill Rd., Fayetteville, NC 28303 [919-864-2080]
_Goldsboro Stake, 1000 Eleventh St., Goldsboro, NC [919-735-0633]
_Greensboro Stake, 3719 Pinetop Rd., Greensboro, NC [919-288-6539]
_Hickory Stake, Highways 127 North, Hickory, NC 28601 [704-324-2823]
_Kinston Stake, 3006 Carey Rd., Kinston, NC 28501 [919-522-4671]
_Raleigh Stake, 5100 Six Forks Rd., Raleigh, NC 27612 [919-781-1662]
_Skyland Stake (Asheville), US 25A, Sweeten Creek and Rosseraggon, Skyland, NC [704-684-6646]
_Wilmington Stake, FHC, 514 South College Rd., Wilmington, NC 28401 [919-799-1339]
_Winston-Salem Stake, 4780 Westchester Dr., Winston-Salem, NC [704-731-7911]

When you get ready to visit these FHC or any of the hundreds of others we will soon mention, call them or write them (including an SASE) inquiring about open hours and exact locations.

Other FHC are to be found in the cities listed below. They may be located by looking in the local telephone directories under the listing CHURCH OF JESUS CHRIST OF LATTER DAY SAINTS or in the yellow pages under CHURCHES-LATTER-DAY SAINTS.

_In AL: Birmingham, Huntsville, in AK: Anchorage, Fairbanks, in AZ: Campe Verde(Cottonwood), Flagstaff, Globe, Holbrook, Mesa, Page, Phoenix, Prescott, St. David, Safford, St. Johns, Show Low, Snowflake, Tucson, Winslow, Yuma, in AR: Little Rock,
_In CA: Anaheim, Bakersfield, Barstow, Blythe(Needles), Camarillo, Cerritos(Santa Fe Springs, Lakewood), Covina (West Covina), Cypress-(Buena Park), El Centro, Escondido, Eureka, Fairfield, Fresno, Garden Grove, Glendale, Gridley, Hacienda Heights, Hemet, La Crescenta(La Canada), Lancaster, Long Beach, Los Angeles(Alhambra, Canyon Country), Menlo Park, Mission Viejo, Modesto, Monterey(Seaside), Napa, Newbury Park, Oakland, Orange, Palmdale, Palm Springs(Cathedral City), Pasadena(East Pasadena), Redding, Ridgecrest, Riverside, Sacramento(Carmichael), San Bernardino, San Diego, San Jose, San Luis Obispo, Santa Barbara(Goleta), Santa Clara, Santa Maria, Santa Rosa, Simi Valley, Southern CA(Los Angeles), Stockton, Upland, Ventura, Whittier,
_In CO: Arvada, Boulder, CO Springs, Columbine(Littleton), Cortez, Denver(Northglenn), Durango, Ft. Collins, Grand Junction, LaJara, Littleton, Meeker(Glenwood Springs), Montrose, Pueblo, in CT: Hartford, in DE: Wilmington(Newark), in FL: Cocoa, Gainesville(Alachua), Hialeah/Ft. Lauderdale, Jacksonville(Orange Park), Lakeland, Marianna, Miami, Orlando(Fern Park), Pensacola, St. Petersburg, Tallahassee, Tampa, West Palm Beach(Boca Raton), in GA: Macon, Marietta(Powder Spring),

Sandy Springs(Dunwoody), in HI: Hilo, Honolulu, Kaneohe, Kona(Kailua), Laie,
_In ID: Bear Lake(Montpelier), Blackfoot(Moreland), Boise, Burley, Caldwell, Driggs, Firth, ID Falls, Iona, Lewiston, Malad, Meridian(Boise), Moore(Arco), Nampa, Pocatello, Post Falls, Salmon, Shelley, Twin Falls, Upper Snake River(Rexburg), in IL: Champaign, Chicago Heights(Lossmoor), Naperville(Downers Grove), Rockford, Wilmette, in IN: Fort Wayne, Indianapolis(Greenwood), in IA: Cedar Rapids, Davenport, Des Moines, in KS: Topeka, Wichita, in KY: Hopkinsville(Benton), Lexington, Louisville, in LA: Baton Rouge, Shreveport,
_In ME: Augusta(Hallowell), in MD: Silver Spring, in MA: Sudbury, in MI: Bloomfield Hills, Grand Blanc, Grand Rapids, Lansing(East Lansing), Midland, Westland, in MN: Minneapolis(Richfield), St. Paul, in MS: Hattiesburg, in MO: Columbia, Kansas City(Shawnee Mission), Liberty, Springfield, St. Louis(Berkeley), in MT: Billings, Bozeman, Butte, Great Falls, Helena, Kalispell, Missoula, in NE: Omaha,
_In NV: Elko, Ely, Fallon, Las Vegas, Logandale, Reno, Sparks, in NJ: East Brunswick, Morristown(Chatham), in NH: Nashua, in NM: Albuquerque-(Los Alamos), Farmington, Gallup, Grants, Los Cruces, Roswell, Santa Fe, in NY: Albany(Loudonville), Buffalo(Williamsville), Ithaca (Vestal), New York City, Plainview(Massapequa), Rochester(Webster), Syracuse, Yorktown(New Canaan, CT), in NC: See above, Charlotte, Fayetteville, Hickory, Kinston, Raleigh(Bailey Road), Wilmington(Hampstead), in OH: Cincinnati, Cleveland(North Olmstead), Columbus(Reynoldsburg), Dayton(Jettering), Kirtland, Toledo(Maumee), in OK: Norman, Oklahoma City, Tulsa,
_In OR: Beaverton, Bend, Coos Bay, Corvallis, Eugene, Grants Pass, Gresham(Fairview), Klamath Falls, LaGrande, Lake Oswego(West Linn), Medford, Nyssa(Ontario), Oregon City, Portland, Prineville, Roseburg, Salem, The Dallas, in PA: Philadelphia(Broomall), Pittsburgh, Reading, State College, York, in SC: Charleston(Hanahan), Columbia(Hopkins), Greenville, in TN: Chattanooga, Kingsport, Knoxville(Bearden), Memphis, Nashville(Madison), in TX: Austin(Georgetown), Beaumont(Nederland), Corpus Christi, Dallas, El Paso, Hurst, Friendswood, Houston-(Bellaire), Longview, Lubbock, Odessa, Plano(Richardson), San Antonio,
_In UT: Beaver, Blanding, Bountiful, Brigham City, Cache(Logan), Castledale(Orangeville), Cedar City, Delta, Duchesne, Fillmore, Heber City, Hurricane, Kanab, Lehi(Salt Lake City), Loa, Moroni, Mount Pleasant, Nephi, Ogden, Parowan, Price, Richfield, Roosevelt, Rose Park(Salt Lake City), Sandy, Santaquin, South Jordan(Riverton), St. George, Springville, Tremonton, UT Valley(Provo), Uintah(Vernal), in VA: Annandale, Charlottesville, Fairfax(Springfield), Norfolk(VA Beach), Oakton, Richmond, Roanoke,
_In WA: Bellevue, Bellingham(Ferndale), Bremerton, Ephrata(Quincy), Everett, Kennewick, Longview, Moses Lake, Mount Vernon, Olympia,

Pasco, Pullman, Puyallup(Sumner), Richland, Seattle, Spokane, Tacoma, Vancouver, Walla Walla, Wenatchee(East Wenatchee), Yakima, in <u>WI</u>: Appleton, Beloit(Belvidere), Milwaukee, in <u>WY</u>: Afton, Casper, Cody, Evanston, Gillette(Sheridan), Green River, Kemmerer, Lovell, Rock Springs, Worland, Wyoming(Cheyenne).

The FHL is constantly adding new branches, so this list will probably be out-of-date by the time you read it. An SASE and a $2 fee to the FHL (address in the 1st paragraph above) will bring you the most-recent listing of FHC.

When you go to a FHC, you need to <u>first</u> look up the NC surnames of interest to you in the following indexes:
_The NC Section of the INTERNATIONAL GENEALOGICAL INDEX (IGI).
_The Surname Portion of the FAMILY HISTORY LIBRARY CATALOG (FHLC).
_THE FAMILY REGISTER.
_The AIS INTEGRATED CENSUS INDEXES for 1790/1800/10, for 1820, for 1830, for 1840, and for the 1850 Eastern States.
_The Subject Portion of the FAMILY HISTORY LIBRARY CATALOG (FHLC), under the heading Family Group Records.

The <u>second</u> set of index investigations you should make is to look at all entries under NC, and then all entries under the NC counties of interest to you:
_The Locality Portion of the FAMILY HISTORY LIBRARY CATALOG (FHLC).
You will find extensive listings of these types of records: administrative, business, census, church, county/town histories, court, family histories, genealogical collections, land, military, newspaper, probate, tax, town, vital record (birth, marriage, death), and will. The only other place that some of these records are available is the county itself (or the NCSA), so this is an exceptionally useful source. When you find entries which you think are applicable to your progenitor(s), copy down the reference numbers and names of the records. These data will permit the FHC librarian to borrow for you the microfilm(s) containing the detailed information from the FHL. The cost is only a few dollars per roll, and when your microfilms arrive (usually 3-6 weeks), you will be notified so that you can return and examine them. A <u>third</u> action you should take is to ask the FHC librarian for a form (Temple Ordinance Indexes Request) to request from the FHL an examination of the Temple Index Bureau Records and the Family Group Records Archive. The above three actions will lead you to many of the materials mentioned in Chapter 2 and many of the records listed under the counties and towns in Chapter 4.

When you go to the FHL or a FHC, <u>first</u> ask for the NC international genealogical index microfiche and examine it for the name of your ancestor, then if you are at FHL, request the records. If you are at FHC, ask them to

borrow the microfilm containing the record from FHL. The cost is only a few dollars, and when your microfilm arrives (usually 4-6 weeks), you will be notified so that you can return and examine it. Second, ask for the surname catalog at FHL or the microfilm copy of it at FHC. Examine it for all listings of the surname of your ancestor. If you think any of the references relate to your ancestral line, and if you are at FHL, request the records. If you are at FHC, ask them to borrow the record for you. Third, ask for the NC locality catalog. Request the catalog at FHL or a microfilm copy of the catalog at FHC. Examine all listings under the main heading of NORTH CAROLINA. Then examine all listings under the subheading of the county you are interested in. These listings follow those for the state of NC. Toward the end of each of the county listings, there are listed materials relating to cities and towns in the county. Be sure not to overlook them. If you are at FHL, you can request the materials which are of interest to you. If you are at FHC, you may have the branch librarian borrow them for you. A large number of the books and records referred to in Chapter 2 and those listed under the counties in Chapter 4 will be found in the NC locality catalog.

If you happen to be at FHL, there are several other important indexes that you should examine thoroughly. Included among them are the Pedigree Index File, Temple Index Bureau, and the Family Group Records Archive (if the Temple Index Bureau indicates). Further details concerning the records in FHL and FHC along with instructions for finding and using them will be found in:
_J. Cerny and W. Elliott, THE LIBRARY, Ancestry Publishing, Salt Lake City, UT, 1988.

We cannot leave this section without reminding you that the NCSA has most of the NC microfilms held by the FHL, a truly large number of rolls with an exceptional volume of records. The microfilms in the NCSA are listed under the counties in a card catalog at the NCSA, which will give you easy access to them.

8. Regional libraries (RL)

In the state of NC there are a number of regional libraries (RL) which have genealogical collections. Their holdings are larger than those of most local libraries (LL), but are smaller than the holdings of NCSL. As might be expected, the materials in each RL are best for the immediate and surrounding counties. Among the best of these RL are:
_(Asheville) Asheville-Buncombe Library System, 67 Haywood St., Asheville, NC 28801.
_(Boone) Belk Library, Appalachian State University, Boone, NC 28608.
_(Charlotte) Public Library of Charlotte and Mecklenburg County, 310 North Tryon St., Charlotte, NC 28202.

_(Cullowhee) Hunter Library, Western Carolina University, Cullowhee, NC 28723.
_(Danville, VA) Danville Public Library, 511 Patton St., Danville, VA 24541.
_(Elizabeth City) East Albemarle Regional Library, 205 East Main St., Elizabeth City, NC 27909.
_(Greensboro) Greensboro Public Library, 201 North Greene St., Greensboro, NC 27402.
_(Greenville) Joyner Library, East Carolina University, Greenville, NC 27858.
_(Halifax) Halifax County Library, Granville St., Halifax, NC 27839.
_(North Wilkesboro) Wilkes County Regional Library, 913 C St., North Wilkesboro, NC 28659.
_(Salisbury) Rowan Public Library, 201 West Fisher St., Salisbury, NC 28144.
_(Wilmington) New Hanover County Public Library, 201 Chestnut St., Wilmington, NC 28401.
_(Winston-Salem) Forsythe County Public Library, 660 West Fifth St., Winston-Salem, NC 27101.

When a visit is made to any of these libraries, your *first* endeavor is to search the card catalog. You can remember what to look for with the acronym SLANT. This procedure should give you very good coverage of the library holdings which are indexed in card catalog.

The *second* endeavor at any of these libraries is to ask about any special archives, indexes, catalogs, collections, manuscripts, or materials which might be pertinent to your search. You should make it your aim particularly to inquire about Bible, cemetery, church, map, manuscript, military, mortuary, and newspaper materials. In some cases, microform (microfilm, microfiche, microcard) records are not included in the regular card catalog but are separately indexed. It is important that you be alert to this possibility.

In addition to the RL mentioned above, there are several libraries in NC which have highly-specialized collections which are pertinent to facets of NC genealogy. Many of these have been listed in section 7 of Chapter 2 which names church record centers. Other specialized collections are mentioned in:
_J. B. Howell, SPECIAL COLLECTIONS IN LIBRARIES OF THE SOUTHEAST, Southeastern Library Association, Jackson, MS, 1978.
_AMERICAN LIBRARY DIRECTORY, Bowker, New York, NY, latest edition.

9. Local libraries (LL)

Listed under the 100 NC counties in Chapter 4 are most of the important local libraries (county, city, consolidated, college, university) in the state. These libraries are of a very wide variety, some having sizable holdings of gene-

alogical materials, some having practically none. However, you must never overlook a LL in a county or city of your interest since quite often they have local records or collections available nowhere else. In addition, local librarians are frequently very knowledgeable concerning genealogical sources in their areas. Further, they are also usually acquainted with people in the county who are experts in the county's history and genealogy. Thus, both local libraries and local librarians can be of exceptional value to you.

When you visit a LL, the general procedure described previously should be followed: <u>First</u>, search the card catalog. Look under the headings summarized by SLANT: subject, location, author, name, title, doing them in the order L-N-S-A-T. Then, <u>second</u>, inquire about special indexes, catalogs, collections, materials, and microforms. Also ask about any other local sources of data such as cemetery records, church records, maps and atlases, genealogical and historical societies, mortuary records, and old newspaper records and indexes.

If you choose to write a LL, please remember that the librarians are very busy people. Always send them an SASE and confine your questions to one straight-forward item. Librarians are usually glad to help you if they can employ indexes to answer your question, but you must not expect them to do research for you. In case research is required, they will usually be able to supply you with a list of researchers which you may hire.

10. <u>Large genealogical libraries</u> (LGL)

Spread around the US there are a number of large genealogical libraries (LGL) which have at least some NC genealogical source materials. In general, those libraries nearest NC (GA, KY, SC, TN, VA) are the ones that have the larger NC collections, but there are exceptions. Among these LGL are:

  In <u>AL</u>: Birmingham Public Library, Library at Samford University in Birmingham, AL Archives and History Department in Birmingham, in <u>AZ</u>: Southern AZ Genealogical Society in Tucson, in <u>AR</u>: AR Genealogical Society in Little Rock, AR History Commission in Little Rock, Little Rock Public Library, in <u>CA</u>: CA Genealogical Society in San Francisco, Los Angeles Public Library, San Diego Public Library, San Francisco Public Library, Sutro Library in San Francisco,

  In <u>CO</u>: Denver Public Library, in <u>CT</u>: CT State Library in Hartford, Godfrey Memorial Library in Middletown, in <u>FL</u>: FL State Library in Tallahassee, Miami-Dade Public Library, Tampa Public Library, in <u>GA</u>: Atlanta Public Library, in <u>ID</u>: ID Genealogical Society, in <u>IL</u>: Newberry Library in Chicago, in <u>IN</u>: IN State Library in Indianapolis, Public Library of Fort Wayne, in

IA: IA State Department of History and Archives in Des Moines, in KY: KY Historical Society Library in Frankfort

In LA: LA State Library in Baton Rouge, in ME: ME State Library in Augusta, in MD: MD State Library in Annapolis, MD Historical Society in Baltimore, in MA: Boston Public Library, New England Historic Genealogical Society in Boston, in MI: Detroit Public Library, in MN: Minneapolis Public Library, in MS: MS Department of Archives and History in Jackson, in MO: Kansas City Public Library, St. Louis Public Library,

In NE: NE State Historical Society in Lincoln, Omaha Public Library, in NV: Washoe County Library in Reno, in NY: NY City Public Library, NY Genealogical and Biographical Society in NY City, in OH: Cincinnati Public Library, OH State Library in Columbus, Western Reserve Historical Society in Cleveland, in OK: OK State Historical Society in Oklahoma City, in OR: Genealogical Forum of Portland, Portland Library Association, in PA: Historical Society of PA in Philadelphia, Carnegie Library of Pittsburgh,

In SC: The South Caroliniana Library in Columbia, in SD: State Historical Society in Pierre, in TN: TN State Library and Archives in Nashville, in TX: Dallas Public Library, Fort Worth Public Library, in UT: Brigham Young University Library in Provo, in VA: VA State Library and VA Historical Society Library in Richmond, in WA: Seattle Public Library, in WV: WV Department of Archives and History in Charleston, in WI: Milwaukee Public Library, State Historical Society in Madison.

LIST OF ABBREVIATIONS

A	=	Agricultural census records
C	=	Civil War Union veterans census records
CH	=	Courthouse(s)
FHC	=	Family History Center(s), Branches of FHL
FHL	=	Family History Library
I	=	Industrial census records
LDU	=	Library, Duke University
LGL	=	Large genealogical library(ies)
LL	=	Local library(ies)
LUNC	=	Library, University of NC
M	=	Mortality census records
N	=	Early NC census-like lists
NA	=	National Archives
NC	=	North Carolina
NCSA	=	NC State Archives
NCSL	=	NC State Library
P	=	Pensioner census records, Revolutionary War
R	=	Regular census records
RBNA	=	Regional Brances of the National Archives
RL	=	Regional library(ies)
S	=	Slaveholder census records

Chapter 4

RESEARCH PROCEDURE & COUNTY LISTINGS

1. Finding the county

Now that you have read Chapters 1-3, you should have a good idea of NC history, its genealogical records, and the locations and availability of these records. Your situation is that now you can begin to use these resources. The single most important thing to discover about a NC ancestor is the county (or counties) in which he or she lived. This is because the basis of most NC genealogical records is the county. If your ancestor lived in NC in or after 1900, this information is probably available to you from older members of your family. There are also the completely indexed 1900 and 1910 censuses (section 6, Chapter 2), and the state-wide birth and death records for the period after 1913 (sections 4 and 13, Chapter 2). However, it is often the case that for a NC ancestor before 1900, all you know is that he or she lived somewhere in the state. If you happen to know the county, you are fortunate because this permits you to proceed without working through the problem of locating it. You may skip directly to section 2 of this chapter. If you don't know the county, discovery of it is your first priority.

Should your ancestor's period be 1790-1910, the federal census records for 1790, 1800, 1810, 1820, 1830, 1840, 1850, 1860, 1870, 1880, 1900, and 1910 will be of a great deal of help (section 6, Chapter 2). Indexes are available for all of these, but the 1880 index is only partial. If these fail to locate your forebear, then you need to look into a number of other state-wide indexes which could list her or him. Among the most useful of these for the period 1790-1910 are:
_Bible record indexes in NCSA, NCSL, LUNC, LDU.
_Biographies (section 3, Chapter 2).
_Cemetery record indexes in NCSA.
_DAR LIBRARY CATALOG (section 12, Chapter 2).
_Genealogical indexes (section 18, Chapter 2).
_Marriage bond index in NCSA.
_Military record indexes (sections 27 and 28, Chapter 2).
Microfilm copies of many of these are in FHL (FHC).

If your ancestor's period falls in the 1663-1790 era, particular attention needs to be paid to the following sources which are the most likely ones to contain references to his or her county location. These are all state-wide listings or indexes:
_Bible record indexes in NCSA, NCSL, LUNC, LDU, DAR Library (section 2, Chapter 2).
_Biographies (section 3, Chapter 2).

_Cemetery index in NCSA (section 5, Chapter 2).
_NC State early census records (section 6, Chapter 2).
_Colonial record compilations (section 10, Chapter 2).
_NC State court records (section 11, Chapter 2).
_DAR LIBRARY CATALOG (section 12, Chapter 2).
_NC Genealogical indexes (section 18, Chapter 2).
_Early NC land grant indexes (section 22, Chapter 2).
_NC Marriage bond index in NCSA (section 24, Chapter 2).
_Military record indexes (sections 25 and 26, Chapter 2).
_Early NC will indexes (section 35, Chapter 2).
Microfilm copies of many of these are in FHL (FHC).

As you can see from the above considerations, the earlier the period in which you think your ancestor was in NC, the greater your need to look into the resources of NCSA. The key items for the period 1790-1910 are the censuses and their indexes. These are to be found in NCSA, NCSL, LUNC, FHL (FHC), the National Archives, Branches of the National Archives, many LGL, and some RL. The key items for the period 1663-1790 are the indexes and early records of the Land Grant Office, which are located in the NC Secretary of State's Office, NCSA, and FHL (FHC) The earlier ones are also in books by Hofmann. Once you locate in the many indexes and records mentioned above a person you think to be your ancestor, you may then dig into the records of the appropriate county. Sometimes you will run into several names which could be your ancestor. In such cases, you will need to look into the various county records in order to sort the names out.

2. Recommended approaches

Having identified the county of your ancestor's residence, you are in position to begin to ferret out the details. To start, you need to turn to section 3 of this chapter and to the section on your forebear's county which is presented in the following pages. In section 3, you will find a summary of the most important state-wide records which are likely to refer to your ancestor. In the county section, you will find a summary of the most important county records which could give you data on your progenitor. The listings are meant to give you a good idea of what is available and what you should look for. They include original records, copies of the original records, and indexes to the original records. Details have been given in Chapter 2. You should make a thorough examination of all the records which apply to your ancestor's dates in the state and county, since this will give you the best chance of finding the maximum amount of information.

The best approach (if you are near NC) is one in which (1) you examine all the holdings of LL, LGL, and any RL near you, then (2) you go to

Raleigh to use the materials in NCSA and NCSL, and perhaps to Chapel Hill and Durham to employ the collections of LUNC and LDU, and then (3) you go to the county seat and look into the LL and the CH, if you deem the latter necessary. A modification of this would be to hire researchers to do the work for you at some or all of NCSA, NCSL, LUNC, LDU, LL, and perhaps CH.

The second best approach (if you are near UT) is one in which (1) you examine all the holdings of LL and LGL near you, then (2) you go to Salt Lake City and use the holdings of the FHL, then (3) you hire a researcher to examine the materials in NCSA and NCSL (and perhaps LUNC and LDU) which you have not seen at FHL, then (4) you hire a researcher to look into the records at the LL and the CH (if called for). When you hire a researcher, be careful to explain exactly what records you have already seen. This will avoid needless duplication of effort and extra expense on your part.

Another approach (if you are not near NC or UT) is one in which (1) you examine all the holdings of LL, LGL, and perhaps RL, near you, then (2) you go to the nearest FHC, order the microfilms you need, wait for them to come, return to FHC to read them, then (3) you hire a researcher to examine the materials in NCSA and NCSL (and perhaps LUNC and LDU) which you have not seen in FHC, then (4) you hire a researcher to look into the records at the LL and CH (if called for). When you hire a researcher, carefully explain exactly what records you have already examined, so as to avoid unnecessary duplication and expense.

In selecting an approach, whether it be one of the above or one at which you arrive by consideration of Chapter 3, you need to think about three items carefully. The first is expense. In visiting NCSA and NCSL (and perhaps LUNC and LDU) or FHL, at least 2 or 3 full working days should be planned for, usually more. This means you will have travel costs plus at least 2 nights' lodging. To visit a county seat (LL, and perhaps CH) requires at least a portion of a day. So travel costs and 1 nights' lodging will be involved, although this could be combined with the trip to NCSA and NCSL, which might cut the expense somewhat. In visiting a FHC, your initial visit for index-checking and microfilm ordering will require about half a day, but your return visits will take more time depending on how many microfilms you order and whether they come together or piecemeal. Thus, travel and perhaps lodging costs for several trips could be involved, plus the cost of borrowing the films. This will run several dollars per film, and in many cases, between 40 and 80 films might be needed for full coverage. This means that the film cost could easily be a couple of hundred dollars. All of this travel, lodging, and film rental must be weighed over against the cost of hiring a researcher or making a trip to FHL and/or NCSA-NCSL-LL-CH. Of course, your own desire to look at the records for yourself may be an important consideration.

The second item is a reminder about interlibrary loans. With the exception of the microfilms of FHC, very few libraries and even fewer archives will lend out their genealogical holdings on interlibrary loan. This is almost always the case for microfilms and usually the case for books. This means that the amount of information you may obtain through interlibrary loan is ordinarily quite limited.

The third item is also a reminder, this being a restatement of what was said in Chapter 3. You will have noticed that correspondence with librarians and archivists of NCSA, NCSL, LUNC, LDU, FHL, FHC, RL, LGL, LL and county employees has not been mentioned in the above paragraphs. This is because these helpful and hard-working federal, state, local, and private employees seldom have time to do detailed work for you because of the demanding duties of their offices. In many cases, these people are willing to look up one specific item for you (a marriage date, a deed record, a will, an entry in a land grant index, a military pension) if an overall index is available. But please don't ask them for detailed data. If you do write them, enclose a long SASE, a check for $5 with the payee line left blank, a brief (no more than one-third page) request for a specific item, and a request that if they do not have the time, that they hand your letter and check to a researcher who can do the work. In requesting military records from the National Archives (service, pension, or bounty land), Form NATF-80 must be used.

3. State-wide records

In this section, a summary of the most-important readily-available state-wide records of NC is given. This listing is to remind you of the sorts of things you should look for at the state level. These state-wide records have been discussed in some detail in Chapter 2, and practically all of them are available in NCSA and NCSL. Many are to be found on microfilm at FHL (FHC). Those which are indexed, or partially indexed, or arranged alphabetically, or partially arranged alphabetically are indicated by an asterisk *.

First, we will list important original or microfilm governmental records in NCSA. These records are especially important for the earlier years of NC, when many types of records now kept by counties were then kept by the state. Secretary of State records: accounts & receipts (1738-1920), estate administrators* (1685-1800), estate inventories & sales* (1733-98), guardian (1741-1918), land entries (1825-1921), council minutes, wills, and inventories (1677-1712), chancery proceedings and wills (1712-54), estate records* (1712-98), estate inventories (1728-41, 1749-54, 1777-84), officers' commission book (1841-77), militia officer and justice of peace appointments (1777-1823), Continental line land records (1782-1826), land entries, warrants, & surveys (1700-1897), entry takers' records (1756-1907), land grants (1721-1874), land grant

index* (1679-1959), land patents (1706-74), land warrants (1681-1706, 1752-80, 1783-1846), western lands now TN* (1777-1807), military land warrants (1783-1841), powers of attorney (1749-1899), quit rents (1739-58), wills* (1663-1783).

Colonial Court records: apprentice (1695-1736), bills of sale (1686-1736), chancery papers (1689-1775), dockets (1704-62), minutes (1680-1767), deeds & land papers (1685-1753), estate records* (1669-1759), jury lists (1700-59), miscellaneous (1677-1775), tax lists (1702-55). District Court records: Edenton dockets, minutes, & estate papers* (1756-1813), Fayetteville dockets, minutes, & papers (1761-1829), Halifax minutes, papers, & petitions (1764-1805), Hillsboro dockets, minutes, estates*, & papers (1764-1806), Morganton estates* & papers (1764-1806), New Bern dockets, minutes, estates*, & papers (1753-1806), Salisbury dockets, minutes, estates*, & papers (1755-1820), Wilmington dockets, minutes, & papers (1755-1808). State Superior Court records: Ashe County dockets (1821-67), Beaufort County minutes (1822-68), Camden County dockets & minutes (1807-68), Chatham County minutes (1821-42), Craven County dockets & minutes (1806-69), Currituck County dockets & minutes (1808-75), Onslow County papers (1852), Pamlico County records (1893), Pasquotank County dockets & minutes (1807-61, 1866-81), Stokes County dockets, minutes, & miscellaneous (1807-1917).

Adjutant General's records: militia returns, rosters, appointments, reports, orders, letterbooks, inventories, records (1771-1950). Governor's Papers: notary commission book (1827-35), claims (1754-64), council bonds, deeds, records (1735-69), elections (1769-83), land grants (1784, 1798-1800, 1810-18, 1832-5), taxables, militia, & magistrates (1754-70), council of state minutes & papers (1679-1953). Treasurers and Comptrollers' records: accounts (1731-1935), Indian (1712-1957), land, estates, & surveys* (1760-1901), military papers (1747-1942), claims (1733-1906). Military Collection: naval records (1700-1962), troop returns (1747-1893), Spanish Invasion records (1742-8), War of Regulation records (1768-85), Frontier and Indian War records (1758-89), Revolutionary War records* (1776-89), War of 1812 records* (1812-5), Mexican War records* (1847-8), Civil War records* (1861-5), Spanish-American War records* (1898-9). Legislative Papers: military*, petitions*, tax lists*, miscellaneous (1689-1935). Granville's Land Office records: land grants* (1729-76). Supreme Court records: original cases* (1800-1908).

Second, we will list other important record categories which have state-wide applicability. Details were given in Chapter 2. Other records: Baptist*, Bible*, biography*, birth*, business, Catholic, cemetery*, census*, colonial compilations*, DAR*, death*, divorce, Episcopal, family*, Friends*, genealogical indexes*, genealogical periodicals, genealogical

societies, German Reformed, higher court records, historical societies, immigrants*, Jewish, Lutheran, manuscript*, marriage*, military*, Moravian*, naturalization*, newspaper*, Presbyterian, published genealogies*.

4. The format of the listings

In the 106 sections to follow, summaries of the most important readily available records of the NC counties are given. These records are for the most part those available in NCSA, NCSL, and FHL (FHC). Some others may in some instances be available at the CH. Take a look at the Alamance County materials which we will use to illustrate the format for these summaries. First, the name of the county is given, then the county seat with its zip code in parentheses. Next comes the date of formation and the territory, county, or counties out of which it was formed. This should alert you to track your ancestor back through the parent counties if he or she was living there at the time of formation. Following this, if appropriate, information is given regarding disastrous events in which records were destroyed, regarding county name changes, regarding dissolution of counties, and regarding the present location of records. Then a reference to a very useful guide (GUIDE) to the county records of NC is given. This reference book, which is available from NCSA, lists in great detail the records of each county. It is an absolute must that you consult it for the counties of your interest:

_Staff of NCSA, GUIDE TO RESEARCH MATERIALS IN THE NC STATE ARCHIVES, SECTION B: COUNTY RECORDS, NCSA, Raleigh, NC, 1990.

The next section under each county lists various governmental county records which started before 1912, along with the dates of their availabilities. The record designations in general refer to labels on various items (books, boxes, files, folders, microfilms) and to the major contents of these items. The dates given in parentheses indicate the span of years in which you may expect to find sizable records, although every year may not necessarily be represented. Two very important notes regarding these governmental county records need to be recognized. First, you must bear in mind that the general record categories may in certain instances represent a wide variety of separate record types. The most important of these are court dockets (which may be of these types: execution, state, trial, appearance, criminal, civil, crown, prosecution, reference, petition, appeal, allowance, recognizance, miscellaneous), court records (civil papers, criminal papers, proceedings, fees, writs, orders, costs, petitions), estate administrators (accounts, bonds, appointments, papers), estate executors (accounts, appointments, bonds, papers), guardian (accounts, appointments, bonds, papers), land miscellaneous (attachments, executions, levies), marriages (bonds, licenses, registers, records), miscellaneous

(orders, decrees, aliens, adoptions, elections, slaves, corporations, partnerships, military, pension, officials, oaths, claims, insolvencies, jurors, inquests, paupers, merchants, papers, licenses), naturalizations (declarations, petitions, final papers), tax (lists, scrolls, reports, records, polls, taxables, receipts), and wills (original, recorded, probate records). This emphasizes the importance of looking at the details in the guide (GUIDE) mentioned above, the importance of looking into the precise listings in the card catalog in NCSA, the importance of examining all NC and county indexes at FHC, and the importance of examining all records. Second, please remember that many types of records occur under other labels; for example, in early years, estate records may be in with the court minutes, as may land records. Or, for another example, in early records administrator and executor information may be filed in the will book. Again, the only way not to miss these valuable materials is to examine all records.

Following this, there appears a section listing other records which are valuable for the county and can be sought in NCSA, NCSL, LUNC, LDU, FHL, FHC, RL, LGL, and LL. The listings largely indicate records available before 1912. In the census listings N indicates a NC state census, R a regular census, A an agricultural census, I an industrial census, M a mortality census, S a slaveholder census, P the special Revolutionary War pension census, and C the 1890 Union Civil War veteran census. For example, 1870 RAIM means that regular, agricultural, industrial, and mortality censuses are available for 1870. You will also notice that Baptist, cemetery, county history, DAR, Friends, landowner map, Lutheran, newspaper, Presbyterian, town history, and WPA inventory records are available for Alamance County. In this section, you will also find an indication of those counties which have in them genealogical societies, and historical societies.

The last sections under each county give you important libraries and indicate to you one or more of the better county histories. When an asterisk appears after the name of a library*, this means that the library has notable holdings of genealogically-related materials.

5. Alamance County

County seat: Graham (27253), formed in 1849 from Orange County, see GUIDE, pages 1-3.
Court house records: bonds of apprentices (1878-1918), bonds of bastardy (1877-1917), court dockets (1846-68), court minutes (1849- 1920), court records (1870-1939), deeds (1849-1945), estate accounts (1869-1951), estate administrators (1882-1963), estate executors (1869-1902), estate inventories (1849-1963), estate records (1856- 1949), estate settlements (1870-1951), estate widows' dowers & allotments (1878-1963), guardian (1849-68, 1878-1963), marriages

(1853-68, 1870-1963), miscellaneous (1849-1963), schools (1877-1948), wills (1849-1963).

Other records: Baptist, cemetery, census (1850RAIMS, 1860RAIMS, 1870RAIM, 1880RAIM, 1890C, 1900R, 1910R), county history, DAR, Friends, landowner map (1893), Lutheran, newspaper, Presbyterian, town history, WPA inventory. Libraries: Central NC Regional Library, 342 South Spring St., Burlington, NC 27215; McEwen Library, Elon College, Elon College, NC 27244. County histories: S. W. Stockard, HISTORY OF ALAMANCE COUNTY, Capital Printing Co., Raleigh, NC, 1900; W. Whitaker, CENTENNIAL HISTORY OF ALAMANCE COUNTY, 1849-1949, Dowd, Charlotte, NC, 1949.

6. Albemarle County formed in 1663 as one of the original counties, discontinued as local unit in 1668/70 when it was subdivided into Chowan, Currituck, Pasquotank, and Perquimans Precincts (early name for counties), see GUIDE, page 4. Records: miscellaneous (1678-1737), petitions (1680).

7. Alexander County County seat: Taylorsville (27253), formed in 1847 from Iredell, Caldwell, and Wilkes Counties, court records burned in 1865, many records lost, see GUIDE, pages 5-6.

Court house records: bonds of bastardy (1865-1900), bonds of officials (1855-1908), court dockets (1861-8), court minutes (1861-1964), court records (1853-1952), deeds (1847-1954), divorce (1867-1905), estate accounts (1869-1968), estate administrators (1868-1914, 1919-68), estate executors (1868-1914, 1919-68), estate records (1856-1968), guardian (1866-1914, 1919-68), land divisions (1863-1942), land entries (1847-1941), land miscellaneous (1847-1957), marriages (1867-1968), miscellaneous (1852-68), roads (1863-1916), wills (1847-1949).

Other records: cemetery, census (1850RAIMS, 1860RAIMS, 1870RAIM, 1880RAIM, 1890C, 1900R, 1910R), county history, historical society, Lutheran, Methodist, WPA inventory. Library: Alexander County Public Library, 115 First Avenue, SW, Taylorville, NC 28681. County histories: A. L. Crouse, HISTORICAL SKETCHES OF ALEXANDER COUNTY, Crouse and Son, Hickory, NC, 1905; P. L. Pittard, PROLOGUE: A HISTORY OF ALEXANDER COUNTY; W. E. White, A HISTORY OF ALEXANDER COUNTY, Alexander County Historical Society, Taylorsville, NC, 1947.

8. Alleghany County

County seat: Sparta (28675), formed in 1859 from Ashe County, court house fire in 1932, a few records lost, see GUIDE, pages 7-9.

Court house records: bonds of apprentices (1863-1909), bonds of bastardy (1863-1910), bonds of officials (1859-79), court dockets (1863-72), court minutes (1862-1955), court records (1862-1957), deeds (1859-1971), divorce (1862-1932), estate accounts (1870-1970), estate administrators (1911-70), estate inventories (1862-9), estate records (1859-1928), guardian (1864-1940), land entries (1870-1962), land miscellaneous (1859-1908), lunacies (1901-70), marriages (1862-1961), miscellaneous (1859-1970), tax (1907-27), wills (1859-).

Other records: Baptist, cemetery, census (1860RAIMS, 1870RAIM, 1880RAIM, 1890C, 1900R, 1910R), county history, genealogical society, historical society, WPA inventory. Library: Alleghany County Public Library, Sparta, NC 28675. County histories: ALLEGHANY COUNTY CENTENNIAL HISTORY AND SOUVENIR BOOKLET, 1859-1959, published 1959; A. B. Cox, FOOTPRINTS ON THE SANDS OF TIME, Star, Sparta, NC, 1900, pp. 76-103; THE HERITAGE OF ALLEGHANY COUNTY, Hunter, Winston-Salem, NC, 1986.

9. Anson County

County seat: Wadesboro (28170), formed in 1750 from Bladen County, court house fire in 1868, many records lost, see GUIDE, pages 10-12.

Court house records: bonds of apprentices (1873-91), bonds of bastardy (1870-1903), bonds of officials (1889-95), court dockets (1837-1909), court minutes (1771-1962), court records (1864-1908), deeds (1749-1962), divorce (1872-1925), estate accounts (1868-1944), estate administrators (1868-1963), estate executors (1868-1963), estate inventories (1849-55), estate records (1805-1953), estate settlements (1850-5, 1875-1945), guardian (1868-1963), land entries (1851-1927), land miscellaneous (1755-1909), miscellaneous (1755-1960), petitions (1768, 1779-9), schools (1873-1919), tax (1763, 1815, 1887), wills (1751-1962).

Other records: Baptist, cemetery, census (1790R, 1800R, 1810R, 1820RI, 1830R, 1840RP, 1850RAIMS, 1860RAIMS, 1870RAIM, 1880RAIM, 1890C, 1900R, 1910R), county history, county map, DAR, Episcopal, family, historical society, Methodist, newspaper. Library: Allen Library, 120 South Greene St, Wadesboro, NC 28170. County history: Anson County Bicentennial Corporation, TORCHLIGHT ON THE PEE DEE, 1747-1949, Dunn, New Bern, NC, 1949; M. L. Medley, HISTORY OF ANSON COUNTY, Anson County Historical Society, Wadesboro, NC, 1976.

10. Archdale County — formed in 1705 from Bath County, name changed to Beaufort County in 1712, see Beaufort County for records.

11. Ashe County — County seat: Jefferson (28640), formed in 1799 from Wilkes County, court house fire in 1865, many records lost, see GUIDE, pages 13-15.
Court house records: bonds of apprentices (1876-1923), bonds of bastardy (1828-1910), bonds of officials (1821-1907), court dockets (1807-68), court minutes (1806-1959), court records (1805-1934), deeds (1799-1966), divorce (1822-1912), estate accounts (1869- 1966), estate administrators (1868-1966), estate executors (1868- 1966), estate inventories (1806-66), estate records (1819-1935), estate sales (1806-66), estate settlements (1869-1966), guardian (1829- 1966), land ejectments (1827-1911), land entries (1803-1906), land grants (1799-1954), land miscellaneous (1826-1911), land processions (1979-83), marriages (1828-81), miscellaneous (1801-1966), roads (1846-1909), schools (1881-1966), tax (1815, 1915-45), wills (1800-1966).
Other records: Baptist, cemetery, census (1800R, 1810R, 1820RI, 1830R, 1840RP, 1850RAIMS, 1860RAIMS, 1870RAIM, 1880RAIM, 1890C, 1900R, 1910R), county history, Episcopal, newspaper, WPA inventory. County history: A. L. Fletcher, ASHE COUNTY, A HISTORY, Ashe County Research Association, Jefferson, NC, 1963.

12. Avery County — County seat: Newland (28657), formed in 1911 from Caldwell, Mitchell, and Watauga Counties, see GUIDE, pages 16-17.
Court house records: court dockets (1930-58), court minutes (1911-68), deeds (1911-70), estate accounts (1912-68), estate administrators (1911-68), estate executors (1911-68), estate settlements (1912-68), estate widows' dowers & allotments (1913-25), guardian (1911-68), land entries (1912-57), land miscellaneous (1914-69), lunacies (1911-68), marriages (1911-70), miscellaneous (1911-68), wills (1911-68).
Other records: Bible, cemetery, county history, WPA inventory. Libraries: Avery County Library, Newland, NC 28657; Carlson Library, Lees-McRae College, Banner Elk, NC 28604. County history: H. Cooper, HISTORY OF AVERY COUNTY, Biltmore Press, Asheville, NC, 1964.

13. Bath County

formed in 1696 from territory south of the Albemarle River. Divided into Archdale, Pamptecough, and Wickham Precincts (early counties) in 1705, and thus discontinued, see GUIDE, page 18. Records are in with those of Beaufort County.

14. Beaufort County

County seat: Washington (27889), formed in 1712 when Archdale County changed its name, see GUIDE, pages 19-21.

Court house records: court dockets (1744-5, 1756-61, 1794- 1868, 1870-85), court minutes (1785-1960), court records (1785- 1938), deeds (1696-1959), divorce (1868-1902), estate accounts (1868-1960), estate administrators (1867-1960), estate executors (1868-1960), estate records (1760-1949), estate settlements (1862- 1960), guardian (1794-1960), land divisions (1736-1909), land entries (1778-95, 1882-1926), land grants (1798-1816), land miscellaneous (1750-1947), land partitions (1736-1909), marriages (1847-1960), miscellaneous (1755-1960), roads (1843-69), schools (190-57), tax (1755, 1764-1927), wills (1720-1960).

Other records: cemetery, census (1790R, 1800R, 1810R, 1820RI, 1830R, 1840RP, 1850RAIMS, 1860RAIMS, 1870RAIM, 1880RAIM, 1890C, 1900R, 1910R), city history, county history, Episcopal, family, newspaper, Presbyterian, WPA inventory. Libraries: Beaufort, Hyde, Martin Regional Library, 158 North Market St., Washington, NC 27889; Brown Library,* 122 Van Norden St., Washington, NC 27889. County history: C. W. Reed, BEAUFORT COUNTY, TWO CENTURIES OF ITS HISTORY, Raleigh, NC, 1962; U. F. Loy and P. M. Worthy, WASHINGTON AND THE PAMLICO, Washington-Beaufort County Bicentennial Commission, Washington, NC, 1976.

15. Bertie County

County seat: Windsor (27983), formed in 1722 from Chowan County, see GUIDE, pages 22-24.

Court house records: bonds of apprentice (1750-1889), bonds of bastardy (1739-1880), bonds of officials (1755-1875), coroner (1810-1914), court dockets (1728-1900), court minutes (1724-1915), court records (1734-1905), deeds (1721-1924), estate accounts (1868-1961), estate administrators (1762-9, 1848-1971), estate records (1728-1870), estate settlements (1866-1936), guardian (1730--1931), justices of peace (1754-1873), land entries (1778-94), land miscellaneous (1723-1890), marriages (1762-1960), miscellaneous (1718-1960), petitions (1773, 1779), roads (1749-1903), schools (1847-95), tax (1741-1903), wills (1749-1961).

Other records: cemetery, census (1785N, 1790R, 1800R, 1810R, 1820RI, 1830R, 1840RP, 1850RAIMS, 1860RAIMS, 1870RAIM, 1880-

RAIM, 1890C, 1900R, 1910R), city history, county history, DAR, Episcopal, landowner maps (1863-4), newspaper, town history, WPA inventory. Library: Lawrence Memorial Public Library, 204 Dundee, Windsor, NC 27983. County histories: F. R. Johnson and T. C. Parramore, THE DAILY ROANOKE CHOWAN NEWS ROANOKE CHOWAN STORY, Parker, Rich Square, NC, 1962; A. D. Watson, BERTIE COUNTY, A BRIEF HISTORY, NCSA, Raleigh, NC, 1982.

16. Bladen County

County seat: Elizabethtown (28337), formed in 1734 from New Hanover County, court house fires in 1800 and 1893, many records lost, see GUIDE, pages 25-26.

Court house records: court dockets (1761-2), court minutes (1866-1961), deeds (1738-1961), estate accounts (1868-1961), estate administrators (1901-12), estate divisions (1899-1941), estate settlements (1885-1923), guardian (1893-1912, 1922-61), land entries (1893-1943), marriages (1868-1961), miscellaneous (1868-1961), tax (1763, 1781-8, 1883, 1895-9), wills (1766-1961).

Other records: Baptist, Bible, cemetery, census (1790R, 1800R, 1810R, 1820RI, 1830R, 1840RP, 1850RAIMS, 1860RAIMS, 1870RAIM, 1880RAIM, 1890C, 1900R, 1910R), county history, DAR, family, landowner map (1885), newspaper, Presbyterian, WPA inventory. Library: Bladen County Public Library, Cypress and Queen Streets, Elizabethtown, NC 28337. County history: C. E. Crawford, BLADEN COUNTY, Elizabethtown, NC, 1957.

17. Brunswick County

County seat: Bolivia (28422), formed in 1764 from New Hanover and Bladen Counties, many records destroyed in 1865, see GUIDE, pages 27-29.

Court house records: bonds of apprentices (1810-1907), bonds of bastardy (1810-1930), bonds of officials (1794-1904), court dockets (1820-68), court minutes (1782-1944), court records (1790-1926), deeds (1764-1952), divorce (1869-1905), estate accounts (1868-1928), estate administrators (1868-1963), estate executors (1868-1963), estate records (1783-1963), estate settlements (1868-1963), guardian (1819-1963), land entries (1853-1958), land grants (1788-1815), land miscellaneous (1898-1929), land surveys (1905-20), marriages (1804-1905), miscellaneous (1786-1963), schools (1841-54, 1872-1935), tax (1769, 72, 84, 1815, 1873-1925), wills (1764-1963).

Other records: Baptist, Bible, cemetery, census (1790R, 1800R, 1810R, 1820RI, 1830R, 1840RP, 1850RAIMS, 1860RAIMS, 1870RAIM, 1880RAIM, 1890C, 1900R, 1910R), county history, DAR, historical society, landowner map (1910), Methodist, newspaper, Presbyterian, town

history WPA inventory. Library: Brunswick County Library, 109 West Moore St., Southport, NC 28461. County history: Brunswick County Historical Society, BICENTENNIAL, BRUNSWICK COUNTY, The Society, Bolivia, NC, 1964; L. Lee, HISTORY OF BRUNSWICK COUNTY, Heritage Press, Charlotte, NC, 1980.

18. Buncombe County

County seat: Asheville (28807), formed in 1791 from Burke and Rutherford Counties, court house fires in 1830 and 1865, many records lost, see GUIDE, pages 30-32.

Court house records: bonds of apprentices (1794-1919), bonds of bastardy (1824-1928), court dockets (1807-87), court minutes (1792-1948), court records (1808-1944), deeds (1791-1962), divorce (1830-1918), estate accounts (1868-- 1964), estate administrators (1868-1963), estate executors (1868-90), estate inventories (1822-4, 1845-69, 1899-1961), estate records (1815- 1924), estate settlements (1864-1964), guardian (1829-1962), land ejectments (1818-1905), land entries (1794-1832), land grants (1795-1871), land miscellaneous (1798-1920), marriages (1842-1963), miscellaneous (1791-1962), naturalizations 1906, 1909-10), wills (1826-1964).

Other records: cemetery, census (1800R, 1810R, 1820RI, 1830R, 1840RP, 1850RAIMS, 1860RAIMS, 1870RAIM, 1880RAIM, 1890C, 1900R, 1910R), city directory, city history, county history, DAR, Episcopal, family, genealogical society, newspaper, Presbyterian, town history, WPA inventory. Libraries: Asheville-Buncombe County Library,* 67 Haywood St., Asheville, NC 28801; Presbyterian Study Center Library and Archives, 318 Georgia Terrace, Montreat, NC 28757. County history: F. A. Sondley, HISTORY OF BUNCOMBE COUNTY, Advocate, Asheville, NC, 1930; D. C. Ward and C. D. Biddix, THE HERITAGE OF OLD BUNCOMBE COUNTY, Hunter Publishing Co., Winston-Salem, NC, 1981.

19. Burke County

County seat: Morganton (28655), formed in 1777 from Rowan County, court house fire in 1865, many records lost, see GUIDE, pages 33-35.

Court house records: court minutes (1791-1964), deeds (1777- 1963), divorce (1828-1911), estate accounts (1868-1963), estate administrators (1868-1963), estate executors (1868-1963), estate inventories (1832-1963), estate records (1832-69), estate sales (1832-1963), estate settlements (1869-1963), guardian (1785-1963), land ejectments (1784-1868), land entries (1770-1945), land miscellaneous (1779-1925), land surveys (1905-45), marriages (1780-1939), miscellaneous (1776-1963), petitions (1778-9), roads (1787-1897), schools (1843-7, 1885-1963), tax (1782-1843, 1875-88, 1894), wills (1740-1963).

Other records: Baptist, cemetery, census (1790R, 1800R, 1810R, 1820RI, 1830R, 1840RP, 1850RAIMS, 1860RAIMS, 1870RAIM, 1880RAIM, 1890C, 1900R, 1910R), county history, DAR, Episcopal, newspaper, Presbyterian, WPA inventory. Library: Burke County Public Library, 204 South King St., Morganton, NC 28655. County histories: T. G. Walton, SKETCHES OF PIONEERS IN BURKE COUNTY HISTORY, Morganton, NC, 1961; E. W. Phifer, BURKE COUNTY, A BRIEF HISTORY, NCSA, Raleigh, NC, 1979; E. W. Phifer, BURKE, THE HISTORY OF A NC COUNTY, 1777-1920, The Author, Morganton, NC, 1977; Burke County Historical Society, THE HERITAGE OF BURKE COUNTY, Hunter Publishing Co., Winston-Salem, NC, 1981.

20. Bute County

formed in 1764 from Granville County, in 1779 was abolished by division into Warren and Franklin Counties, see records of these counties, especially Warren, see GUIDE, page 36. Records: court dockets (1764-79), court minutes (1767-79), deeds (1764-7), estate administrators (1766-8), estate inventories (1760-79), guardians (1770-8), justices of peace (1764-9), land entries (1778-9), marriage (1764-79), tax (1771), wills (1764-79).

21. Cabarrus County

County seat: Concord (28025), formed in 1792 from Mecklenburg County, court house fire in 1876, a few records lost, see GUIDE, pages 37-39.

Court house records: bonds of apprentices (1875-1901), bonds of bastardy (1869-1918), court dockets (1793-1909), court minutes (1793-1963), court records (1824-1944), deeds (1792-1964), divorce (1866-1930), estate accounts (1846-1965), estate administrators (1875-1966), estate executors (1868-1911, 1926-66), estate inventories (1869-1965), estate records (1793-1953), estate sales (1921-66), estate settlements (1846-1965), guardian (1847-1962), land miscellaneous (1818-1945), marriages (1792-1966), miscellaneous (1794-1966), naturalizations (1909-21), roads (1837), schools (1841-1966), tax (1860-1921), wills (1794-1966).

Other records: cemetery, census (1800R, 1810R, 1820RI, 1830R, 1840RP, 1850RAIMS, 1860RAIMS, 1870RAIM, 1880RAIM, 1890C, 1900R, 1910R), county history, DAR, Episcopal, family, German Reformed, Lutheran, newspaper, Presbyterian, Reformed, WPA inventory. Libraries: Cannon Memorial Library, 27 Union St. North, Concord, NC 28025; Cannon Memorial Library, 1050 Mountain St., Kannapolis, NC 28081.
County histories: C. Hammer, Jr., RHINELANDERS ON THE YADKIN, Rowan, Salisbury, NC, 1965; J. K. Rouse, HISTORICAL SHADOWS OF CABARRUS COUNTY, Crabtree, Charlotte, NC, 1970.

22. Caldwell County

County seat: Lenoir (28645), formed in 1841 from Burke and Wilkes Counties, see GUIDE, pages 40-42.

Court house records: bonds of apprentices (1841-1906), bonds of bastardy (1843-1925), bonds of officials (1841-1917), court dockets (1841-68), court minutes (1841-1954), court records (1838-1932), deeds (1841-1968), divorce (1850-1925), estate accounts (1868-1966), estate administrators (1868-1966), estate executors (1868-1966), estate inventories (1847-67, 1885-1962), estate records (1841-1934), estate sales (1847-67, 1885-1962), estate settlements (1868-1966), guardian (1842-1966), land ejectments (1841-1904), land entries (1841-1954), land miscellaneous (1841-1934), marriages (1841-1968), miscellaneous (1841-1952), roads (1841-1913), schools (1885-1952), sheriffs' records (1841-1903), tax (1841-53), wills (1841-1966).

Other records: Baptist, cemetery, census (1850RAIMS, 1860-RAIMS, 1870RAIM, 1880RAIM, 1890C, 1900R, 1910R), county history, newspaper, Presbyterian, WPA inventory. Library: Caldwell County Public Library, 120 Hospital Ave., SW, Lenoir, NC 28645. County history: W. W. Scott, ANNALS OF CALDWELL COUNTY, News-Topic, Lenoir, NC, 1930; THE HERITAGE OF CALDWELL COUNTY, Hunter, Winston-Salem, NC, 1987.

23. Camden County

County seat: Camden (27921), formed in 1777 from Pasquotank County, fire in Civil War, some records lost, many missing, see GUIDE, pages 43-44.

Court house records: bonds of apprentices (1871-86), bonds of bastardy (1871-9), court dockets (1807-1912, 1929-60), court minutes (1807-1925), court records (1802-1929), deeds (1777-1927), estate accounts (1866-1918), estate administrators (1853-1916), estate records (1790-1929), estate settlements (1862-1960), estate widows' dowers (1894-1918), guardian (1800-1925), land miscellaneous (1807-1925), land processions (1874-1904), marriages (1848-1960), miscellaneous (1786-1928), naturalizations (1786-1928), roads (1879-1903, 1917-31), schools (1861-77), tax (1782, 1790-5, 1815, 1848-1918), wills (1777-1960).

Other records: cemetery, census (1790R, 1800R, 1810R, 1820RI, 1830R, 1840RP, 1850RAIMS, 1860RAIMS, 1870RAIM, 1880RAIM, 1890C, 1900R, 1910R), county history, DAR, historical society, WPA inventory. Library: Pasquotank-Camden Library, 205 East Main St., Elizabeth City, NC 27909. County history: J. F. Pugh, THREE HUNDRED YEARS ALONG THE PASQUOTANK: A BIOGRAPHICAL HISTORY OF CAMDEN COUNTY, The Author, Old Trap, NC, 1957.

24. Carteret County

County seat: Beaufort (28516), formed in 1722 from Craven County, see GUIDE, pages 45-7.

Court house records: bonds of bastardy (1771-1906), bonds of officials (1755-1909), court dockets (1731-1881), court minutes (17231919), court records (1741-1938), deeds (1722-1961), divorce (1877-1939), estate accounts (1868-1922), estate administrators (1884-1936), estate executors (1868-1936), estate records (1744-1957), estate sales (1922-61), estate settlements (1880-1922), guardian (1789-1962), land entries (1778-1958), land miscellaneous (1743-1948), marriages (1746-1961), miscellaneous (1722-1961), naturalizations (1910-11), petitions (1777, 1779), roads (1811-1911), schools (1841-58, 1871-2), tax (1745-1899), wills (1744-1961).

Other records: cemetery, census (1790R, 1800R, 1810R, 1820RI, 1830R, 1840RP, 1850RAIMS, 1860RAIMS, 1870RAIM, 1880RAIM, 1890C, 1900R, 1910R), county history, DAR, Episcopal, Friends, historical society, Methodist, newspaper, town history, WPA inventory. Library: Carteret County Public Library, 210 Turner St., Beaufort, NC 28516. County history: A. Lefferts and others, CARTERET COUNTY, University of NC Press, Chapel Hill, NC, 1926; THE HERITAGE OF CARTERET COUNTY, Hunter, Winston-Salem, NC, 1986.

25. Caswell County

County seat: Yanceyville (27379), formed in 1777 from Orange County, some records lost during Reconstruction, see GUIDE, pages 48-51.

Court house records: bonds of apprentices (1777-1921), bonds of bastardy (1785-1905), bonds of officials (1777-1907), court dockets (1777-1868), court minutes (1777-1934), court records (1777-1944), deeds (1777-1963), divorce (1818-1928), estate accounts (1867-1963), estate administrators (1864-1949), estate executors (1868-), estate inventories (1777-1931), estate records (1777-1941), estate settlements (1777-1931), guardian (1777-1949), land ejectments (1779-1878), land entries (1778-95, 1841-63), land grants (1771-1963), land miscellaneous (1778-1918), marriages (1777-1963), miscellaneous (1777-1963), powers of attorney (1785-1876), roads (17851923), schools (1816-27, 1859, 1882-1935), tax (1771-1917), wills (1777-1963).

Other records: Baptist, Bible, cemetery, census (1785N, 1790R, 1800R, 1810R, 1820RI, 1830R, 1840RP, 1850RAIMS, 1860RAIMS, 1870RAIM, 1880RAIM, 1890C, 1900R, 1910R), county history, DAR, family, historical society, landowner map (1868), Methodist, newspaper, Presbyterian, WPA inventory. Library: Hyconeechee Regional Library,* 317 Main St., E., Yanceyville, NC 27379. County history: W. S. Powell, A HISTORY OF CASWELL COUNTY, Moore Publishing, Durham, NC, 1977.

26. Catawba County

County seat: Newton (28658), formed in 1842 from Lincoln County, many records missing, cause not known, see GUIDE, pages 52-54.

Court house records: bonds of bastardy (1868-1911), court dockets (1843-68), court minutes (1843-1960), court records (1858-1926), deeds (1842-1955), divorce (1869-1927), estate accounts (1843-1966), estate administrators (1843-1966), estate executors (1843-1966), estate inventories (1843-1966), estate records (1874-1922), estate sales (1843-68), estate settlements (1868-1966), estate widows' dowers & allotments (1875-1907), guardian (1843-1966), land divisions (1875-1907), land miscellaneous (1864-1906), marriages (1842-1968), miscellaneous (1851-1952), roads (1873-1911), schools (1885-1968), tax (1843-1965), wills (1843-1966).

Other records: Bible, cemetery, census (1850RAIMS, 1860RAIMS, 1870RAIM, 1880RAIM, 1890C, 1900R, 1910R), Congregational, DAR, family, historical society, landowner map (1886), Lutheran, Methodist, newspaper, Presbyterian, Reformed, WPA inventory. Libraries: Ivey Memorial Library, 420 Third Ave., NW, Hickory, NC 28601; Catawba County Library, 115 West C St., Newton, NC 28658; Catawba County Historical Museum Library,* 1716 South College Dr., Newton, NC 28658. County history: C. J. Preslar, A HISTORY OF CATAWBA COUNTY, Rowan, Salisbury, NC, 1954.

27. Chatham County

County seat: Pittsboro (27312), formed in 1770 from Orange County. some records missing, cause not known, see GUIDE, pages 55-58.

Court house records: bonds of apprentices (1787-1930), bonds of bastardy (1869-1931), bonds of officials (1771-1907), court dockets (1774- 1902), court minutes (1774-1900), court records (1757-1940), deeds (1771-1952), divorce (1829-1934), estate account (1850-1917), estate administrators (1867-1958), estate executors (1867-1958), estate inventories (1795-1868), estate records (1771-1948), estate sales (1795-1941), estate settlements (1869-1913), guardian (1784-1959), justices of peace (1855-77), land ejectments (1787-1962), land entries (1843-1913), marriages (1772-1960), miscellaneous (1772-1971, 1922-6), roads (1921), tax (1787-1815, 1902-8), wills (1771-1924).

Other records: Baptist, cemetery, census (1790R, 1800R, 1810R, 1820RI, 1830R, 1840RP, 1850RAIMS, 1860RAIMS, 1870RAIM, 1880-RAIM, 1890C, 1900R, 1910R), county history, DAR, Episcopal, family, Friends, landowner map (1870), Lutheran, Methodist, newspaper, WPA inventory. Library: Pittsboro Memorial Library, 204 West St., Pittsboro, NC 27312. County history: W. Hadley and others, CHATHAM COUNTY, 1771-1971, Moore, Durham, NC, 1971.

28. Cherokee County

County seat: Murphy (28906), formed in 1839 from Macon County, court house fires in 1865 and 1895, some records lost, see GUIDE, pages 59-61.

Court house records: bonds of apprentices (1896, 1906), bonds of bastardy (1866-1912), bonds of officials (1866-1948), court minutes (1865-1945), court records (1846-1926), deeds (1839-1967), divorce (1869-1942), estate accounts (1868-1966), estate administrators (1914-56), estate executors (1868-1925), estate records (1843-1940), estate settlements (1871-1966), guardian (1869-1936, 1947-66), land entries (1883-1931), land miscellaneous (1838-57, 1869-1946), marriages (1837-9, 1868-1906), miscellaneous (1843-1967), roads (1874-1927), schools (1926-67), tax (1867-1946), wills (1869-1966).

Other records: Baptist, cemetery, census (1840RP, 1850RAIMS, 1860RAIMS, 1870RAIM, 1880RAIM, 1890C, 1900R, 1910R), county history, DAR, newspaper, WPA inventory. Library: Murphy Public Library, 101 Blumenthal St., Murphy, NC 28906. County history: M. W. Freel, OUR HERITAGE: THE PEOPLE OF CHEROKEE COUNTY, 1540-1955, Miller, Asheville, NC, 1956.

29. Chowan County

County seat: Edenton (27932), formed in 1670 from Albemarle County, some records destroyed in 1848, see GUIDE, pages 62-65.

Court house records: births (1750-1817), bonds of apprentices (1737-1909), bonds of bastardy (1736-1933), bonds of officials (1737-1921), court dockets (1757-1868), court minutes (1715-1910), court records (1720-1933), deaths (1750-1817), deeds (1695-1928), divorce (1823-1960), estate accounts (1707-1912), estate administrators (1748-1966), estate divisions (1770-1868), estate executors (1811-1966), estate inventories (1735-1868), estate records (1728-1960), estate settlements (1859-1927), estate widows' dowers & allotments (1841- 58), guardian (1751-1966), justices of peace (1722-1877), land divisions (1841-58), land ejectments (1767-1879), land entries (1794- 1881), land miscellaneous (1708-1923), land levies (1849-1911), marriages (1741-1958), miscellaneous (1670-89, 1709-1935), petitions (1758, 1773, 1815-41), roads (1725-1912), schools (1839-97), strays (1906-19), tax (1717-1909), wills (1694-1969).

Other records: Baptist, cemetery, census (1785N, 1790R, 1800R, 1810R, 1820RI, 1830R, 1840RP, 1850RAIMS, 1860RAIMS, 1870RAIM, 1880RAIM, 1890C, 1900R, 1910R), county history, DAR, Episcopal, family, Methodist, newspaper, WPA inventory. Library: Shepard-Pruden Memorial Library, 106 West Water St., Edenton, NC 27932. County histories: T. C. Parramore, CRADLE OF THE COLONY: THE HISTORY OF CHOWAN COUNTY AND EDENTON, The Author, Edenton, NC, 1967.

30. Clay County

County seat: Hayesville (28904), formed in 1861 from Cherokee County, fire in 1870, all records lost, see GUIDE, pages 66-67.

Court house records: bonds of apprentices (1871-1910), bonds of bastardy (1879), bonds of officials (1879-1939), court minutes (1870- 1966), court records (1868-1942), deeds (1870-1970), estate accounts (1870-1966), estate administrators (1870-1966), estate executors (1877-1966), estate sales (1933-66), estate settlements (1873-1946), estate widows' dowers & allotments (1871-1931), guardian (1869- 1966), land entries (1871-1929), land processions (1881-91), marriages (1870-1970), miscellaneous (1869-1966), roads (1871-1903), wills (1870-1966).

Other records: Baptist, cemetery, census (1870RAIM, 1880RAIM, 1890C, 1900R, 1910R), county history, WPA inventory. Library: Moss Memorial Library, Hayesville, NC 28904. County histories: Clay County Historical Committee, CLAY COUNTY, 1861-1961, The Committee, Hayesville, NC, 1961; H. Billings, ALL DOWN THE VALLEY, Viking Press, New York, NY, 1952.

31. Cleveland County

County seat: Shelby (28150), formed in 1841 from Rutherford and Lincoln Counties, see GUIDE, pages 68-70.

Court house records: bonds of apprentices (1841-88), bonds of bastardy (1841-1919), bonds of officials (1841-1909), court dockets (1841-68), court minutes (1841-1950), court records (1838-1921), deeds (1841-1959), estate accounts (1868-1964), estate administrators (1898-1956), estate executors (1868-1964), estate records (1795-1915), estate settlements (1849- 1960), guardian (1841-1910), land entries (1888-1925), land processions (1841-59), marriages (1851-1965), miscellaneous (1841-1960), roads (1838-91), tax lists (1918), wills (1841-1965).

Other records: Baptist, cemetery, census (1850RAIMS, 1860-RAIMS, 1870RAIM, 1880RAIM, 1890C, 1900R, 1910R), county history, DAR, historical society, landowner map (1886), newspaper, WPA inventory. Libraries: Cleveland County Memorial Library,* 104 Howie Dr., Shelby, NC 28151; Mauney Memorial Library,* 100 South Piedmont Ave., Kings Mountain, NC 28086. County histories: L. B. Weathers, THE LIVING PAST OF CLEVELAND COUNTY, The Star, Shelby, NC, 1956; Shelby Daily Star, OUR HERITAGE, A HISTORY OF CLEVELAND COUNTY, The Star, Shelby NC, 1976; THE HERITAGE OF CLEVELAND COUNTY, Hunter, Winston-Salem, NC 1987.

32. Columbus County

County seat: Whiteville (28472), formed in 1808 from Bladen and Brunswick Counties, see GUIDE, pages 71-73.

Court house records: bonds of apprentices (1874-91), bonds of officials (1868-81, 1891-1914), court dockets (1842-68), court minutes (1817-1960), court records (1858-60), deeds (1808-1966), estate accounts (1869-1967), estate administrators (1869-1967), estate divisions (1887-1967), estate executors (1869-1967), estate records (1812-1923), estate settlements (1869-1967), guardian (1844-1967), marriages (1867-1967), miscellaneous (1869-1967), schools (1885--1936), tax (1869, 1881-1917, 1925), wills (1808-1967).

Other records: cemetery, census (1810R, 1820RI, 1830R, 1840-RP, 1850RAIMS, 1860RAIMS, 1870RAIM, 1880RAIM, 1890C, 1900R, 1910R), city history, county history, newspaper, Presbyterian, town history, WPA inventory. Libraries: Columbus County Public Library, 407 N. Powell Blvd., Whiteville, NC 28472; Southeastern Community College Library,* Whiteville, NC 28472. County histories: J. A. Rogers, COLUMBUS COUNTY, News Reporter, Whiteville, NC, 1946; A. C. W. Little, COLUMBUS COUNTY RECOLLECTIONS & RECORDS, Columbus County Bicentennial Committee, Whiteville, NC, 1980.

33. Craven County

County seat: New Bern (28560), in 1712 Archdale County was renamed Craven, see GUIDE, pages 74-77.

Court house records: bonds of apprentices (1748-1910), bonds of bastardy (1803-80), bonds of officials (1757-1867), coroner (1782-1905), court dockets (1754-1869), court minutes (1712-5, 1730-1914), court records (1756-1920), deeds (1728-1960), divorce (1828-95), estate accounts (1829-1960), estate administrators (1829-1947), estate divisions (1803-68), estate executors (1869-1910), estate inventories (1729-1867), estate records (1736-1945), estate settlements (1869-1930), guardian (1766-1960), land ejectments (1787-1872), land entries (1770-1903), land grants (1710-1835), land patents (1780-1859), land surveys (1785-1901), marriages (1740-1960), miscellaneous (1757-1929), petitions (1740, 1778), powers of attorney (1786-99), roads (1767-1868), schools (1841-61), sheriffs' records (1811-54), tax (1720-1904), wills (1737-1960).

Other records: cemetery, census (1790R, 1800R, 1810R, 1820RI, 1830R, 1840RP, 1850RAIMS, 1860RAIMS, 1870RAIM, 1880RAIM, 1890C, 1900R, 1910R), Christian Church, city history, county history, DAR, Episcopal, family, genealogical society, Methodist, newspaper, Presbyterian, WPA inventory. Library: Craven, Pamlico, Carteret Regional Library, 400 Johnson St., New Bern, NC 28560. County history: Garden

Club of NC, NEW BERN, CRADLE OF NC, Edwards and Broughton, Raleigh, NC, 1941.

34. Cumberland County

County seat: Fayetteville (28301), formed in 1754 from Bladen County, see GUIDE, pages 80-81.

Court house records: bonds of apprentices (1812-1909), bonds of bastardy (1760-1910), bonds of officials (1779-1954), court dockets (1774-1888), court minutes (1755-1942), court records (1759-1946), deeds (1754-1942), estate accounts (1868-1962), estate administrators (1769-1906), estate divisions (1808-60), estate executors (1868-1906), estate inventories (1890-1962), estate records (1759-1930), estate sales (1825-8), estate settlements (1865-1916), guardian (1795-1956), land grants (1754-1947), land miscellaneous (1784-1955), land surveys (1904-10), marriages (1800-1962), miscellaneous (1758-1965), naturalizations (1894-1904), petitions (1772), roads (1825-55, 1863-1909), sheriffs' records (1821-32), tax (1755, 1767, 1777-1884), wills (1757-1962).

Other records: Baptist, Bible, FHC, cemetery, census (1790R, 1800R, 1810R, 1820RI, 1830R, 1840RP, 1850RAIMS, 1860RAIMS, 1870RAIM, 1880RAIM, 1890C, 1900R, 1910R), Christian Church, city history, county history, DAR, Episcopal, family, landowner map (1880), Methodist, newspaper, Presbyterian, WPA inventory. Library: Cumberland County Public Library, 300 Maiden Lane., Fayetteville, NC 28301. County histories: J. H. Myrover, SHORT HISTORY OF CUMBERLAND COUNTY AND THE CAPE FEAR SECTION, The Author, Fayetteville, NC, 1905; J. A. Oates, THE STORY OF FAYETTEVILLE AND THE UPPER CAPE FEAR, Womens' Club, Fayetteville, NC, 1972.

35. Currituck County

County seat: Currituck (27253), formed in 1670 from Albemarle County, many early records missing, cause not known, see GUIDE, pages 82-83.

Court house records: bonds of apprentices (1868-84), bonds of bastardy (1830-), court dockets (1806-1925), court minutes (1799-1832, 1838-1916), court records (1810-1923), deeds (1735-1928), estate accounts (1841-1906), estate administrators (1795-1927), estate executors (1868-1919), estate inventories (1830-1906), estate records (1812-1926), estate sales (1830-1918), estate settlements (1869-99), guardian (1830-1928), land divisions (1877-1911), land entries (1872-1955), land miscellaneous (1810-1915), miscellaneous (1787-1915), tax lists (1714-21, 1755, 1779), wills (1772-1960).

Other records: cemetery, census (1790R, 1800R, 1810R, 1820RI, 1830R, 1840RP, 1850RAIMS, 1860RAIMS, 1870RAIM, 1880RAIM,

1890C, 1900R, 1910R), county history, WPA inventory. Library: Currituck County Public Library, Highway 158, Barco, NC 27917. County history: CURRITUCK COUNTY in The State, August 8, 1942.

36. Dare County

County seat: Manteo (27954), formed in 1870 from Currituck, Tyrell, and Hyde Counties, see GUIDE, pages 84-85.

Court house records: bonds of bastardy (1869-1957), court minutes (1870-1967), court records (1869-1968), deeds (1870-1966), estate accounts (1870--1967), estate administrators (1870-1966), estate divisions (1869-1915), estate executors (1870-1966), estate records (1832-1964), estate settlements (18671926), estate widows' dowers & allotments (1869-1915), guardian (1866-1967), land entries (1870-1959), land partitions (1869-1915), land surveys (1905-23), marriages (1870-1967), miscellaneous (1871-1966), schools (1896-1963), tax (1881-1905, 1915, 1925, 1935, 1945), wills (1870-1967).

Other records: cemetery, census (1870RAIM, 1880RAIM, 1890C, 1900R, 1910R), county history, DAR, town history, WPA inventory. Library: Dare County Library, Virginia Dare Highway, Manteo, NC 27954. County history: D. Stick, DARE COUNTY, A HISTORY, NCSA, Raleigh, NC, 1970.

37. Davidson County

County seat: Lexington (27292), formed in 1822 from Rowan County, see GUIDE, pages 86-89.

Court house records: bonds of apprentices (1824-1919), bonds of bastardy (1823-1904), bonds of officials (1827-1930), court dockets (1823-68), court minutes (1823-1955), court records (1822-1941), deeds (1822-1953), divorce (1831-1914), estate accounts (1830-1961), estate administrators (1868-1966), estate executors (1868-1966), estate inventories (1830-97), estate records (18221945), estate sales (1830-97), estate settlements (1830-1960), estate widows' dowers & allotments (1915-52), guardian (1823-1967), land divisions (1835-1956), land ejectments (1822-90), land entries (1874-1916), land miscellaneous (1817-1937), land processions (1827-1920), marriages (1822-1967), miscellaneous (1824-1959), roads (1823-1907), schools (1860-1963), tax (1823-82), wills (1823-1966).

Other records: Baptist, cemetery, census (1830R, 1840RP, 1850-RAIMS, 1860RAIMS, 1870RAIM, 1880RAIM, 1890C, 1900R, 1910R), Christian Church, county history, DAR, family, genealogical society, historical society, landowner map (1890), Lutheran, newspaper, Presbyterian, Reformed, WPA inventory. Library: Davidson County Public Library,* 224 South Main St., Lexington, NC 27292. County histories: J. C. Leonard, CENTENNIAL HISTORY OF DAVIDSON COUNTY, Edwards and Broughton, Raleigh, NC, 1927; M. J. Sink and M. G. Matthews, PATHFINDERS PAST

AND PRESENT, A HISTORY OF DAVIDSON COUNTY, Hall, High Point, NC, 1972; Genealogical Society of Davidson County, THE HERITAGE OF DAVIDSON COUNTY, Hunter Publishing Co., WinstonSalem, NC, 1982.

38. Davie County

County seat: Mocksville (27028), formed in 1836 from Rowan County, see GUIDE, pages 90-92.

Court house records: bonds of apprentices (1837-1925), bonds of bastardy (1837-97), bonds of officials (1830-96), court dockets (1837-68), court minutes (1837-1905), court records (1829-1906), deeds (1837-1967), estate accounts (1855-1967), estate administrators (1837-1967), estate executors (1868-1937), estate records (1837-1967), estate sales (1846-54), estate settlements (1840-1904), guardian (1836-1967), land entries (1837-1910), land miscellaneous (1792-1914), land processions (1840-84), marriages (1851-1967), miscellaneous (1813-1967), roads (1837-1909), schools (1839-1967), tax (1838-96, 1905, 1915), wills (1837-1967).

Other records: Baptist, cemetery, census (1840RP, 1850RAIMS, 1860RAIMS, 1870RAIM, 1880RAIM, 1890C, 1900R, 1910R), DAR, family, landowner map (1887), Lutheran, Methodist, newspaper, Presbyterian, WPA inventory. Library: Davie County Public Library,* 371 North Main St., Mocksville, NC 27028. County histories: J. W. Wall, HISTORY OF DAVIE COUNTY, Davie County Historical Publishing Assn., Mocksville, NC, 1969; J. W. Wall, DAVIE COUNTY, A BRIEF HISTORY, NCSA, Raleigh, NC, 1976.

39. Dobbs County

formed in 1758 from Johnston County, discontinued and divided into Glasgow and Lenoir Counties in 1791, see GUIDE, page 93. Records: deed (1765-91), estate probates (1763-72), justices of peace (1760-91), miscellaneous (1765-9), petitions (1786-90), tax (1769, 1780).

40. Duplin County

County seat: Kenansville (28349), formed in 1750 from New Hanover County, for early deeds see Sampson County, many records missing, cause not known, see GUIDE, pages 94-96.

Court house records: bonds of apprentices (1871-1916), court dockets (1824-68), court minutes (1784-1930), court records (1866-8), deeds (1784-1940, see Sampson County for 1752-84), estate accounts (1769-1800, 1830-1962), estate administrators (1846-1962), estate executors (1868-78), estate inventories (1769-1800, 1830-1936), estate records (1779-1930), estate sales (1830-76), estate settlements (1869-1961), guardian (1781-1962), land divisions (1800-1960), land entries (1896-1941), land miscellaneous (1775-1922), land processions (1859-77), land surveys (1784-

1962), marriages (1755-1962), miscellaneous (1773-1962), petitions (1779), schools (1872-1935), tax (1783-1843, 1895-1925), wills (1759-1962).

Other records: Baptist, cemetery, census (1785N, 1790R, 1800R, 1810R, 1820RI, 1830R, 1840RP, 1850RAIMS, 1860RAIMS, 1870RAIM, 1880RAIM, 1890C, 1900R, 1910R), county history, DAR, historical society, Methodist, newspaper, Presbyterian, WPA inventory. Libraries: Duplin County Library, Kenansville, NC 28349; James Sprunt College Library,* Kenansville, NC 28349. County history: F. W. McGowen and others, FLASHES OF DUPLIN'S HISTORY AND GOVERNMENTS, Kenansville, NC, 1971.

41. Durham County

County seat: Durham (27701), formed in 1881 from Orange and Wake Counties, see GUIDE, pages 97-99.

Court house records: bonds of apprentices (1882-1913), court minutes (1884-1959), court records (1881-1936), deeds (1881-1961), estate accounts (1881-1946), estate administrators (1881-1965), estate executors (1881-1965), estate records (1881-1968), estate settlements (1882-1966), estate widows' dowers & allotments (1881-1969), guardian (1881-1966), justices of peace (1889-1900), marriages (1881-1969), miscellaneous (1881-1966), tax (1882-1902, 1905, 10, 15, 25, 35, 45), wills (1881-1968).

Other records: Baptist, Catholic, cemetery, census (1900R, 1910R), city history, county history, DAR, Episcopal, landowner map (1887), Methodist, newspaper, WPA inventory. Libraries: Perkins Library,* Duke University, Durham, NC 27706; Durham County Library, 300 North Roxboro St., Durham, NC 27702. County histories: W. K. Boyd, THE STORY OF DURHAM, Duke University Press, Durham, NC, 1925; W. C. Dula and A. C. Simpson, DURHAM AND HER PEOPLE, Seeman, Durham, NC, 1951.

42. Edgecombe County

County seat: Tarboro (27886), formed in 1741 from Bertie County, for early deeds see Halifax County, see GUIDE, pages 100-103.

Court house records: bonds of apprentices (1875-1924), bonds of bastardy (1771-1909), bonds of officials (1874-5), court dockets (1745-6, 1753-1868), court minutes (1744-6, 1757-1924), court records (1753-1918), deeds (1759-1920, see Halifax County for 1741-59), divorce (1835-1901), estate accounts (1730-53, 1783-1930), estate administrators (1797-1961), estate executors (1868-1961), estate inventories (1730-53, 1783-1930), estate records (1748-1917), estate sales (1730-53, 1783-96), estate settlements (1868-1961), guardian (1787-1961), land entries (1795-

1853), land miscellaneous (1742-1913), marriages (1760-1961), miscellaneous (1849-1963), petitions (1777), roads (1761-1912), schools (1846-60, 1883-1907), tax (1815, 1852-66), wills (1750-1961).

Other records: Baptist, Bible, cemetery, census (1785N, 1790R, 1800R, 1810R, 1820RI, 1830R, 1840RP, 1850RAIMS, 1860RAIMS, 1870RAIM, 1880RAIM, 1890C, 1900R, 1910R), city history, county history, DAR, Episcopal, family, landowner maps (1864, 1905), Lutheran, newspaper, Presbyterian, WPA inventory. Libraries: Edgecombe County Memorial Library, 909 Main St., Tarboro, NC 27886; High Point Public Library, 411 South Main St., High Point, NC 27261. County histories: J. K. Turner and J. L. Bridgers, HISTORY OF EDGECOMBE COUNTY, Edwards and Broughton, Raleigh, NC, 1920; J. W. Watson, KINFOLKS OF EDGECOMBE COUNTY, Rocky Mount, NC, 1969; A. D. Watson, EDGECOMBE COUNTY, A BRIEF HISTORY, NCSA, Raleigh, NC, 1979.

43. Forsyth County

County seat: Winston-Salem (27102), formed in 1849 from Stokes County, see GUIDE, pages 104-107.

Court house records: bonds of apprentices (1850-1920), bonds of bastardy (1849-79), bonds of officials (1877), court dockets (1849-85), court minutes (1849-1949), court records (1851-1930), deeds (1849-1965), estate accounts (1868-82), estate administrators (1849-1968), estate executors (1849-1968), estate inventories (1849-68), estate sales (1917-68), guardian (1849-1968), land processions (1884-6), lunacies (1852-1960), marriages (1849-1967), miscellaneous (1849-1968), naturalizations (1891-1921), petitions (1891-1949), roads (1850-79), schools (1883-90), tax lists (1846-68), wills (1849-1969).

Other records: Baptist, Bible, cemetery, census (1850RAIMS, 1860RAIMS, 1870RAIM, 1880RAIM, 1890C, 1900R, 1910R), Christian Church, city directory, city history, county history, DAR, family, Friends, Lutheran, Methodist, Moravian, newspaper, Presbyterian, WPA inventory. Libraries: Forsyth County Public Library,* 660 West Fifth St., Winston-Salem, NC 27101; Reynolds Library, Wake Forest University, Winston-Salem, NC 27109. County histories: A. L. Fries, FORSYTH COUNTY, Stewart's Printing, Winston-Salem, NC, 1898; A. L. Fries, S. T. Wright, and J. E. Hendricks, FORSYSTH, THE HISTORY OF A COUNTY ON THE MARCH, University of NC, Chapel Hill, NC, 1976.

44. Franklin County

County seat: Louisburg (27549), formed in 1779 from Bute County, see GUIDE, pages 108-110.

Court house records: bonds of bastardy (1784-1906), bonds of officials (1820-98), court dockets (1785-1868, 1903-15), court minutes (1785-68, 1884-1945), court records (1774-1934), deeds (1776-1951), divorce

(1820-1930), estate accounts (1848-1964), estate administrators (1866-1964), estate executors (1872-1964), estate inventories (1785-1915), estate records (1781-1934), estate sales (1922-36), estate settlements (1869-1964), estate widows' dowers & allotments (1925-64), guardian (1793-1964), land ejectments (1804-99), land entries (1778-1898), land miscellaneous (1793-1931), marriages (1789-1964), miscellaneous (1783-1964), schools (1885-1941), tax (1771, 1785-1904, 1915, 1925), wills (1785-1964).

Other records: Baptist, cemetery, census (1785N, 1790R, 1800R, 1810R, 1820RI, 1830R, 1840RP, 1850RAIMS, 1860RAIMS, 1870RAIM, 1880RAIM, 1890C, 1900R, 1910R), county history, Episcopal, landowner map (1867), Methodist, newspaper, WPA inventory. Libraries: Franklin County Library, 906 North Main St., Louisburg, NC 27549; Robbins Library, Louisburg College, 502 North Main St., Louisburg, NC, 27549. County history: E. H. Davis, HISTORICAL SKETCHES OF FRANKLIN COUNTY, Edwards and Broughton, Raleigh, NC, 1948.

45. Gaston County

County seat: Gastonia (28052), formed in 1846 from Lincoln County, court house fire in 1874, some records lost, see GUIDE, pages 111-13.

Court house records: bonds of apprentices (1869-1919), bonds of bastardy (1849-1905), bonds of officials (1868-89), court dockets (1847-68), court minutes (1847-1948), court records (1860-1912), deeds (1846-1961), divorce (1859-1910), estate accounts (1869-1963), estate administrators (1869-1963), estate executors (1869-1961), estate inventories (1863-9), estate records (1846-1928), estate sales (1863-9), estate settlements (1869-1963), guardian (1849-1963), land grants (1845-91), marriages (1848-1963), miscellaneous (1847-1963), roads (1859-1912), schools (1885-1964), tax (1847-1902), wills (1847-1963).

Other records: Baptist, cemetery, census (1850RAIMS, 1860RAIMS, 1870RAIM, 1880RAIM, 1890C, 1900R, 1910R), city history, county history, DAR, family, Lutheran, newspaper, Presbyterian, town history, WPA inventory. Library: Gaston-Lincoln Regional Library, 1555 E. Garrison Blvd., Gastonia, NC 28054. County histories: R. F. Cope and M. W. Wellman, THE COUNTY OF GASTON, Gaston County Historical Society, Charlotte, NC, 1961; M. S. Puett, HISTORY OF GASTON COUNTY, Charlotte Observer, Charlotte, NC, 1939; J. H. Separk, GASTONIA AND GASTON COUNTY, 1846-1949, Gastonia, NC, 1940.

46. Gates County

County seat: Gatesville (27938), formed in 1779 from Chowan, Hertford, and Perquimans Counties, see GUIDE, pages 114-16.

Court house records: bonds of apprentices (1846-1917), court minutes (1779-1964), deeds (1779-1964), estate accounts (1869-1964), estate administrators

(1804-47, 1868-1964), estate executors (1804-41, 1868-1964), estate inventories (1806-67), estate records (1765-1920), estate sales (1806-67), estate settlements (1867-1964), guardian (1785-1964), land divisions (1810-11), land ejectments (1795-1911), land entries (1811-7, 1831-3), land miscellaneous (1776-1908), land surveys (1894-1922), marriages (1779-1964), miscellaneous (1780-1964), roads (1779-1912), schools (1841-61, 1885-1927), tax (1782-1868, 1874-1935) ,wills (1779-1964).

Other records: Baptist, cemetery, census (1785N, 1790R, 1800R, 1810R, 1820RI, 1830R, 1840RP, 1850RAIMS, 1860RAIMS, 1870RAIM, 1880RAIM, 1890C, 1900R, 1910R), Christian Church, Congregational, county history, Episcopal, Methodist, WPA inventory. Library: Gates County Library, Gatesville, NC 27938. County history: I. S. Harrell, GATES COUNTY TO 1860, Trinity College Historical Society, Annual Publication 12 (1916), pp. 56-106.

47. Glasgow County

formed in 1791 from Dobbs County, name changed to Greene County in 1799. See Greene County for records.

48. Graham County

County seat: Robbinsville (28771), formed in 1872 from Cherokee County, see GUIDE, pages 117-18.

Court house records: bonds of officials (1872-1914), court minutes (1873-1960), court records (1872-1931), deeds (1873-1967), estate accounts (1873-1966), estate administrators (1879-1966), estate settlements (1886-1903, 1928-61), guardian (1877-98, 1910-66), land entries (1872-1961), marriages (1873-1970), miscellaneous (1872-1953), schools (1877-1948), tax (1874-1921), wills (1873-1966).

Other records: cemetery, census (1880RAIM, 1890C, 1900R, 1910R), county history, WPA inventory. Library: Graham County Library, Knight St., Robbinsville, NC 28771. County history: M. W. Freel, OUR HERITAGE: THE PEOPLE OF CHEROKEE COUNTY, 1540-1955, Miller, Asheville, NC, 1956.

49. Granville County

County seat: Oxford (27565), formed in 1746 from Edgecombe County, see GUIDE, pages 119-22.

Court house records: bonds of apprentices (1749-1913), bonds of bastardy (1746-1910), court minutes (1754-1929), deeds (1746-1961), divorce (1819-95), estate accounts (1868-1961), estate administrators (1868-1961), estate executors (1868-1933), estate inventories (1849-1963),

estate records (1746-1919), estate settlements (1868-1961), guardian (1758-1940), justices of peace (1749-1902), land ejectments (1788-1886), land entries (1778-1904), land miscellaneous (1748-1918), marriages (1758-1961), miscellaneous (1742-1961), naturalizations (1909-29), petitions (1772), powers of attorney (1749-1877), schools (1842-86), tax (1748-1935), wills (1762-1962).

Other records: Baptist, cemetery, census (1785N, 1790R, 1800R, 1810R, 1820RI, 1830R, 1840RP, 1850RAIMS, 1860RAIMS, 1870RAIM, 1880RAIM, 1890C, 1900R, 1910R), Christian Church, city history, county history, Episcopal, family, landowner map (1868), Methodist, newspaper, Presbyterian, town history, WPA inventory. Library: Thornton Library,* Main and Spring Sts., Oxford, NC 27565. County histories: J. R. Caldwell, A HISTORY OF GRANVILLE COUNTY, 1746-1800, PhD Thesis, University of NC, Chapel Hill, NC, 1950; W. S. Ray, COLONIAL GRANVILLE AND ITS PEOPLE, Genealogical Publishing Co., Baltimore, MD, 1965; Z. H. Gwynn, KINFOLKS OF GRANVILLE COUNTY, 1765-1826, Watson, Rocky Mount, NC, 1974.

50. Greene County

County seat: Snow Hill (28580), in 1799 Glasgow was renamed Greene, court house fire in 1876, many records lost, see GUIDE, pages 123-25.

Court house records: bonds of apprentices (1869-88, 1911-2), bonds of officials (1860-1937), court dockets (1861-2, 1866-1911), court minutes (1869-1966), court records (1868-1967), deeds (1857-1966), divorce (1875-1959), estate accounts (1868-1956), estate administrators (1869- 1920), estate executors (1869-1920), estate inventories (1869-1966), estate records (1839-45), estate settlements (1869-1952), guardian (1857-1966), land entries (1906-13), marriages (1875-1966), miscellaneous (1800-1967), schools (1911-67), tax (1816, 1875-1955), wills (1846-1966).

Other records: cemetery, census (1800R, 1810R, 1820RI, 1830R, 1840RP, 1850RAIMS, 1860RAIMS, 1870RAIM, 1880RAIM, 1890C, 1900R, 1910R), Christian Church, county history, landowner map (1864), newspaper, WPA inventory. Library: Greene County Public Library, 229 Kingold Blvd., Snow Hill, NC 28580. County history: J. M. Creech, HISTORY OF GREENE COUNTY, Gateway Press, Baltimore, MD, 1980.

51. Guilford County

County seat: Greensboro (27402), formed in 1770 from Rowan and Orange Counties, court house fire in 1872, a few records lost, see GUIDE, pages 126-29.

Court house records: bonds of apprentices (1817-1922), bonds of bastardy (1816-77), bonds of officials (1774-1892), court dockets (1779-1879), court minutes (1781-1964), court records (1790-1935), deeds (1771-1957), divorce (1820-1929),

estate accounts (1857-1962), estate administrators (1868-1947), estate executors (1844-1957), estate inventories (1820-79), estate records (1775-1970), estate sales (1836-68, 1872-9), estate settlements (1820-1962), estate widows' dowers & allotments (1866-1962), guardian (1775-1968), land miscellaneous (1806-1941), lunacies (1826-1925), marriages (1771-1961), miscellaneous (1796-1968), petitions (1772-3), powers of attorney (1805-1929), roads (1799-1890), schools (1872-1965), tax lists (1786, 1815), wills (1771-1969).

Other records: Baptist, Bible, cemetery, census (1790R, 1800R, 1810R, 1820RI, 1830R, 1840RP, 1850RAIMS, 1860RAIMS, 1870RAIM, 1880RAIM, 1890C, 1900R, 1910R), city directory, city history, county history, DAR, family, Friends, genealogical society, historical society, landowner map (1910), Lutheran, Methodist, newspaper, Presbyterian, Reformed, WPA inventory. Libraries: Greensboro Public Library,* 201 North Greene St., Greensboro, NC 27402; Guilford College Library, 5800 West Friendly Ave., Greensboro, NC 27410; High Point Public Library, 411 South Main St., High Point, NC 27261. County histories: Guilford County Bicentennial Commission, GUILFORD COUNTY, The Commission, Greensboro, NC, 1971; S. W. Stockard, HISTORY OF GUILFORD COUNTY, Gaut-Ogden, Knoxville, TN, 1902; A. E. Weatherly, THE FIRST 100 YEARS OF HISTORIC GUILFORD, Greensboro Printing Co., Greensboro, NC, 1972; B. P. Robinson, THE HISTORY OF GUILFORD COUNTY TO 1890, Guilford County Bicentennial Committee, Greensboro, NC, 1978.

52. Halifax County

County seat: Halifax (27839), formed in 1758 from Edgecombe County, some early records missing, cause not known, see GUIDE, pages 131-32.

Court house records: bonds of apprentices (1722-1855), bonds of bastardy (1858, 1872-99), court dockets (1759-70, 1822-69), court minutes (1784-1940), court records (1765-1829, 1860-1922), deeds (1732-1934, includes Bertie and Edgecombe records), divorce (1870-1922), estate accounts (1868-1954), estate administrators (1826-49, 1868-1946), estate executors (1868-1963), estate inventories (1773-9, 1828-62), estate records (1762-1924), estate sales (1773-9, 1828-62), estate settlements (1870-1950), guardian (1808-1963), land entries (1844-59), marriages (1770-1963), miscellaneous (1761-1963), petitions (1768), schools (1909-51), tax (1782-1834, 1860-3, 1915, 1925, 1935), wills (1759-1963).

Other records: Baptist, cemetery, census (1785N, 1790R, 1800R, 1810R, 1820RI, 1830R, 1840RP, 1850RAIMS, 1860RAIMS, 1870RAIM, 1880RAIM, 1890C, 1900R, 1910R), county history, DAR, Episcopal, family, historical society, landowner map (1864), Methodist, newspaper, WPA inventory. Library: Halifax County Library,* Granville St., Halifax, NC 27839. County history: W. C. Allen, HISTORY OF HALIFAX COUNTY, Cornhill, Boston, MA, 1918.

53. Harnett County

County seat: Lillington (27546), formed in 1855 from Cumberland County, court house fires in 1892 and 1894, many records lost, see GUIDE, pages 133-34.

Court house records: bonds of officials (1893-1918), court minutes (1898-1956), deeds (1855-1955), estate accounts (1884-1956), estate administrators (1892-1959), estate executors (1892-1954), estate inventories (1908-62), estate settlements (1889-1957), estate widows' dowers & allotments (1893-1938), guardian (1892-1967), land divisions (1898-1921), land partitions (1898-1921), marriages (1892-1967), miscellaneous (1892-1967), schools (1857-1960), tax (1900-6, 1915), wills (1883-1967).

Other records: Bible, cemetery, census (1860RAIMS, 1870RAIM, 1880RAIM, 1890C, 1900R, 1910R), Christian Church, county history, DAR, family, newspaper, Presbyterian, WPA inventory. Library: Harnett County Library, 601 Main St., Lillington, NC 27546. County history: M. Fowler, THEY PASSED THIS WAY, Harnett County Centennial, Lillington, NC, 1955.

54. Haywood County

County seat: Waynesville (28786), formed in 1808 from Buncombe County, see GUIDE, pages 135-38.

Court house records: bonds of apprentices (1812-61), bonds of bastardy (1814-1936), bonds of officials (1812-1942), court dockets (1809-82), court minutes (1809-1966), court records (1810-1948), deeds (1808-1966), divorce (1829-1944), estate accounts (1866-1966), estate administrators (1867-1966), estate executors (1867-1966), estate inventories (1866-75), estate records (1808-1939), estate sales (1866-75), estate settlements (1869-1966), guardian (1815-1966), land entries (1809-87), marriages (1808-1965), miscellaneous (1820-), roads (1811-1932), schools (1830-1950), tax (1820, 1933), wills (1808-1966).

Other records: Baptist, cemetery, census (1810R, 1820RI, 1830R, 1840RP, 1850RAIMS, 1860RAIMS, 1870RAIM, 1880RAIM, 1890C, 1900R, 1910R), county history, Methodist, newspaper, WPA inventory. Library: Haywood County Public Library,* 402 South Haywood St., Waynesville, NC 28786. County histories: W. C. Allen, ANNALS OF HAYWOOD COUNTY, The Author, Waynesville, NC, 1935; W. C. Medford, THE EARLY HISTORY OF HAYWOOD COUNTY, Waynesville, NC, 1961; W. C. Medford, THE MIDDLE HISTORY OF HAYWOOD COUNTY, Waynesville, NC, 1968.

55. Henderson County

County seat: Hendersonville (28739), formed in 1838 from Buncombe County, see GUIDE, pages 139-41.

Court house records: bonds of apprentices (1875-85), bonds of bastardy (1840-1956), bonds of officials (1839-1931), court dockets (1839-68), court minutes (1839-1949), court records (1838-1966), deeds (1759-1968), divorce (1842-1931), estate accounts (1870-1967), estate administrators (1868-1968), estate executors (1868-1967), estate records (1838-1933), estate settlements (1869-1968), guardian (1838-1967), justices of peace (1853-1955), land ejectments (1838-1957), land miscellaneous (1840-1959), marriages (1838-1967), miscellaneous (1838-1967), roads (1842-1954), schools (1885-1967), tax (1841-1955), wills (1841-1967).

Other records: Baptist, cemetery, census (1840RP, 1850RAIMS, 1860RAIMS, 1870RAIM, 1880RAIM, 1890C, 1900R, 1910R), county history, DAR, Episcopal, newspaper, WPA inventory. Library: Henderson County Public Library, 301 North Washington St., Hendersonville, NC 28739. County histories: S. S. Patton, THE STORY OF HENDERSON COUNTY, Miller, Asheville, NC, 1947; L. Ray, POSTMARKS: A HISTORY OF HENDERSON COUNTY, 1787-1968, Adams, Chicago, IL, 1970.

56. Hertford County

County seat: Winton (27986), formed in 1759 from Bertie, Chowan, Northampton, and Gates Counties, court house fires in 1830 and 1862, most records lost in 1832, many in 1862, see GUIDE, pages 142-43.

Court house records: bonds of apprentices (1861-8), bonds of bastardy (1865-98), court dockets (1830-68, 1879-87), court minutes (1830-1950), court records (1855-1914), deeds (1775-1960), divorce (1871-1914), estate accounts (1830-40, 1847-1963), estate administrators (1868-1963), estate executors (1866-1963), estate inventories (1895-1963), estate records (1858-1914), estate settlements (1868-1963), guardian (1823-45, 1858-1962), marriages (1868-1963), miscellaneous (1866-1963), petitions (1759), tax (1779-84, 1815, 1842-71), schools (1877-1948), wills (1763-5, 1830-1963).

Other records: Baptist, cemetery, census (1790R, 1800R, 1810R, 1820RI, 1830R, 1840RP, 1850RAIMS, 1860RAIMS, 1870RAIM, 1880RAIM, 1890C, 1900R, 1910R), county history, Episcopal, Jewish, landowner map (1863-4), Methodist, newspaper, town history, WPA inventory. Library: Albemarle Regional Library, Winton, NC 27986. County history: B. B. Winborne, COLONIAL AND STATE POLITICAL HISTORY OF HERTFORD COUNTY, Edwards and Broughton, Raleigh, NC, 1906.

57. Hoke County

County seat: Raeford (28376), formed in 1911 from Cumberland and Robeson Counties, see GUIDE, pages 144-5.

Court house records: court dockets (1930-42), court minutes (1911-66), deeds (1911-70), estate accounts (1911-60), estate administrators (1911-66), estate executors (1911-66), estate settlements (1911-65), guardian (1911-66), land entries (1913-29), marriages (1911-70), miscellaneous (1911-70), schools (1911-70), tax (1915, 1925), wills (1911-66).

Other records: cemetery, county history, DAR, family, Presbyterian, WPA inventory. Library: Hoke County Library, 334 North Main St., Raeford, NC 28376. County history: Hoke County Golden Jubilee Committee, SOUVENIR PROGRAM, CONTAINING A HISTORY OF HOKE COUNTY, The Committee, Raeford, NC, 1961.

58. Hyde County

County seat: Swanquarter (27885), formed in 1705 from Bath County and named Wickham County, in 1712 name of Wickham County was changed to Hyde, court house fire in 1789, some records lost, early deeds are in Beaufort County, see GUIDE, pages 146-48.

Court house records: bonds of apprentices (1771-1912), bonds of bastardy (1740-1896), court dockets (1744-69), court minutes (1736-7, 1744-1921), court records (1713-1899), deeds (1736-1937), divorce (1829-98), estate accounts (1869-1921), estate administrators (1868-1960), estate executors (1868-1960), estate inventories (1781-5), estate records (1745-1904), estate settlements (1856-1905), guardian (1745-1960), land entries (1778-95, 1891-2), land grants (1779-1857), marriages (1742-1958), miscellaneous (1735-1960), roads (1767-1888), tax (1741-1897), wills (1760-1960). Other records: cemetery, census (1785N, 1790R, 1800R, 1810R, 1830R, 1840RP, 1850RAIMS, 1860RAIMS, 1870RAIM, 1880RAIM, 1890C, 1900R, 1910R), church, county history, DAR, historical society, WPA inventory. Library: George Library, Swanquarter, NC 27885. County history: Hyde County Historical Society, HYDE COUNTY HISTORY, The Society, Swanquarter, NC, 1976.

59. Iredell County

County seat: Statesville (28677), formed in 1788 from Rowan County, court house fire in 1854, many records lost, see GUIDE, pages 149-51.

Court house records: bonds of bastardy (1860-1913), bonds of officials (1846-1903), coroner (1854-1906), court dockets (1791-1868), court minutes (1789-1954), court records (1808-1932), deeds (1788-1965), divorce (1855-1913), estate accounts (1788-1965), estate administrators (1846-1965), estate executors (1868-76, 1888-1931), estate inventor-

ies (1843-68), estate records (1790-1944), estate sales (1843-68, 1921-65), estate settlements (1868-95), estate widows' dowers & allotments (1867-1965), guardian (1803-1965), land ejectments (1853-1906), land entries (1789-94, 1855-1905), land miscellaneous (1843-1948), marriages (1788-1965), miscellaneous (1788-1965), schools (1885-1950), tax (1790-1910), wills (1788-1965).

Other records: Baptist, FHC, cemetery, census (1790R, 1800R, 1810R, 1820RI, 1830R, 1840RP, 1850RAIMS, 1860RAIMS, 1870RAIM, 1880RAIM, 1890C, 1900R, 1910R), county history, DAR, family, funeral, genealogical society, Lutheran, Methodist, newspaper, WPA inventory. Library: Iredell County Library, 135 East Water St., Statesville, NC 28677. County history: Genealogical Society of Iredell County, THE HERITAGE OF IREDELL COUNTY, Hunter Publishing Co., Winston-Salem, NC, 1980.

60. Jackson County

County seat: Sylva (28779), formed in 1851 from Haywood and Macon Counties, many records missing, reason not known, see GUIDE, pages 152-53.

Court house records: court minutes (1853-1957), deeds (1853-1970), estate administrators (1870-1966), estate executors (1868-1966), estate inventories (1863-75), estate settlements (1868-1966), guardian (1870-1966), land entries (1853-1968), land probate (1872-94), marriages (1853-1970), miscellaneous (1865-1970), tax lists (1872-89, 1910-21), wills (1853-1966).

Other records: cemetery, census (1860RAIMS, 1870RAIM, 1880RAIM, 1890C, 1900R, 1910R), county history, WPA inventory. Library: Jackson County Public Library, 51 West Main St., Sylva, NC 28779. County history: C. A. Hoyle, PANORAMA OF PROGRESS, JACKSON COUNTY CENTENNIAL, Jackson County Centennial Committee, Sylva, NC, 1951.

61. Johnston County

County seat: Smithfield (27577), formed in 1746 from Craven County, many records missing, reason not known, see GUIDE, pages 154-57.

Court house records: bonds of apprentices (1850-1911), bonds of bastardy (1850-95), court dockets (1785-1869), court minutes (1759-1929), court records (1769-1936), deeds (1749-1939), divorce (1853-1926), estate accounts (1808-1946), estate administrators (1849-1940), estate executors (1868-1923), estate records (1771-1962), estate settlements (1868-1924), estate widows' dowers & allotments (1793-1817, 1902-49), guardian (1793-1962), land divisions (1789-1961), land entries (1778-1926), land grants (1779-82), land miscellaneous (1772-1954), land partitions (1793-1817), land probate (1869-80), marriages (1746-1961), miscel-

laneous (1764-1962), schools (1885-1938), tax (1784-1915), wills (1760-1961).

Other records: Baptist, cemetery, census (1785N, 1790R, 1800R, 1810R, 1820RI, 1830R, 1840RP, 1850RAIMS, 1860RAIMS, 1870RAIM, 1880RAIM, 1890C, 1900R, 1910R), Christian Church, county history, DAR, Episcopal, family, genealogical society, historical society, Methodist, newspaper, town history, WPA inventory. Library: Public Library of Johnston County and Smithfield, 305 Market St., Smithfield, NC 27577. County history: W. M. Sanders, Jr., and G. Y. Ragsdale, JOHNSTON COUNTY, ECONOMIC AND SOCIAL, Observer, Smithfield, NC, 1922.

62. Jones County

County seat: Trenton (28585), formed in 1778 from Craven County, court house fire in 1862, some records lost, see GUIDE, pages 158-60.

Court house records: bonds of apprentices (1847-1902), bonds of bastardy (1812-1914), court dockets (1807-68), court minutes (1807-1964), court records (1786, 1800, 1853-1944), deeds (1779-1964), divorce (1871-1905), estate accounts (1803-1954), estate administrators (1792-9, 1869-1964), estate divisions (1809-1957), estate executors (1792-9, 1868-1964), estate inventories (1803-1929), estate records (1786-1938), estate settlements (1809-1957), guardian (1792-9, 1844-1964), land ejectments (1853-1905), land entries (1779-1959), land grants (17803, 1788-95), marriages (1851-1964), miscellaneous (1785-1964), schools (1873-9, 1885-1964), tax (1779, 1785-6, 1866), wills (1779-1964).

Other records: Baptist, cemetery, census (1785N, 1790R, 1800R, 1810R, 1820RI, 1830R, 1840RP, 1850RAIMS, 1860RAIMS, 1870RAIM, 1880RAIM, 1890C, 1900R, 1910R), Christian Church, county history, Episcopal, historical society, Methodist, WPA inventory. Library: Trenton Public Library, Lakeside Dr., Trenton, NC 28585. County history: S. B. Henderson, JONES COUNTY, FACT AND FOLKLORE, The Author, Trenton, NC, 1979.

63. Lee County

County seat: Sanford (27330), formed in 1907 from Chatham and Moore Counties, see GUIDE, pages 161-62.

Court house records: bonds of apprentices (1911-23), court dockets (1908-68), court minutes (1908-59), deeds (1908-70), estate accounts (1907-34), estate administrators (1908-68), estate executors (1908-68), estate settlements (1912-26), guardian (1908-36), land surveys (1908-28), lunacies (1908-69), marriages (1908-70), miscellaneous (1908-69), schools (1908-70), wills (1908-68).

Other records: Baptist, cemetery, census (1910R), Christian Church, county history, DAR, Methodist, newspaper, Presbyterian, WPA

inventory. Library: Lee County Library, 107 Hawkins Ave., Sanford, NC 27330. County history: LEE COUNTY, The State, March 13, 1954.

64. Lenoir County

County seat: Kinston (28501), formed in 1791 from Dobbs County, court house fires in 1878 and 1880, most records lost, see GUIDE, pages 163-65.

Court house records: bonds of apprentices (1885-1917), bonds of officials (1802-1937), court minutes (1800-1953), court records (1874-1939), deeds (1792-1964), divorce (1878-1933), estate accounts (1880-1966), estate administrators (1879-1955), estate divisions (1866-1956), estate executors (1894-1955), estate records (1830-1966), estate settlements (1880-1966), estate widows' dowers & allotments (1868-1958), guardian (1879-1955), land entries (1879-1915), land maps (1870-1966), land miscellaneous (1791-), marriages (1791-1966), miscellaneous (1792-1840, 1848-1954), roads (1826-1904), schools (1884-1957), tax lists (1880-1937), wills (1869-1966).

Other records: FHC, cemetery, census (1800R, 1810R, 1820RI, 1830R, 1840RP, 1850RAIMS, 1860RAIMS, 1870RAIM, 1880RAIM, 1890C, 1900R, 1910R), Christian Church, county history, Episcopal, landowner map (1864), newspaper, town history, WPA inventory. Libraries: Kinston-Lenoir County Public Library, 510 North Queen St., Kinston, NC 28501; Lenoir Community College Library,* Kinston, NC 28501. County histories: T. C. Johnson and C. R. Holloman, THE STORY OF KINSTON AND LENOIR COUNTY, Edwards and Broughton, Raleigh, NC, 1954; W. S. Powell, ANNALS OF PROGRESS, THE STORY OF LENOIR COUNTY, NCSA, Raleigh, NC, 1963; The Lenoir County Historical Association, THE HERITAGE OF LENOIR COUNTY, Hunter Publishing Co., Winston-Salem, NC, 1981.

65. Lincoln County

County seat: Lincolnton (28092), formed in 1778 from Tryon County, many records missing, cause not known, see GUIDE, pages 166-69.

Court house records: bonds of apprentices (1783-1917), bonds of bastardy (1784-1893), bonds of officials (1769-1883, 1902-21), court dockets (1783-1870), court minutes (1779-1960), court records (1779-1918), deeds (1779-1964, see Tryon County also), divorce (1811-1921), estate accounts (1831-1969), estate administrators (1868-1964), estate executors (1869-1964), estate inventories (1812-9, 1831-68), estate records (1779-1925), estate sales (1812-9, 1921-64), estate settlements (1833-1969), guardian (1777-1925), land ejectments (1800-95), land entries (1783-95), land grants (1763- 1807), land levies (1838-46), lunacies (1868-1964), marriages (1779- 1964), miscellaneous (1779-

1965), roads (1781-1869), schools (1845-65, 1883-1964), tax (1784-1886), wills (1779-1964).

Other records: cemetery, census (1790R, 1800R, 1810R, 1820RI, 1830R, 1840RP, 1850RAIMS, 1860RAIMS, 1870RAIM, 1880RAIM, 1890C, 1900R, 1910R), church, county history, family, Lutheran, newspaper, Reformed, town history, WPA inventory. Library: Lincoln County Public Library,* 306 West Main St., Lincolnton, NC 28092. County history: W. L. Sherrill, ANNALS OF LINCOLN COUNTY, Observer, Charlotte, NC, 1937.

66. Macon County

County seat: Franklin (28734), formed in 1828 from Haywood County, many records missing, cause not known, see GUIDE, pages 170-72.

Court house records: bonds of bastardy (1838-97), court dockets (1829-70), court minutes (1829-1963), court records (1828-1926), deeds (1828-1966), divorce (1835-1913), estate accounts (1868-1966), estate administrators (1868-1930), estate executors (1868-1966), estate inventories (1866-88), estate records (1831-1920), estate settlements (1870-1966), guardian (1845-1966), land ejectments (1833-90), land entries (1836-7), land grants (1826, 1836-1919), land miscellaneous (1837-1924), land surveys (1905-27), marriages (1828-1966), miscellaneous (1829-1966), roads (1829-1905), schools (1835-1966), tax (1857-68), wills (1830-1966).

Other records: Baptist, cemetery, census (1830R, 1840RP, 1850RAIMS, 1860RAIMS, 1870RAIM, 1880RAIM, 1890C, 1900R, 1910R), county history, Episcopal, Methodist, newspaper, Presbyterian, WPA inventory. Library: Macon County Public Library, 45 Wayah St., Franklin, NC 28734. County history: C. D. Smith, A BRIEF HISTORY OF MACON COUNTY, Franklin Press, Franklin, NC, 1891.

67. Madison County

County seat: Marshall (28753), formed in 1851 from Buncombe and Yancey Counties, see GUIDE, pages 173-75.

Court house records: bonds of apprentices (1874-1914), bonds of bastardy (1874-1910), bonds of officials (1894-1969), court minutes (1851-1955), deeds (1851-1969), divorce (1854-1926), estate accounts (1873-1968), estate administrators (1851-1968), estate executors (1851-1968), estate inventories (1852-62), estate records (1851-1943), estate settlements (1868-1968), guardian (1855-1968), land ejectments (1851-1907), land levies (1851-1932), marriages (1851-1969), miscellaneous (1851-1969), roads (1854-1937), tax lists (1862, 1887), wills (1851-1969).

Other records: Baptist, cemetery, census (1860RAIMS, 1870RAIM, 1880RAIM, 1890C, 1900R, 1910R), county history, DAR, family, histori-

cal society, town history, WPA inventory. Library: Madison County Public Library, Main St., Marshall, NC 28753. County history: M. W. Wellman, THE KINGDOM OF MADISON, University of NC Press, Chapel Hill, NC, 1973.

68. Martin County

County seat: Williamston (27892), formed in 1774 from Halifax and Tyrrell Counties, court house fire in 1884, some records lost, see GUIDE, pages 176-78.

Court house records: court minutes (1838-1939), deeds (1774-1963), divorce (1882-1903), estate accounts (1869-1963), estate administrators (1827-1963), estate executors (1827-1928), estate inventories (1905-63), estate records (1820-1906), estate sales (190563), estate widows' dowers & allotments (1885-1963), guardian (1866-1963), land entries (1866-1900), land miscellaneous (1779-1917), schools (1884-1963), tax (1779, 1885-1915), wills (1774-1963).

Other records: Baptist, cemetery, census (1785N, 1790R, 1800R, 1810R, 1820RI, 1830R, 1840RP, 1850RAIMS, 1860RAIMS, 1870RAIM, 1880RAIM, 1890C, 1900R, 1910R), Christian Church, county history, Episcopal, historical society, landowner map (1864), newspaper, WPA inventory. Libraries: Martin Memorial Library, East Grace St., Williamston, NC 27892; Beaufort, Hyde, Martin Regional Library, 158 North Market St., Washington, NC 27889. County history: S. G. N. Hughes, MARTIN COUNTY HERITAGE, Martin County Historical Society and Hunter Publishing Co., Winston-Salem, NC, 1980.

69. McDowell County

County seat: Marion (28752), formed in 1842 from Burke and Rutherford Counties, see GUIDE, pages 179-182.

Court house records: bonds of apprentices (1842-1917), bonds of bastardy (1842-1912), bonds of officials (1843-1922), court dockets (1843-1968), court minutes (1843-1957), court records (1843-1936), deeds (1842- 1961), divorce (1849-1911), estate accounts (1869-1968), estate executors (1868-1968), estate inventories (1859-1967), estate records (1842-1968), estate settlements (1872-1968), guardian (1843-1968), land ejectments (1843-1915), land entries (1843-1956), land miscellaneous (1843-1921), land surveys (1905-14), lunacies (1848-1951), marriages (1842-1968), military pensions (1852-1939), miscellaneous (1843-1957), roads (1843-1909), schools (1873-1968), tax (1842-1934), wills (1843-1968).

Other records: cemetery, census (1850RAIMS, 1860RAIMS, 1870-RAIM, 1880RAIM, 1890C, 1900R, 1910R), county history, DAR, family, historical society, newspaper, Presbyterian, WPA inventory. Library: McDowell County Public Library, 100 West Court St., Marion, NC 28752.

County history: M. B. Fossett, HISTORY OF McDOWELL COUNTY, McDowell County Bicentennial Committee, Marion, NC, 1976.

70. Mecklenburg County

County seat: Charlotte (28202), formed in 1762 from Anson County, see GUIDE, pages 183-85.

Court house records: bonds of apprentices (1871-1920), court dockets (1774-1868), court minutes (1774-1960), court records (1782-1910), deeds (1763-1963), divorce (1805-1910), estate accounts (1785-1965), estate administrators (1868-1964), estate executors (1868-1964), estate records (1762-1965), estate sales (1827-30), estate settlements (1785-1965), guardian (1781-1964), land entries (1778-1855), land grants (1789-1845), land miscellaneous (1767-1912), marriages (1783-1962), miscellaneous (1762-1965), petitions (1772, 1778), tax (1777-8, 1797-1824, 18434, 1915-6), wills (1763-1965).

Other records: Baptist, Bible, FHC, cemetery, census (1790R, 1800R, 1810R, 1820RI, 1830R, 1840RP, 1850RAIMS, 1860RAIMS, 1870RAIM, 1880RAIM, 1890C, 1900R, 1910R), city directory, county history, DAR, Episcopal, family, historical society, landowner map (1893), Lutheran, Methodist, newspaper, Presbyterian, WPA inventory. Library: Public Library of Charlotte and Mecklenburg County,* 310 North Tryon St., Charlotte, NC 28202. County histories: J. B. Alexander, HISTORY OF MECKLENBURG COUNTY, Observer, Charlotte, NC, 1902; L. Blythe and C. R. Brockermann, HORNETS' NEST, THE STORY OF CHARLOTTE AND MECKLENBURG COUNTY, Public Library of Charlotte, Charlotte, NC, 1961; D. A. Tompkins, A HISTORY OF MECKLENBURG COUNTY, Observer, Charlotte, NC, 1903, 2 volumes.

71. Mitchell County

County seat: Bakersville (28705), formed in 1861 from Burke, Caldwell, McDowell, Watauga, and Yancey Counties, court house move in 1907, some records lost, see GUIDE, pages 186-88.

Court house records: court minutes (1861-1966), deeds (1861-1970), divorce (1861-1970), estate accounts (1875-1968), estate administrators (1871-1968), estate executors (1871-1968), estate records (1861-1946), estate widows' dowers & allotments (1908-38), guardian (1866-1968), land entries (1901-50), land miscellaneous (1861-1936), lunacies (1899-1964), marriages (1861-1969), miscellaneous (1861-1968), schools (1901-28), tax (1861-1969), wills (1861-1969).

Other records: cemetery, census (1870RAIM, 1880RAIM, 1890C, 1900R, 1910R), city history, county history, DAR, family, newspaper, Presbyterian, WPA inventory. Libraries: Mitchell County Library, Bakersville, NC 28705; Avery, Mitchell, Yancey Regional Library, 304 Walnut St.,

Spruce Pine, NC 28777. County history: County Board of Education, DISCOVERING MITCHELL COUNTY, The Board, Bakersville, NC, 1939/40.

72. Montgomery County

County seat: Troy (27371), formed in 1779 from Anson County, court house fire in 1835, many records lost, see GUIDE, pages 189-91.

Court house records: bonds of apprentices (1840-97), bonds of bastardy (1844-97), bonds of officials (1837-1918), court dockets (1821-68), court minutes (1807-24, 1843-1912), court records (1833-1940), deeds (1779-1964), divorce (1856-1907), estate accounts (1847-1964), estate administrators (1868-1964), estate executors (1868-1946), estate inventories (1849-58), estate records (1818-1970), estate sales (1842-8, 1861-8), estate settlements (1849-58, 1868-1964), guardian (1843-1964), land ejectments (1840-92), land entries (1837-1955), land miscellaneous (1779-1924), land tax sales (1845-70), marriages (1779-1964), miscellaneous (1785-1962), roads (1839-1926), schools (1872-1926), tax (1782-6, 1843-6, 1851-68, 1873-1916), wills (1785-1970).

Other records: Baptist, cemetery, census (1785N, 1790R, 1800R, 1810R, 1820RI, 1830R, 1840RP, 1850RAIMS, 1860RAIMS, 1870RAIM, 1880RAIM, 1890C, 1900R, 1910R), county history, DAR, family, newspaper, Presbyterian, town history, WPA inventory. Library: Montgomery County Public Library, West Main St., Troy, NC 27371. County history: M. S. Lassiter, PATTERN OF TIMELESS MOMENTS, A HISTORY OF MONTGOMERY COUNTY, Board of Commissioners, Troy, NC, 1976; THE HERITAGE OF MONTGOMERY COUNTY, Hunter, Winston-Salem, NC, 1989.

73. Moore County

County seat: Carthage (28327), formed in 1784 from Cumberland County, court house fire in 1889, many records lost, see GUIDE, pages 192-94.

Court house records: court dockets (1786-1953), court minutes (1784-1956), court records (1829-1924), deeds (1889-1966), divorce (1887-1915), estate accounts (1868-1965), estate administrators (1787-1963), estate executors (1787-1916), estate settlements (18691965), estate widows' dowers & allotments (1889-1964), guardian (1870-1965), land entries (1889-1958), land grants (1787-1965), land owners (1815), marriages (1851-1965), miscellaneous (1784-1965), schools (1872-1941), tax lists (1815, 1852-8, 1889-1931), wills (1784-1965).

Other records: Baptist, cemetery, census (1790R, 1800R, 1810R, 1820RI, 1830R, 1840RP, 1850RAIMS, 1860RAIMS, 1870RAIM, 1880RAIM, 1890C, 1900R, 1910R), county history, DAR, family, landowner map (1885), Methodist, newspaper, Presbyterian, town history, WPA inventory. Library: Moore County Library, Dowd St., Carthage, NC 28327.

County histories: B. P. Robinson, A HISTORY OF MOORE COUNTY, 1747-1847, Moore County Historical Association, Southern Pines, NC, 1956; M. W. Wellman, THE COUNTY OF MOORE, 1847-1947, Moore County Historical Association, Southern Pines, NC, 1962.

---

74. Nash County

County seat: Nashville (27856), formed in 1777 from Edgecombe County, see GUIDE, pages 195-98.

Court house records: bonds of apprentices (1793-1931), bonds of bastardy (1779-1883), bonds of officials (1778-1888), court dockets (1779-1880), court minutes (1778-1963), court records (1777-1908), deeds (1777-1963), divorce (1789-1878), estate accounts (1818-27, 1869-1964), estate administrators (1857-1964), estate executors (1868-1964), estate inventories (1821-68), estate records (1777-1909), estate sales (1821-68), estate settlements (1869-1964), estate widows' allotments (1883-1918), guardian (1784-1918), land entries (1777-94, 1838-1909), land miscellaneous (1777-1911), marriages (1777-1964), miscellaneous (1778-1963), roads (1768-1887), schools (1843-1956), tax (1782-1902), wills (1778-1964).

Other records: Baptist, cemetery, census (1785N, 1790R, 1800R, 1810R, 1820RI, 1830R, 1840RP, 1850RAIMS, 1860RAIMS, 1870RAIM, 1880RAIM, 1890C, 1900R, 1910R), Christian Church, city history, historical society, landowner map (1864), newspaper, WPA inventory. Library: Braswell Memorial Library,* 344 Falls Road, Rocky Mount, NC 27804. County history: T. E. Ricks, NASH COUNTY HISTORICAL NOTES, Nash County Historical Association, Nashville, NC, 1976.

---

75. New Hanover County

County seat: Wilmington (28401), formed in 1729 from Craven County, court house fires in 1798, 1819, and 1840, a few records lost, see GUIDE, pages 199-202.

Court house records: births (1903-10), bonds of apprentices (1797-1899), bonds of bastardy (1818-1906), bonds of officials (1766-1908), coroner (1768-1880), court dockets (1750-1868), court minutes (1738-1939), court records (1758-1940), deaths (1903-10), deeds (1729-1954), divorce (1858-1945), estate accounts (1868-1940), estate administrators (1841-1946), estate executors (1841-79), estate inventories (1829-1913), estate records (1741-1939), estate settlements (1869-84), estate widows' dowers & allotments (1800-1934), guardian (1763-1946), land ejectments (1784-1898), land entries (1778-1948), land miscellaneous (1748-1950), marriages (1741-1963), miscellaneous (1756-1943), naturalizations & citizenships (1842-1908), roads (1798-1868), schools (1841-1913), tax (1755, 1762-3, 1782, 1799-1925), wills (1734-1961).

Other records: Baptist, Biography, FHC, cemetery, census (1785N, 1790R, 1800R, 1810R, 1820RI, 1830R, 1840RP, 1850RAIMS, 1860-RAIMS, 1870RAIM, 1880RAIM, 1890C, 1900R, 1910R), city directory, city history, county history, DAR, Episcopal, family, Jewish, landowner map (1869, 1886), Lutheran, Methodist, newspaper, Presbyterian, WPA inventory. Library: New Hanover County Public Library, 201 Chestnut St., Wilmington, NC 28401. County histories: W. L. DeRosset, PICTORIAL AND HISTORICAL NEW HANOVER COUNTY AND WILMINGTON, The Author, Wilmington, NC, 1938; E. L. Lee, NEW HANOVER COUNTY, A BRIEF HISTORY, NCSA, Raleigh, NC, 1971; A. M. Waddell, HISTORY OF NEW HANOVER COUNTY, 1725-1800, Wilmington, NC, 1909.

76. Northampton County

County seat: Jackson (27845), formed in 1741 from Bertie County, a few records missing, see GUIDE, pages 203-5.

Court house records: bills of sale (1779-1875), bonds of apprentices (1797-1918), bonds of bastardy (1783-1894), bonds of officials (1787-1899), court dockets (1802-68), court minutes (1792-1932), court records (1771-1926), deeds (1741-1961), divorce (1818-1951), estate accounts (1868-1961), estate administrators (1881-34, 1868-1961), estate executors (1923-61), estate inventories (1781-1868), estate records (1785-1929), estate sales (1781-1868), estate settlements (1861-1907), guardian (1781-1926), land ejectments (1782-1869), land miscellaneous (1741-1924), marriages (1811-1961), miscellaneous (1773-1961), powers of attorney (1740, 1808-79), roads (1789-1867), tax (1754-62, 1784-1879), wills (1760-1961).

Other records: Baptist, cemetery, census (1785N, 1790R, 1800R, 1810R, 1820RI, 1830R, 1840RP, 1850RAIMS, 1860RAIMS, 1870RAIM, 1880RAIM, 1890C, 1900R, 1910R), county history, DAR, Episcopal, Friends, landowner maps (1863-4), newspaper, Presbyterian, WPA inventory. Library: Northampton County Memorial Library, Jackson, NC 27845. County history: Northampton County Bicentennial Committee, FOOTPRINTS IN NORTHAMPTON, The Committee, Jackson, NC, 1976.

77. Onslow County

County seat: Jacksonville (28540), formed in 1734 from New Hanover County, court house damage by storms in 1752 and 1786, many records lost, see GUIDE, pages 206-8.

Court house records: bonds of apprentices (1757-1907), bonds of bastardy (1764-1909), bonds of officials (1781-1913), court dockets (1745-1882), court minutes (1734-1926), court records (1759-1929), deeds (1734-1961), divorce (1866-1906), estate accounts (1868-1961), estate administrators (1824-54, 1869-1913), estate executors (1869-1912), estate inventories (1780-6,

1845-62), estate records (1735-1914), estate sales (1780-6, 1845-62), estate settlements (1829-45, 1869-1961), guardian (1775-1912), land ejectments (1790-1901), land entries (1781-1955), land grants (1712-1928), land miscellaneous (1753-1908), land partitions (1870-1909), marriages (1745-1961), miscellaneous (1732-1950), roads (1827-53), tax (1754-1912), wills (1757-1961).

Other records: Baptist, cemetery, census (1785N, 1790R, 1800R, 1810R, 1820RI, 1830R, 1840RP, 1850RAIMS, 1860RAIMS, 1870RAIM, 1880RAIM, 1890C, 1900R, 1910R), Christian Church, county history, DAR, family, historical society, WPA inventory. Library: Onslow County Public Library, 58 Doris Ave., Jacksonville, NC 28540. County history: J. P. Brown, THE COMMONWEALTH OF ONSLOW, A HISTORY, Dunn, New Bern, NC, 1960; THE HERITAGE OF ONSLOW COUNTY, Hunter, Winston-Salem, NC, 1988.

78. Orange County

County seat: Hillsboro (27278), formed in 1752 from Bladen, Granville, and Johnston Counties, see GUIDE, pages 209-12.

Court house records: bills of sale (1778-1886), bonds of apprentices (1780-1905), bonds of bastardy (1782-1908), bonds of officials (1782-1928), coroner (1785-1911), court dockets (1772-1884), court minutes (1752-1944), court records (1771-1943), deeds (1755-1962), divorce (1824-1908), estate accounts (1758-85, 1800-1949), estate administrators (1868-1962), estate executors (1870-62), estate inventories (1758-85, 1800-1951), estate records (1754-1944), estate sales (1758-85, 1800-1962), estate settlements (1826-30, 1868-1954), guardian (1782-1962), land ejectments (1782-1902), land miscellaneous (1752-1940), marriages (1779-1962), miscellaneous (1767-1962), petitions (1768, 1772-3), powers of attorney (1781-1909), roads (1786-1909), schools (1859-1962), tax (1755, 1779-1827, 1860, 1866, 1902-15), wills (1752-1962).

Other records: Baptist, cemetery, census (1790R, 1800R, 1810R, 1820RI, 1830R, 1840RP, 1850RAIMS, 1860RAIMS, 1870RAIM, 1880RAIM, 1890C, 1900R, 1910R), city history, county history, DAR, Episcopal, family, historical society, landowner map (1861), Methodist, newspaper, Presbyterian, town history, WPA inventory. Libraries: Orange County Public Library, 300 W. Tryon St., Hillsborough, NC 27278; Library of the University of NC,* Chapel Hill, NC 27514. County history: H. T. Lefler and P. Wager, ORANGE COUNTY, 1752-1952, Orange Printshop, Chapel Hill, NC, 1953.

79. Pamlico County

County seat: Bayboro (28515), formed in 1872 from Beaufort and Craven Counties, see GUIDE, pages 213-14.

Court house records: bonds of bastardy (1874-1910), bonds of officials (1872-1928), court minutes (1872-1947), court records (1872-1935), deeds (1872-1968), divorce (1874-1915), estate accounts (1872-1968), estate administrators (1872-1968), estate executors (1872-1968), estate records (1872-1939), estate settlements (1881-1968), estate widows' dowers & allotments (1899-1945), guardian (1872-1968), land entries (1872-1961), land miscellaneous (1876-1919), marriages (1872-1968), miscellaneous (1872-1962), schools (1885-1968), tax lists (1875-1920), wills (1872-1968).

Other records: cemetery, census (1880RAIM, 1890C, 1900R, 1910R), county history, newspaper, WPA inventory. Libraries: Pamlico County Library, County High School, Bayboro, NC 28515; Craven, Pamlico, Carteret Regional Library, 400 Johnson St., New Bern, NC 28560. County history: Pamlico County Centennial Committee, PAMLICO COUNTY, 1872-1972, Morgan, Greenville, NC, 1972.

80. Pasquotank County

County seat: Elizabeth City (27909), formed in 1670 from Albemarle County, court house fire in 1862, many early records missing, cause not known, see GUIDE, pages 215-18.

Court house records: births (1691-1822), bonds of apprentices (1716-1898), bonds of bastardy (1740-1917), bonds of officials (1741-1882), court dockets (1745-1881), court minutes (1737-1908), court records (1712-1929), deaths (1691-1822), deeds (1700-1915), divorce (1838-1919), estate accounts (1797-1919), estate administrators (1798-1943), estate inventories (1795-1854), estate records (1712-1931), estate sales (1797-1868), estate settlements (1868-1928), estate widows' dowers & allotments (1881-1960), guardian (1719-1931), justices of peace (1720-1899), land ejectments (1746-1901), land entries (1778-93, 1831-8), land miscellaneous (1728-1946), land petitions (1744-1904), marriages (1691-1960), miscellaneous (1703-1960), powers of attorney (1711-1907), roads (1734-1920), schools (1757-1914), tax (1709-1925), wills (1709-1966).

Other records: Baptist, cemetery, census (1785N, 1790R, 1800R, 1810R, 1820RI, 1830R, 1840RP, 1850RAIMS, 1860RAIMS, 1870RAIM, 1880RAIM, 1890C, 1900R, 1910R), county history, DAR, Episcopal, Friends, historical society, Methodist, newspaper, Presbyterian, WPA inventory. Library: Pasquotank-Camden Library, 205 East Main St., Elizabeth City, NC 27909. County histories: J. B. Flora, AN HISTORICAL SKETCH OF ANCIENT PASQUOTANK COUNTY, 1586-1793, Chamber of Commerce, Elizabeth City, NC, 1950; J. E. Wood, BRIEF SKETCH OF

PASQUOTANK COUNTY, Chamber of Commerce, Elizabeth City, NC; PASQUOTANK HISTORICAL SOCIETY YEARBOOK. The Society, Elizabeth City, NC, 1955.

81. Pender County

County seat: Burgaw (28425), formed in 1875 from New Hanover County, see GUIDE, pages 219-20.

Court house records: bonds of officials (1875-86), court minutes (1875-1968), deeds (1875-1968), estate accounts (1875-1968), estate administrators (1875-1967), estate executors (1903-67), estate inventories (1875-1968), estate sales (1875-1968), estate widows' dowers & allotments (1875-1922), guardian (1875-1967), land entries (1875-1963), lunacies (1903-60), marriages (1875-1968), miscellaneous (1875-1968), wills (1875-1968).

Other records: Baptist, cemetery, census (1880RAIM, 1890C, 1900R, 1910R), county history, DAR, Methodist, Presbyterian, WPA inventory. Library: Pender County Library, 103 Cowan St., Burgaw, NC 28425. County history: M. Bloodworth, HISTORY OF PENDER COUNTY, Dietz, Richmond, VA, 1947.

82. Perquimans County

County seat: Hertford (27944), formed in 1670 from Albemarle County, a few early records missing, see GUIDE, pages 221-24.

Court house records: births (1659-1820), bonds of apprentices (1737-1892), bonds of bastardy (1756-1905), bonds of officials (1720-1908), coroner (1794-1892), court dockets (1777-1868), court minutes (1688-1915), court records (1709-1912), deeds (1681-1940), divorce (1824-1912), estate accounts (1803-1909), estate administrators (1842-1960), estate divisions (1841-61), estate executors (1806-1960), estate inventories (1804-1933), estate records (1714-1930), estate sales (1804-1933), estate settlements (1865-1939), guardian (1709-1965), land ejectments (1737-1887), land entries (1834-76), land miscellaneous (1709-1907), land plats (1808-42), marriages (1659-1960), miscellaneous (1709-1921), roads (1711-1910), tax (1712-21, 1742-1875), wills (1711-1960).

Other records: Baptist, cemetery, census (1785N, 1790R, 1800R, 1810R, 1820RI, 1830R, 1840RP, 1850RAIMS, 1860RAIMS, 1870RAIM, 1880RAIM, 1890C, 1900R, 1910R), county history, Episcopal, Friends, historical society, newspaper, town history, WPA inventory. Library: Perquimans County Library, 110 West Academy St., Hertford, NC 27944. County histories: E. G. Winslow, HISTORY OF PERQUIMANS COUNTY, Edwards and Broughton, Raleigh, NC, 1931; Perquimans County Historical Society, YEARBOOK, The Society, Hertford, NC, 1970; W. G. Newby,

TOWN OF HERTFORD BICENTENNIAL AND HISTORICAL DATA OF PERQUIMANS COUNTY, Dunn, New Bern, NC, 1958.

83. Person County

County seat: Roxboro (27573), formed in 1791 from Caswell County, see GUIDE, pages 225-28.

Court house records: bonds of apprentices (1801-1925), bonds of bastardy (1793-1891), bonds of officials (1792-1903), court dockets (1792-1869), court minutes (1792-1966), court records (1775-1924), deeds (1791-1966), divorce (1829-1913), estate accounts (1868-1966), estate administrators (1870-1966), estate records (1795-1920), estate settlements (1869-1966), guardian (1810-1920), justices of peace (1795-1837), land entries (1872-99), land miscellaneous (1792-1902), marriages (1791-1966), miscellaneous (1792-1966), powers of attorney (1785-1900), schools (1841-56), tax (1792-1925), wills (1792-1966).

Other records: Baptist, cemetery, census (1800R, 1810R, 1820RI, 1830R, 1840RP, 1850RAIMS, 1860RAIMS, 1870RAIM, 1880RAIM, 1890C, 1900R, 1910R), county history, DAR, family, historical society, newspaper, town history, WPA inventory. Library: Person County Public Library, 307 South Main St., Roxboro, NC 27573. County histories: S. T. Wright, HISTORICAL SKETCH OF PERSON COUNTY, Womack Press, Danville, VA, 1974; H. R. Mathis, ALONG THE BORDER, Coble, Oxford, NC, 1964; THE HERITAGE OF PERSON COUNTY, Hunter, Winston-Salem, NC, 1986.

84. Pitt County

County seat: Greenville (27834), formed in 1760 from Beaufort County, court house fire in 1857, some records lost, see GUIDE, pages 229-31.

Court house records: bonds of apprentices (1911-26), bonds of bastardy (1854-1906), court dockets (1850-70), court minutes (1858-1941), court records (1850-1963), deeds (1762-1962), divorce (1861, 1866-1906), estate accounts (1868-1963), estate administrators (1868-1963) estate executors (1868-1963), estate inventories (1858-71), estate records (1791, 1827-1947), estate sales (1858-71), estate settlements (1858-1952), estate widows' dowers & allotments (1858-1946), guardian (1857-1950), land divisions (1858-1936), land entries (1858-1941), land grants (1779-1800), land miscellaneous (1763-1923), marriages (1826-37, 1866-1961), miscellaneous (1763-1963), petitions (1775), schools (1885-1956), tax lists (1762-1851), wills (1805-8, 1817, 1836-1963).

Other records: Baptist, cemetery, census (1785N, 1790R, 1800R, 1810R, 1820RI, 1830R, 1840RP, 1850RAIMS, 1860RAIMS, 1870RAIM, 1880RAIM, 1890C, 1900R, 1910R), Christian Church, city history, county history, DAR, Episcopal, family, historical society, landowner map

(1864), Methodist, newspaper, Presbyterian, town history, WPA inventory. Libraries: Sheppard Memorial Library, 530 Evans St., Greenville, NC 27858; Joyner Library, East Carolina University, Greenville, NC 27858. County histories: J. G. Duncan, PITT COUNTY POTPOURRI, East Carolina College Library, Greenville, NC, 1966; H. T. King, SKETCHES OF PITT COUNTY, Edwards and Broughton, Raleigh, NC, 1911; THE HERITAGE OF PITT COUNTY, Hunter, Winston-Salem, NC, 1986.

85. Polk County

County seat: Columbus (28722), formed in 1855 from Henderson and Rutherford Counties, 1847-55 records are in Rutherford County, see GUIDE, pages 232-34.

Court house records: bonds of apprentices (1877-1912), court dockets (1855-68), court minutes (1855-1968), court records (1855-1917), deeds (1855-1967), divorce (1856-1909), estate accounts (1869-1968), estate administrators (1868-1939), estate executors (1868-1968), estate records (1855-1913), estate settlements (1868- 1968), guardian (1855-1968), land ejectments (1855-97), land entries (1870-1950), land miscellaneous (1868-1902), marriages (1855-1969), miscellaneous (1856-1968), wills (1855-1968).

Other records: cemetery, census (1860RAIMS, 1870RAIM, 1880-RAIM, 1890C, 1900R, 1910R), city history, county history, Episcopal, newspaper, WPA inventory. Library: Polk County Public Library, 204 Walker St., Columbus, NC 28722. County history: S. S. Patton, SKETCHES OF POLK COUNTY HISTORY, Miller, Asheville, NC, 1950.

86. Randolph County

County seat: Asheboro (27203), formed in 1779 from Guilford County, some records missing, cause not known, see GUIDE, pages 235-38.

Court house records: bonds of apprentices (1779-1923), bonds of bastardy (1780-1930), court dockets (1779-1868), court minutes (1779-1946), court records (1779-1931), deeds (1779-1964), divorce (1804-1927), estate accounts (1868-1964), estate administrators (1868-1964), estate executors (1868-1964), estate records (1781-1928), estate settlements (1867-1964), estate widows' dowers & allotments (1872-1964), guardian (1793-1964), land ejectments (1792-1897), land entries (1802-33), land miscellaneous (1782-1929), marriage (1779-1964), miscellaneous (1779-1964), roads (1783-1898), schools (1840-64, 1881-5, 1910-64), tax (1779-1886), wills (1779-1964).

Other records: Baptist, cemetery, census (1790R, 1800R, 1810R, 1820RI, 1830R, 1840RP, 1850RAIMS, 1860RAIMS, 1870RAIM, 1880-RAIM, 1890C, 1900R, 1910R), county history, DAR, family, Friends, genealogical society, historical society, landowner maps (1873, 1885), Lutheran, Methodist, newspaper, WPA inventory. Library: Randolph Public

Library, 201 Worth St., Asheboro, NC 27203. County histories: J. A. Blair, REMINISCENCES OF RANDOLPH COUNTY, Reece and Elam, Greensboro, NC, 1890; F. Burgess, RANDOLPH COUNTY, ECONOMIC AND SOCIAL, University of NC, Chapel Hill, NC, 1924.

87. Richmond County

County seat: Rockingham (28379), formed in 1779 from Anson County, a few records missing, see GUIDE, pages 239-42.

Court house records: bonds of apprentices (1782-1912), bonds of bastardy (1783-1880), bonds of officials (1785-1924), court dockets (1780-1872), court minutes (1779-1964), court records (1779-1941), deeds (1779-1964), divorce (1816-1910), estate accounts (1869-1964), estate administrators (1865-1964), estate executors (1865-1964), estate inventories (1789-1807, 1823-8, 1848-68), estate records (1778-1933), estate sales (1823-8, 1848-68), estate settlements (1854-1964), guardian (1784-1964), land ejectments (1786-1887), land entries (1780-1945), land grants (1854-1929), land miscellaneous (1779-1931), land partitions (1847-1912), marriages (1779-1964), miscellaneous (1779-1964), roads (1779-1909), schools (1839-1925), tax (1783-1898), wills (1779-1964).

Other records: Bible, cemetery, census (1785N, 1790R, 1800R, 1810R, 1820RI, 1830R, 1840RP, 1850RAIMS, 1860RAIMS, 1870RAIM, 1880RAIM, 1890C, 1900R, 1910R), city history, county history, DAR, Methodist, newspaper, Presbyterian, WPA inventory. Library: Sandhill Regional Library,* 412 E. Franklin St., Rockingham, NC 28379. County history: J. E. and I. C. Huneycutt, A HISTORY OF RICHMOND COUNTY, The Authors, Rockingham, NC, 1976.

88. Robeson County

County seat: Lumberton (28358), formed in 1787 from Bladen County, some records missing, cause not known, see GUIDE, pages 243-46.

Court house records: bonds of apprentices (1820-1904), bonds of bastardy (1813-1910), bonds of officials (1795-1914), court dockets (1836-69), court minutes (1797-1966), court records (1801-1926), deeds (1787-1966), divorce (1841-1920), estate accounts (1870-1961), estate administrators (1868-1966), estate executors (1868-1966), estate inventories (1821-70), estate records (1801-1935), estate sales (1821-70), estate settlements (1869-1914), guardian (1821-1966), justices of peace (1868-1936), land divisions (1857-1926), land ejectments (1824-1900), land entries (1834-54), land grants (1788-97), land miscellaneous (1782-1926), marriages (1803-1966), miscellaneous (1793-1966), roads (1833-1924), schools (1818-1927), tax (1788-1910), wills (1787-1966).

Other records: Baptist, cemetery, census (1790R, 1800R, 1810R, 1820RI, 1830R, 1840RP, 1850RAIMS, 1860RAIMS, 1870RAIM, 1880-RAIM, 1890C, 1900R, 1910R), Christian Church, city history, county history, DAR, Episcopal, landowner map (1884), newspaper, Presbyterian, WPA inventory. Library: Robeson County Public Library,* 101 North Chestnut St., Lumberton, NC 28359. County history: R. C. Lawrence, THE STATE OF ROBESON, Little and Ives, New York, NY, 1939.

89. Rockingham County

County seat: Wentworth (27375), formed in 1785 from Guilford County, court house fire in 1906, some records missing, cause not known, see GUIDE, pages 247-49.

Court house records: bonds of apprentices (1871-1919), bonds of bastardy (1873-8), court dockets (1786-1868), court minutes (1786-1948), court records (1860-3), deeds (1785-1963), divorce (1859-1921), estate accounts (1868-1965), estate administrators (1864-80), estate inventories (1829-68), estate records (1796-1927), estate sales (1829-68), estate settlements (1817-1965), guardian (1804-1965), land entries (1904-29), land miscellaneous (1786-1922), land processions (1836-67), marriages (1785-1965), miscellaneous (1785-1966), powers of attorney (1784-1923), roads (1811-29), schools (1841-1965), tax (1815, 1887-1915), wills (1785-1965).

Other records: Baptist, Bible, cemetery, census (1790R, 1800R, 1810R, 1820RI, 1830R, 1840RP, 1850RAIMS, 1860RAIMS, 1870RAIM, 1880RAIM, 1890C, 1900R, 1910R), city history, county history, DAR, family, landowner map (1912), Methodist, newspaper, Presbyterian, WPA inventory. Libraries: Rockingham Community College Library, Wentworth, NC 27375; Rockingham County Public Library, 527 Boone Rd., Eden, NC 27288. County histories: L. S. Butler, Jr., ROCKINGHAM COUNTY, A BRIEF HISTORY, NCSA, Raleigh, NC, 1982; L. S. Butler, Jr., OUR PROUD HERITAGE, A PICTORIAL HISTORY OF ROCKINGHAM COUNTY, Bassett Printing, Bassett, VA, 1971; THE HERITAGE OF ROCKINGHAM COUNTY, Hunter, Winston-Salem, NC, 1987.

90. Rowan County

County seat: Salisbury (28144), formed in 1753 from Anson County, a few records destroyed in Civil war, see GUIDE, pages 250-53.

Court house records: bonds of apprentices (1779-1891), bonds of bastardy (1757-1904), bonds of officials (1783-1868), court dockets (1753-1885), court minutes (1753-1942), court records (1753-1915), deeds (1753-1962), divorce (1805-1900), estate accounts (1849-1959), estate administrators (1823-30, 1868-1959), estate divisions (1803-68), estate executors (1868-79, 1889-11909, 1926-34), estate inventories (1849-64), estate records (1753-1920), estate settlements (1868-1959), es-

tate widows' dowers (1796-1861), guardian (1764-1828, 1849-79, 1889-1959), justices of peace (1770-1924), land entries (1778-1925), land processions (1803-24, 1879-93), marriages (1753-1962), miscellaneous (1764-1962), naturalizations (1910-4), petitions (1772-3, 1778), roads (1757-1894), schools (1847-1962), tax (1758-1898), wills (1761-1959).

Other records: Baptist, Catholic, cemetery, census (1790R, 1800R, 1810R, 1820RI, 1830R, 1840RP, 1850RAIMS, 1860RAIMS, 1870RAIM, 1880RAIM, 1890C, 1900R, 1910R), county history, DAR, Episcopal, family, Lutheran, Methodist, Moravian, newspaper, Presbyterian, Reformed, town history, WPA inventory. Library: Rowan Public Library,* 201 West Fisher St., Salisbury, NC 28144. County histories: J. S. Brawley, ROWAN COUNTY, A BRIEF HISTORY, NCSA, Raleigh, NC, 1977; J. S. Brawley, THE ROWAN STORY, 1753-1953, Rowan Printing, Salisbury, NC, 1953; J. Rumple, HISTORY OF ROWAN COUNTY, Bruner, Salisbury, NC, 1881.

91. Rutherford County

County seat: Rutherfordton (28139), formed in 1779 from Burke and Tryon Counties, court house fire in 1907, some records lost, see GUIDE, pages 254-56.

Court house records: bonds of apprentices (1872-1919), bonds of bastardy (1872-8), court dockets (1783-1871), court minutes (1779-1964), court records (1783-1946), deeds (1779-1965), divorce (1870-1930), estate accounts (1835-1964), estate administrators (1871-1963), estate executors (1868-1964), estate records (1831-1902), estate settlements (1868-1964), estate widows' dowers & allotments (1884-1964), guardian (1824-1964), land entries (1778-1949), land grants (1782-7), marriages (1779-1965), miscellaneous (1779-1964), roads (1803-68), schools (1880-1942), tax lists (1782-5, 1797, 1830), wills (1782-1964).

Other records: Baptist, cemetery, census (1790R, 1800R, 1810R, 1820RI, 1830R, 1840RP, 1850RAIMS, 1860RAIMS, 1870RAIM, 1880-RAIM, 1890C, 1900R, 1910R), county history, genealogical society, Methodist, newspaper, WPA inventory. Library: Rutherford County Library,* 205 Koone Rd., Spindale, NC 28160. County histories: C. Griffin, THE HISTORY OF OLD TRYON AND RUTHERFORD COUNTIES, 1730-1936, Miller, Asheville, NC, 1937; C. Griffin, HISTORY OF RUTHERFORD COUNTY, 1937-51, Inland, Asheville, NC, 1952.

92. Sampson County

County seat: Clinton (28328), formed in 1784 from Duplin and New Hanover Counties, court house fire in 1921, some records lost, see GUIDE, pages 257-59.

Court house records: bonds of bastardy (1835-1924), court dockets (1784-1869), court minutes (1793-1944), court records (1790-1934), deeds (1752-1965, includes early deeds of

Duplin County), divorce (1869-1921), estate accounts (1830-1958), estate administrators (1908-65), estate divisions (1848-1927), estate executors (1925-65), estate records (1784-1927), estate sales (1848-1927), estate settlements (1869-1961), guardian (1803-1965), land entries (1789-1874), land grants (1780-1874), land miscellaneous (1810-1928), land surveys (1895-1911), marriages (1867-1964), miscellaneous (1785-1965), naturalizations (1911-6), roads (1829-68), schools (1895-1965), tax (1784-1922), wills (1784-1965).

Other records: Bible, cemetery, census (1785N, 1790R, 1800R, 1810R, 1820RI, 1830R, 1840RP, 1850RAIMS, 1860RAIMS, 1870RAIM, 1880RAIM, 1890C, 1900R, 1910R), Christian Church, county history, DAR, family, historical society, Methodist, newspaper, Presbyterian, WPA inventory. Library: Sampson-Clinton Public Library, 217 Graham St., Clinton, NC 28328. County history: Sampson County Club, SAMPSON COUNTY, ECONOMIC AND SOCIAL, University of NC, Chapel Hill, NC, 1917; THE HERITAGE OF SAMPSON COUNTY, Hunter, Winston-Salem, NC, 1985.

93. Scotland County

County seat: Laurinburg (28352), formed in 1899 from Richmond County, see GUIDE, pages 260-61.

Court house records: court minutes (1901-59), court records (1887-1955), deeds (1900-70), divorce (1901-48), estate accounts (1901-66), estate administrators (1901-66), estate records (1887-1951), estate settlements (1901-66), funerals (1904-14), guardian (1901-55), land grants (1900- 50), marriages (1900-70), miscellaneous (1901-70), roads (1904-5), tax (1905, 10, 15, 1923-49, 1955, 1965), wills (1898-1966).

Other records: Baptist, cemetery, census (1900R, 1910R), county history, DAR, landowner map (1908), newspaper, Presbyterian, WPA inventory. Library: Scotland County Memorial Library, 312 West Church St., Laurinburg, NC 28352. County history: SCOTLAND COUNTY, The State, November 21, 1942, September 23, 1944.

94. Stanly County

County seat: Albemarle (28001), formed in 1841 from Montgomery County, a few records missing, cause not known, see GUIDE, pages 262-65.

Court house records: bonds of apprentices (1872-1938), bonds of bastardy (1843-1923), bonds of officials (1848-1918), court dockets (1841-69), court minutes (1841-1955), court records (1841-1925), deeds (1841-1955), divorce (1854-1920), estate accounts (1868-1968), estate administrators (1868-1968), estate executors (1868-1968), estate records (1841-1908), estate settlements (1870-1951), guardian (1841-1968), land ejectments (1841-66), land entries (1841-1939), land miscellaneous

(1841-1963), marriages (1859-1968), miscellaneous (1841-1968), naturalizations (1921-8), roads (1841-1921), schools (1858-63, 1885-1961), tax (1840-1918), wills (1841-1968).

Other records: Baptist, cemetery, census (1850RAIMS, 1860-RAIMS, 1870RAIM, 1880RAIM, 1890C, 1900R, 1910R), county history, DAR, historical society, landowner map (1911), Lutheran, Methodist, newspaper, town history, United Church of Christ, WPA inventory. Library: Stanly County Public Library, 133 East Main St., Albemarle, NC 28001. County history: I. L. Sharpe, STANLY COUNTY, THE STORY OF AN ERA AND AN AREA, 1841-1972, Piedmont Press, Greensboro, NC, 1972.

95. Stokes County

County seat: Danbury (27016), formed in 1789 from Surry County, a few records missing, cause not known, some records are in Forsythe County, see GUIDE, pages 266-69.

Court house records: bonds of apprentices (1790-1907), bonds of bastardy (1790-1932), bonds of officials (1790-1926), coroner (1805-1916), court dockets (1790-1899), court minutes (1790-1940), court records (1790-1944), deeds (1789-1962), divorce (1816-1941), estate accounts (1790-1841, 1861-1965), estate administrators (1790-1817, 1868-1965), estate executors (1868-1965), estate inventories (1790-1841, 1861-9), estate records (1753-1931), estate settlements (1846-1960), guardian (1790-1965), land ejectments (1791-1915), land entries (1779-1926), land grants (1779-1924), land miscellaneous (1784-1932), lunacies (1794-1931), marriages (1790-1965), miscellaneous (1789-1952), roads (1790-1943), schools (1840-1927), tax (1790-1927), wills (1849-1963).

Other records: Baptist, cemetery, census (1790R, 1800R, 1810R, 1820RI, 1830R, 1840RP, 1850RAIMS, 1860RAIMS, 1870RAIM, 1880RAIM, 1890C, 1900R, 1910R), county history, Friends, Moravian, newspaper, WPA inventory. Library: Stokes County Public Library, Danbury, NC 27016. County histories: R. Hunter, STOKES COUNTY, Pepper, Winston-Salem, NC, 1964; J. R. Woodard, THE HERITAGE OF STOKES COUNTY, Stokes County Historical Society and Hunter Publishing Co., Winston-Salem, NC, 1981.

96. Surry County

County seat: Dobson (27017), formed in 1770 from Rowan County, see GUIDE, pages 270-73.

Court house records: bonds of apprentices (1779-1921), bonds of bastardy (1830-1928), bonds of officials (1777-1893), court dockets (1772-1872), court minutes (1778-1940), court records (1771-1929), deeds (1771-1963), divorce (1826-1927), estate accounts (1792-1963), estate administrators (1776-1958), estate executors (1868-1902), estate inventories (1784-1963), estate records (1771-1943), estate sales (1784-1845), estate settlements (1868-1963), guardian

(1784-1963), land ejectments (1798-1905), land entries (1778-1883), land grants (1782-1877), land miscellaneous (1772-1930), land processions (1801-87), marriages (1778-1963), miscellaneous (1771-1963), naturalizations (1910-28), petitions (1778), roads (1722-1931), tax (1771-1888), wills (1771-1963).

Other records: Baptist, cemetery, census (1785N, 1790R, 1800R, 1810R, 1820RI, 1830R, 1840RP, 1850RAIMS, 1860RAIMS, 1870RAIM, 1880RAIM, 1890C, 1900R, 1910R), Church of Christ, county history, DAR, Episcopal, Friends, Moravian, newspaper, town history, WPA inventory. Libraries: Dobson Community Library, 117 West Atkins St., Dobson, NC 27017; Northwestern Regional Library, 111 North Front St., Elkin, NC 28621. County histories: J. G. Hollingsworth, HISTORY OF SURRY COUNTY, Fisher, Greensboro, NC, 1935; Bicentennial Commission Book Committee, THE SURRY COUNTY BOOK, Surry County Historical Society, Elkin, NC, 1978; THE HERITAGE OF SURRY COUNTY, Hunter, Winston-Salem, NC, 1988.

97. Swain County

County seat: Bryson City (28713), formed in 1871 from Jackson and Macon Counties, court house fires in 1879 and 1900, many records lost, see GUIDE, pages 274-75.

Court house records: bonds of apprentices (1873-1918), bonds of bastardy (1871-80), court minutes (1871-1949), deeds (1871-1970), estate accounts (1877-1970), estate administrators (1873-1966), estate executors (1908-27), guardian (1871-1944), land entries (1871-1944), land grants (1872-1917), land surveys (1905-24), lunacies (1909-17), marriages (1871-1959), miscellaneous (1873-1966), schools (1908-70), tax (1910-27), wills (1873-1966).

Other records: Baptist, cemetery, census (1880RAIM, 1890C, 1900R, 1910R), county history, newspaper, WPA inventory. Library: Fontana Regional Library, Bryson City, NC 28713. County history: L. F. Thomasson, SWAIN COUNTY, EARLY HISTORY AND EDUCATIONAL DEVELOPMENT, Bryson City, NC, 1965.

98. Transylvania County

County seat: Brevard (28712), formed in 1861 from Henderson and Jackson Counties, see GUIDE, pages 276-78.

Court house records: bonds of apprentices (1879-1906), bonds of bastardy (1879-80), court dockets (1861-8), court minutes (1861-1968), deeds (1861-1960), estate accounts (1861-1968), estate administrators (1862-1968), estate executors (1862-1968), estate records (1861-1914), estate settlements (1880-1968), guardian (1863-1968), land entries (1865-1959), land surveys (1906-1959), marriages (1861-1970), miscellaneous (1878-1968), tax (1876-7, 1889, 1897, 1905), wills (1863-1968).

Other records: Baptist, census (1870RAIM, 1880RAIM, 1890C, 1900R, 1910R), county history, Episcopal, landowner map (1868), newspaper, WPA inventory. Library: Transylvania County Library, 105 South Broad St.,Brevard, NC 28712. County history: Transylvania Historical Commission, TRANSYLVANIA COUNTY CENTENNIAL HISTORICAL SOUVENIR PROGRAM, The Commission, Brevard, NC, 1961.

99. Tryon County

formed in 1768 from Mecklenburg County, abolished in 1779 and territory was divided into Lincoln and Rutherford Counties, most records are in Lincoln County, see GUIDE, page 279.
Records: court dockets (1772-8), court minutes (1769-79), deeds (1769-79), miscellaneous (1768-79), petitions (1775).

100. Tyrrell County

County seat: Columbia (27925), formed in 1729 from Bertie, Chowan, Currituck, and Pasquotank Counties, a few early records missing, cause not known, see GUIDE, pages 280-82.
Court house records: bonds of apprentices (1742-1886), bonds of bastardy (1793-1879), bonds of officials (1756-1899), court dockets (1754-1962), court minutes (1735-1925), court records (1736-1962), deeds (1729-1961), estate accounts (1865-1961), estate administrators (1904-61), estate executors (1868-78), estate inventories (1802-68), estate records (1739-1895), estate sales (1841-68), estate settlements (1867-1961), guardian (1757-1895, 1905-16), justices of peace (1774-99), land ejectments (1787-1898), land entries (1778-96, 1887-1924), land grants (1779-80), land miscellaneous (1792-1895), land sales (1808-16), lunacies (1900-41), marriages (1742-1961), miscellaneous (1763-1961), petitions (1779), roads (1788-1898), tax (1751-5, 1782-1901, 15, 39), wills (1744-1961).
Other records: cemetery, census (1785N, 1790R,1800R, 1810R, 1820RI, 1830R, 1840RP, 1850RAIMS, 1860RAIMS, 1870RAIM, 1880-RAIM, 1890C, 1900R, 1910R), county history, DAR, Episcopal, WPA inventory. Library: Tyrrell County Public Library, Highway 64, Columbia, NC 27925. County history: D. E. Davis, HISTORY OF TYRRELL COUNTY, Christopher, Norfolk, VA, 1963.

101. Union County

County seat: Monroe (28110), formed in 1842 from Anson and Mecklenburg Counties, a few records missing, cause not known, see GUIDE, pages 283-85.
Court house records: bonds of apprentices (1871-1910), bonds of bastardy (1871-82), court dockets (1843-70), court minutes (1843-1961), court records (1844-1907), deeds

(1842-1968), divorce (1866-1903), estate accounts (1868-1967), estate administrators (1871-1968), estate executors (1868-1968), estate records (1843-1913), estate settlements (1867-1968), guardian (1871-1913), land probate (1852-81), marriages (1842-1966), miscellaneous (1850-1968), naturalizations (1915-28), roads (1849-1905), tax (1842-69), wills (1837-1968).

Other records: Baptist, cemetery, census (1850RAIMS, 1860-RAIMS, 1870RAIM, 1880RAIM, 1890C, 1900R, 1910R), city history, county history, DAR, genealogical society, historical society, landowner map (1907), Methodist, newspaper, Presbyterian, WPA inventory. Library: Union County Public Library,* 316 East Windsor, Monroe, NC 28110. County histories : J. M. Redwine, UNION COUNTY, Monroe, NC, 1954; A. M. Stack and R. F. Beasley, SKETCHES OF MONROE AND UNION COUNTY, News and Times, Charlotte, NC, 1902; H. N. Walden, HISTORY OF UNION COUNTY, Monroe, NC, 1964.

102. Vance County

County seat: Henderson (27536), formed in 1881 from Franklin, Granville, and Warren Counties, see GUIDE, pages 286-87.

Court house records: bonds of apprentices (1882-1922), bonds of officials (1881-1925), court minutes (1881-1963), deeds (1881-1969), estate accounts (1881-1968), estate administrators (1906-68), estate settlements (1883-1968), land surveys (1886-1907), marriages (1881-1969), miscellaneous (1881-1968), schools (1899-1967), tax (1771, 1882-99, 1903, 1925, 35, 45, 55-6, 65), wills (1881-1969).

Other records: cemetery, census (1890C, 1900R 1910R), county history, Episcopal, Methodist, newspaper, WPA inventory. Library: Perry Memorial Library, 134 Rose Ave., Henderson, NC 27536. County histories: R. Y. Dodd, REMINISCENCES, 1811-1911, Henderson, NC, 1941; J. B. Watkins, HISTORIC VANCE COUNTY, Dispatch, Henderson, NC, 1941.

103. Wake County

County seat: Raleigh (27611), formed in 1771 from Cumberland, Johnston, and Orange Counties, court house office fire in 1832, a few records lost, see GUIDE, pages 288-92.

Court house records: bonds of apprentices (1770-1903), bonds of bastardy (1772-1937), bonds of officials (1787-1898), court dockets (1772-1940), court minutes (1771-1930), court records (1771-1947), deaths (1887-1937), deeds (1774-1958), divorce (1831-1952), estate administrators (1858-1916), estate executors (1858-1916), estate inventories (1868-1913), estate records (1716-1941), estate settlements (1868-1918), estate widows' dowers & allotments (1820-54, 1878-1912), guardian (1772-1940), land divisions (1820-1937), land ejectments (1789-1937), land entries (1778-1846),

land miscellaneous (1800-1942), marriages (1771-1868), miscellaneous (1772-1868), naturalizations (1824-1908), roads (1800-1938), schools (1856-1939), tax (1781-1939), wills (1771-1952).

Other records: Baptist, FHC, cemetery, census (1790R, 1800R, 1810R, 1820RI, 1830R, 1840RP, 1850RAIMS, 1860RAIMS, 1870RAIM, 1880RAIM, 1890C, 1900R, 1910R), Christian Church, city directory, city history, county history, DAR, Episcopal, genealogical society, historical society, landowner maps (1870, 1885, 1887), Methodist, newspaper, Presbyterian, town history, WPA inventory. Library: NC State Library,* 109 East Jones St., Raleigh, NC 27611. County histories: H. S. Chamberlain, HISTORY OF WAKE COUNTY, Edwards and Broughton, Raleigh, NC, 1922; E. R. Murray, WAKE, CAPITAL COUNTY OF NC, Capital County Publishing Co., Raleigh, NC, 1983; THE HERITAGE OF WAKE COUNTY, Hunter, Winston-Salem, NC, 1984.

104. Warren County

County seat: Warrenton (27589), formed in 1779 from Bute County, a few records missing, cause not known, see GUIDE, pages 293-95.

Court house records: bonds of apprentices (1779-1867), bonds of bastardy (1784-1895), bonds of officials (1800-75), court dockets (1787-1868), court minutes (1779-1964), court records (1779-1905), deeds (1779-1964), estate accounts (1868-1964), estate administrators (1905-6, 1912-64), estate records (1768-1920), estate settlements (1878-1964), guardian (1792-1819, 1905-6, 1926-64), land miscellaneous (1779-1897), marriages (1779-1964), miscellaneous (1785-1965), roads (1805-15, 1848-66), schools (1853-64, 1872-1964), tax (1779-1877), wills (1779-1964).

Other records: cemetery, census (1785N, 1790R, 1800R, 1810R, 1820RI, 1830R, 1840RP, 1850RAIMS, 1860RAIMS, 1870RAIM, 1880RAIM, 1890C, 1900R, 1910R), city history, county history, DAR, Episcopal, landowner map (1874), newspaper, WPA inventory. Library: Warren County Memorial Library, 117 South Main St., Warrenton, NC 27589. County history: M. W. Wellman, THE COUNTY OF WARREN, University of NC Press, Chapel Hill, NC, 1959.

105. Washington County

County seat: Plymouth (27962), formed in 1799 from Tyrrell County, court house destruction in 1862, court house fires in 1869 and 1881, many records lost, see GUIDE, pages 296-97.

Court house records: court minutes (1822-1959), court records (1815-1932), deeds (1799-1967), divorce (1851, 1873-1903), estate administrators (1873-1951), estate executors (1873-1951), estate records (1799-1939), estate settlements (1873-1931), guardian (1870-

1951), land miscellaneous (1856-1944), marriages (1851-1967), miscellaneous (1867-1967), schools (1841-1926), wills (1856-1967).

Other records: Baptist, cemetery, census (1800R, 1810R, 1820RI, 1830R, 1840RP, 1850RAIMS, 1860RAIMS, 1870RAIM, 1880RAIM, 1890C, 1900R, 1910R), county history, DAR, Episcopal, newspaper, WPA inventory. Library: Pettigrew Regional Library, Adams and Third St., Plymouth, NC 27962. County history: Washington County Historical Society, HISTORIC WASHINGTON COUNTY, The Society, Plymouth, NC, 1971.

106. Watauga County

County seat: Boone (28607), formed in 1849 from Ashe, Caldwell, Wilkes, and Yancey Counties, court house fire in 1873, most records lost, see GUIDE, pages 298-300.

Court house records: bonds of apprentices (1874-1906), bonds of bastardy (1874-1910), bonds of officials (1873-1911), court minutes (1873-1959), court records (1873-1910), deeds (1858-1976), divorce (1874-1908), estate accounts (1873-1968), estate administrators (1873-1968), estate executors (1873-1968), estate records (1858-1948), estate settlements (1873-1968), guardian (1873-1968), land probate (1873-1913), land surveys (1904-53), marriages (1873-1969), miscellaneous (1848-1974), roads (1867-1946), schools (1870-98), tax (1873-1969), wills (1872-1969).

Other records: cemetery, census (1850RAIMS, 1860RAIMS, 1870RAIM, 1880RAIM, 1890C, 1900R, 1910R), county history, DAR, newspaper, WPA inventory. Library: Watauga County Public Library, 106 Water St., Boone, NC 28607. County histories: J. P. Arthur, HISTORY OF WATAUGA COUNTY, Waddey, Richmond, VA, 1915; D. J. Whitener, HISTORY OF WATAUGA COUNTY, Franklin, Kingsport, TN, 1949.

107. Wayne County

County seat: Goldsboro (27530), formed in 1779 from Craven and Dobbs Counties, a few records missing, cause not known, see GUIDE, pages 301-4.

Court house records: bonds of apprentices (1800-1917), bonds of bastardy (1786-1879, 1889), bonds of officials (1790-1925), court dockets (1785-1868), court minutes (1787-1942), court records (1782-1930), deeds (1780-1963), divorce (1822-1930), estate accounts (1807-1953), estate administrators (1820-1965), estate executors (1820-1965), estate inventories (1807-68), estate records (1782-1932), estate sales (1807-68), estate settlements (1878-1953), estate widows' dowers & allotments (1867-1950), guardian (1787-1965), land divisions (1786-1938), land ejectments (1788-1874), land miscellaneous (1773-1958), land plats (1847-1965), marriages (1790-1964), miscellaneous (1785-1965), naturalizations (1908-10), roads (1791-1914), tax (1780-1912), wills (1782-1965).

Other records: cemetery, census (1790R, 1800R, 1810R, 1820RI, 1830R, 1840RP, 1850RAIMS, 1860RAIMS, 1870RAIM, 1880RAIM, 1890C, 1900R, 1810R), Christian Church, city history, county history, Episcopal, Friends, landowner map (1864), Methodist, newspaper, Presbyterian, WPA inventory. Library: Wayne County Public Library,* 1001 East Ash St., Goldsboro, NC 27530. County history: F. A. Daniels, HISTORY OF WAYNE COUNTY, Goldsboro, NC, 1914; THE HERITAGE OF WAYNE COUNTY, Hunter, Winston-Salem, NC, 1987.

108. Wilkes County

County seat: Wilkesboro (28697), formed in 1777 from Surry County, a few records missing, cause not known, see GUIDE, pages 305-8.

Court house records: bonds of apprentices (1778-1916), bonds of bastardy (1777-1911), bonds of officials (1777-1914), court dockets (1778-1866), court minutes (1778-1948), court records (1777-1945), deeds (1778-1964), divorce (1820-1912), estate accounts (1868-1963), estate administrators (1868-1964), estate executors (1868-1964), estate inventories (1778-99), estate records (1777-1945), estate settlements (1805-34, 1852-1963), estate widows' allotments (1871-1963), guardian (1780-1964), land ejectments (1799-1907), land entries (1783-1962), land grants (1777-1944), land miscellaneous (1778-1932), land petitions (1779-1932), land processions (1883-4), land surveys (1906-31), marriages (1778-1964), miscellaneous (1777-1964), roads (1776-1911), schools (1840-1963), tax (1778-1908), wills (1778-1963).

Other records: Baptist, cemetery, census (1785N, 1790R, 1800R, 1810R, 1820RI, 1830R, 1840RP, 1850RAIMS, 1860RAIMS, 1870RAIM, 1880RAIM, 1890C, 1900R, 1910R), county history, DAR, Episcopal, genealogical society, historical society, Methodist, Moravian, newspaper, Presbyterian, WPA inventory. Libraries: Wilkes Community College Library, Wilkesboro, NC 28697; Wilkes County Regional Library,* 913 C St., North Wilkesboro, NC 28659. County histories: J. Crouch, HISTORICAL SKETCHES OF WILKES COUNTY, Crouch, Wilkesboro, NC, 1902; J. J. Hayes, THE LAND OF WILKES, Wilkes County Historical Society, Wilkesboro, NC, 1962; THE HERITAGE OF WILKES COUNTY, Hunter, Winston-Salem, NC, 1986.

109. Wilson County

County seat: Wilson (27893), formed in 1855 from Edgecombe, Johnston, Nash, and Wayne Counties, a few records missing, cause not known, see GUIDE, pages 309-11.

Court house records: bonds of apprentices (1869-1919), bonds of bastardy (1855-1908), bonds of officials (1855-1958), court dockets (1855-68), court minutes (1855-1914), court records (1855-1922), deeds (1855-1935), divorce (1859-1912),

estate accounts (1868-1924), estate administrators (1855-1960), estate executors (1855-68, 1897-1960), estate records (1855-1959), estate settlements (1868-1959), estate widows' dowers & allotments (1855-1923), guardian (1866-1960), land divisions (1855-1923), land miscellaneous (1856- 1962), marriages (1855-1960), miscellaneous (1855-1961), powers of attorney (1859-1961), tax (1858-1935), wills (1855-1960).

Other records: Baptist, cemetery, census (1860RAIMS, 1870RAIM, 1880RAIM, 1890C, 1900R, 1910R), Christian Church, county history, Episcopal, landowner map (1864), newspaper, WPA inventory. Library: Wilson County Central Public Library, Wilson, NC 27894. County history: WILSON COUNTY, The State, March 29, 1941.

110. Yadkin County

County seat: Yadkinville (27055), formed in 1850 from Surry County, see GUIDE, pages 312-14.

Court house records: bonds of apprentices (1850-1939), bonds of bastardy (1851-1934), bonds of officials (1851-1902), court dockets (1851-68), court minutes (1851-1961), court records (1851-1940), deeds (1850-1969), divorce (1851-1931), estate accounts (1856-1969), estate administrators (1868-1969), estate executors (1868-1905), estate inventories (1851-88), estate probate (1872-85), estate records (1850-1920), estate settlements (1872-1969), guardian (1851-1969), land entries (1852-1940), land miscellaneous (1851-1953), marriages (1850-1969), miscellaneous (1850-1969), roads (1850-1922), schools (1853-78), tax (1851-62, 1873-4, 1925, 35, 45, 1950-69), wills (1851-1969).

Other records: Baptist, cemetery, census (1860RAIMS, 1870RAIM, 1880RAIM, 1890C, 1900R, 1910R), county history, Friends, historical society, Moravian, newspaper, WPA inventory. Library: Yadkin County Public Library, 243 East Main St., Yadkinville, NC 27055. County history: W. E. Rutledge, AN ILLUSTRATED HISTORY OF YADKIN COUNTY, 1850-1965, Rutledge and Welborn, Yadkinville, NC, 1965; THE HERITAGE OF YADKIN COUNTY, Hunter, Winston-Salem, NC, 1985.

111. Yancey County

County seat: Burnsville (28714), formed in 1833 from Buncombe and Burke Counties, some records missing, cause not known, see GUIDE, pages 315-17.

Court house records: bonds of apprentices (1874-1912), bonds of bastardy (1866-1914), bonds of officials (1873-1911), court dockets (1824-68), court minutes (1834-1956), court records (1861-1923), deeds (1833-1967), divorce (1866-1914), estate accounts (1855-1967), estate administrators (1833-1961), estate executors (1833-1961), estate inventories (1855-69), estate records

(1835-1915), estate settlements (1855-1923), guardian (1820-1961), land entries (1851-1946), land probate (1847-71), land surveys (1909-33), marriages (1851-1967), miscellaneous (1854-1967), schools (1842-68, 1885-1953), tax (1840-1), wills (1838-1967).

Other records: cemetery, census (1840RP, 1850RAIMS, 1860RAIMS, 1870RAIM, 1880RAIM, 1890C, 1900R, 1910R), county history, WPA inventory. Library: Yancey County Library, 18 Town Square, Burnsville, NC 28714. County history: Teacher Training Class of Burnsville, HISTORY AND GEOGRAPHY OF YANCEY COUNTY, Edwards, Burnsville, NC, 1930.

112. TN records

Before 1790, practically all of the territory which now makes up the state of TN belonged to NC. As you may remember from Chapter 1, enough people had moved into this area such that the District of Washington was established in 1776, and in 1777 it became the NC County of Washington. In 1779, Sullivan County was split off Washington County, and in 1783, two more counties were split off: Davidson and Greene Counties. In 1787, Sullivan County was divided to yield Hawkins County, and Davidson was divided to give Sumner. Then in 1788, Tennessee County was split off Davidson County. The NC Legislature ceded this area (made up of Washington, Sullivan, Davidson, Greene, Hawkins, Sumner, and Tennessee Counties) to the US Government in 1790. In 1796, the territory became the State of TN.

Thus, during the period up to 1790, there were state records of NC relating to the seven counties, and the seven counties also kept their own records. The state records are in NCSA, but the county records were kept by the counties and should be sought in them and at the TN State Archives, 403 Seventh Ave., North, Nashville, TN 37219. Microfilm copies of some of the county records have been obtained from TN by NCSA, and have been added to the collection in Raleigh, NC. Listed below are summaries of the records in NCSA which relate to the area which is now TN and to the seven counties which were formed before 1790. After the name of the entry, its NCSA collection designation is given, and then the applicable dates appear in parentheses.

The TN Area: Land entries, SS 436-9.1 (1783-4), land records SS 737 (1777-1807), suspended land grants, SS 748 (1780-1801), land entries, SS 1080 (1783-92), western land records, T & C Lands 9 (1784-93), military land frauds, T & C Lands 9 (1798-1800), NC governor's and legislative papers, Microfilm (1777-90), officers and magistrates, MC TR4 (1788), Morgan District Continental troops, MC TR4 (1782), Glasgow land frauds, SS 753-6.1 (1798-1800).

Davidson County (formed 1783): Court minutes, microfilms (1783-1803), clerk bonds, T & C Oaths 26 (1787-8), deeds and grants, microfilm (1784-93), land records, SS 736 (1786-92), suspended land grants, SS 748 (1784-96), land grievances, SS 727.7 (1786-94), wills and inventories, microfilm (1784-1805), justices, GO 147 (1788-9), militia officers, GO 147 (1787-9), vouchers for service against Indians, T & C Mil 71-3 (1790), Cumberland Battalion, MC Cumb Bn 1 (1786- 92), settlements T & C County Settlements 37 (1787-92), Revolutionary accounts, T & C Mil 14, 17, 21 (1780, 1792-6).

Greene County (formed 1783): court minutes, Microfilm (1783-96), clerk bonds, T & C Oaths 28 (1783, 1788), land records, SS 736 (1783-94), land entries, TCR 2.405.1 (1783), suspended land grants, SS 748 (1784-96), land grievances, SS 727.7 (1783-1804), justices, GO 147 (1788), militia officers, GO 147 (1786-7), officers and magistrates, MC TR4 (1788), settlements, T & C County Settlements 44 (1783-90).

Hawkins County (formed 1787): clerk bonds, T & C Oaths 28 (1787), register bonds, T & C Oaths 43 (1787-9), sheriff bonds, T & C Oaths 9 (1787-8), deeds, Microfilm (1788-1800), deed index, Microfilm (1780-1861), land surveys, SS 737 (1787), wills, Microfilm (1797-1886), militia officers and justices, GO 147 (1788-9).

Sullivan County (formed 1779): clerk bonds, T & C Oaths 36 (1787), county officers, T & C Oaths 55 (1789), deeds, Microfilm (17751802), land records, SS 736 (1778-96), land caveats, T & C Lands 9 (1782), suspended land grants, SS 748 (1780-99), land grievances, SS 727.9 (1784-90), wills, SS 884 (1781-3), justices and militia officers, GO 147 (1788-9), officers and magistrates, MC TR4 (1788), census, GO 131 (1787), settlements, T & C County Settlements 831 (1787-9), Revolutionary certificates, T & C Mil 35 (1782).

Sumner County (formed 1787): county officers return, T & C Oaths 55 (1789), sheriff bonds, T & C Oaths 18 (1787), tax collector bonds, T & C Oaths 52 (1787), court minutes, Microfilm (1787-1805), land entries, SS 736 (1792), suspended land grants, SS 748 (1797, 1801), justices and militia officers, GO 147 (1787-9), vouchers for service against Indians, T & C Mil 71-3 (1790), settlements, T & C County Settlements 83 (1787-9), Revolutionary accounts, T & C Mil 17, 23 (1780-95).

Tennessee County (formed 1788): suspended grants, SS 748 (1790), justices and militia officers, GO 147 (1789), settlements, T & C County Settlements 85 (1789).

Washington County (formed 1777): court minutes, Microfilms (1779-1806), clerk bonds, T & C Oaths 38 (1778-87), deed index, Mi-

crofilm (1779-1866), land records, SS 737 (1777-97), land caveats, T & C Lands 9 (1782-4), suspended land grants, SS 748 (1779-97), land grievances, SS 727.9 (1779-1801), estate records, Microfilm (1779-1841), tax lists, TCR 1.405.1 (1778-87), justices and military officer, GO 147 (1786-9), officers and magistrates, MC TR4 (1788), wills, Microfilm (1779-1858), settlements, T & C County Settlements 89 (1783-90), Revolutionary certificates, T & C Mil 35 (1782).

For further detail on these records as well as NCSA holdings for TN counties which were formed 1790-6, consult:
_C. F. W. Coker and G. Stevenson, RECORDS RELATING TO TN IN NCSA, Archives Information Circular No 3, NCSA, Raleigh, NC, 1980.

Books by George K. Schweitzer

CIVIL WAR GENEALOGY. A 78-paged book of 316 sources for tracing your Civil War ancestor. Chapters include I: The Civil War, II: The Archives, III: National Publications, IV: State Publications, V: Local Sources, VI: Military Unit Histories, VII: Civil War Events.

GEORGIA GENEALOGICAL RESEARCH. A 235-paged book containing 1303 sources for tracing your GA ancestor along with detailed instructions. Chapters include I: GA Background, II: Types of Records, III: Record Locations, IV: Research Procedure and County Listings (detailed listing of records available for each of the 159 GA counties).

HANDBOOK OF GENEALOGICAL SOURCES. A 217-paged book describing all major and many minor sources of genealogical information with precise and detailed instructions for obtaining data from them.

KENTUCKY GENEALOGICAL RESEARCH. A 154-paged book containing 1191 sources for tracing your KY ancestor along with detailed instructions. Chapters include I: KY Background, II: Types of Records, III: Record Locations, IV: Research Procedure and County Listings (detailed listing of records available for each of the 120 KY counties).

MASSACHUSETTS GENEALOGICAL RESEARCH. A 279-paged book containing 1709 sources for tracing your MA ancestor along with detailed instructions. Chapters include I: MA Background, II: Types of Records, III: Record Locations, IV: Research Procedure and County-Town-City Listings (detailed listing of records available for each of the 14 MA counties and the 351 cities-towns).

NEW YORK GENEALOGICAL RESEARCH. A 240-paged book containing 1426 sources for tracing your NY ancestor along with detailed instructions. Chapters include I: NY Background, II: Types of Records, III: Record Locations, IV: Research Procedure and NY City Record Listings (detailed listing of records available for the 5 counties of NY City), V: Record Listings for Other Counties (detailed listing of records available for each of the other 57 NY counties).

NORTH CAROLINA GENEALOGICAL RESEARCH. A 172-paged book containing 1233 sources for tracing your NC ancestor along with detailed instructions. Chapters include I: NC Background, II: Types of Records, III: Record Locations, IV: Research Procedure and County Listings (detailed listing of records available for each of the 100 NC counties).

PENNSYLVANIA GENEALOGICAL RESEARCH. A 225-paged book containing 1309 sources for tracing your PA ancestor along with detailed instructions. Chapters include I: PA Background, II: Types of Records, III: Record Locations, IV: Research Procedure and County Listings (detailed listing of records available for each of the 67 PA counties).

REVOLUTIONARY WAR GENEALOGY. A 110-paged book containing 407 sources for tracing your Revolutionary War ancestor. Chapters include I: Revolutionary War History, II: The Archives, III: National Publications, IV: State Publications, V: Local Sources, VI: Military Unit Histories, VII: Sites and Museums.

SOUTH CAROLINA GENEALOGICAL RESEARCH. A 190-paged book containing 1107 sources for tracing your SC ancestor along with detailed instructions. Chapters include I: SC Background, II: Types of Records, III: Record Locations, IV: Research Procedure and County Listings (detailed listing of records available for each of the 47 SC counties and districts).

TENNESSEE GENEALOGICAL RESEARCH. A 136-paged book containing 1073 sources for tracing your TN ancestor along with detailed instructions. Chapters include I: TN Background, II: Types of Records, III: Record Locations, IV: Research Procedure and County Listings (detailed listing of records available for each of the 96 TN counties).

VIRGINIA GENEALOGICAL RESEARCH. A 187-paged book containing 1273 sources for tracing your VA ancestor along with detailed instructions. Chapters include I: VA Background, II: Types of Records, III: Record Locations, IV: Research Procedure and County Listings (detailed listing of records available for each of the 100 VA counties and 41 major cities).

WAR OF 1812 GENEALOGY. A 69-paged book of 289 sources for tracing your War of 1812 ancestor. Chapters include I: History of the War, II: Service Records, III: Bounty Land and Pension Records, IV: National and State Publications, V: Local Sources, VI: Military Unit Histories, VII: Sites and Events.

All of the above books may be ordered from Dr. George K. Schweitzer at the address given on the title page. Or send a long SASE for a FREE descriptive leaflet on any or all of the books.

Presented To

LaPORTE BRANCH LIBRARY

By

LaPORTE-BAY AREA
HERITAGE SOCIETY

Harris County Public Library

NORTH CAROLINA GENEALOGICAL RESEARCH

by

George K. Schweitzer, Ph.D., Sc.D.
407 Regent Court
Knoxville, TN 37923-5807

Wordprocessing by
Anne M. Smalley